THE ART WORLD

LAW, BUSINESS & PRACTICE IN CANADA

AARON MILRAD & ELLA AGNEW

Merritt Publishing Company Limited
Toronto   New York   Vancouver

PUBLISHED BY MERRITT PUBLISHING COMPANY LIMITED
Toronto, New York, Vancouver

DISTRIBUTED IN CANADA
BY JOHN WILEY AND SONS CANADA LIMITED

This book is a general introduction to
a number of complex legal and business topics.
Any specific concerns should be resolved by
seeking professional advice.

CATALOGUING IN PUBLICATIONS DATA
Milrad, Aaron.
The art world.
Includes index.

ISBN 0-920886-04-3

1. Law and art.
2. Art – Collectors and collecting – Canada.
3. Art industries and trade – Canada. 1. Agnew, Ella.
11. Title.

KE3968.M54   344.71097   C80-094283-3

In Memoriam
Jack Bush

CONTENTS

CHAPTER 4
NON-PROFIT STRUCTURES AND
THEIR USES FOR THE VISUAL ARTS

CHAPTER 8
THE CORPORATE COLLECTOR:
TAXATION AND GIFTING

CHAPTER 9
THE ARTIST: BUSINESS ARRANGEMENTS
AND TAXATION

FOREWORD

During the past decade, considerable attention has been devoted to management concerns in the performing arts. Similar concern has been focussed on the problems of gallery and museum management in the visual arts. But little has been done for the individual artist whose needs require, perhaps, more attention than any other group in the artistic community.

"Individual" is the key word here. Performing artists have, for years, had the protection of professional associations and even trade unions. Composers have also been represented by such agencies as CAPAC in Canada and ASCAP in the United States. Writers turn to ACTRA or have agents to represent them to publishers.

But the individual painter, sculptor or printmaker has, with few exceptions, had little support or even information available for the protection of his professional rights. While the Canadian Artists Representation has made some headway in information distribution and in the area of royalty payments, no concerted effort has been undertaken to articulate to the visual artist a full range of the protections available.

Likewise, too little has been said on the rights and, more important, on the responsibilities of dealers, private and corporate collectors and public galleries. Compiled here for the first time are a series of essays which treat in some detail the legal problems inherent in the ownership of a work of art. The myth of casual ownership and the commonly held views of residual rights are exploded and treated in a forthright manner. Art schools and university art departments now have a text which can stimulate discourse on the rights and responsibilities of artists, art dealers and art patrons. Even attorneys have here a text with which to acquaint themselves with the problems and pitfalls of the fine art marketplace.

This volume is the first significant step in Canada to fill what has been for years a gaping void into which many artists and collectors have fallen. Armed with the insights and procedures set forth in the following pages, Canada's artists can now join their colleagues in the creative and performing arts in seeking opportunities for fiscal stability and in demanding their economic and legal rights in the cultural marketplace, while patrons and dealers can begin to approach that marketplace with a sense of sophisticated responsibility toward the makers of art.

Business transactions are at least two-way dialogues. With an enlightened cultural community, the visual arts in this nation will flourish, aesthetically and financially. No longer need the artist claim that the largest subsidy for Canadian art comes from the producer of that art.

Joseph G. Green, Dean
Faculty of Fine Arts
York University
Toronto

PREFACE

The idea for this book originated after Aaron Milrad attended a meeting of the Practising Law Institute of the American Bar Association in New York City in the early part of 1973. Lawyers and museum people involved with the law affecting the art world were invited to attend the seminar. All, except Milrad, were American. At the meeting, problems of the artist, the private dealer, the collector, and the public museum were discussed in some depth from the lawyer's point of view. Almost all of the law discussed in the seminars related to only the American experience. So, after returning from New York, Milrad made enquiries to determine whether any book existed dealing with Canadian jurisprudence and the Canadian art world. Nothing was found, and so Milrad began discussing the idea of a book with artists, private art dealers, museum people and collectors.

The initial reactions from most of these people were, "just how relevant would such a book be?" "Is there enough material to put such a book together?" In fact, our problem was in limiting the amount of material, and selecting what would be most useful to people interested in the Canadian art scene.

It is not difficult to understand the original reaction encountered, for only in the past few years have dealings in painting and sculpture in Canada grown in both number and dollar volume to the point where many of the problems inherent in the field need professional advice. Today, it is not uncommon to find works by living Canadian artists selling for $50,000 or more, and older Canadian paintings selling for up to half a million dollars. The day of the inexpensive painting is fast disappearing.

In addition, there is now a greater awareness of the arts by provincial, federal and municipal governments. The Canada Council contributes many thousands of dollars to the visual arts. Provincial government bodies are making large contributions as well. Not long ago, the Parliament of Canada enacted the Cultural Property Export and Import Act, dealing with the importation into Canada of cultural property illegally exported from foreign states, and the exportation of works of art from Canada to foreign countries. The Government of Canada has recognized the importance of Canadian culture, and of preserving the country's cultural history and heritage for future Canadians. The federal government has also allowed, and in some cases expanded, tax deductions to the private sector for gifts of works of art to art institutions, museums, and universities.

For a period of time, the Department of Public Works in Ottawa also set aside up to one percent of the cost of all Capital Government Construction for works of art. This in turn led to numerous commissions to Canadian artists for federal buildings not only in Ottawa but across the country. The Canada Council

"Art Bank" has also become a major art purchaser in Canada.

The Provinces of Alberta and Quebec have passed Provincial Cultural Heritage Laws preventing the export of works of art determined to be important to those provinces. Municipalities such as Toronto and Montreal have art programs which include the purchase of art for municipal purposes.

Corporations have also actively entered the art field, and many major corporations such as banks or oil companies are now developing substantial art collections.

In the past few years, Toronto has become an international centre of art. The dollar volume of art sales per year in Toronto is now in the millions of dollars, and transactions that were once informal arrangements must now be dealt with in a much more professional manner. Montreal is an important art centre with many prestigious galleries. Edmonton has a very important collection of contemporary art, and Vancouver is in the process of establishing a major new museum. It can be expected that western centres will become increasingly prominent in the Canadian art world, and perhaps the international sphere, within the next few years. Consequently, an understanding of the legal aspects of Canadian art dealings is imperative.

The purpose of this book is to deal with some of the major legal problems that face the various groups that make up the Canadian art world. For instance, for the private dealer, questions arise about the sale of art on a time-purchase basis. What risk does the dealer take by selling works "on time"? What risk does the artist take when he transfers a work of art to a dealer on a "consignment basis," and the dealer, in turn, has resold it on a time-purchase contract? Who bears the loss if the dealer goes bankrupt? Who bears the loss if the collector goes bankrupt before paying for the work? Who, then, owns the painting?

This, in turn, leads to questions involving the art collector. What are his rights against a gallery as to warranties of authenticity for a painting that turns out to be a forgery? What risks does he take by buying at an auction? What are the tax consequences of a gift made by a collector to a public institution? What tax benefits will be available to him?

Then there are questions affecting the public institution that accepts a work of art as a donation. For instance, does the institution have the right to sell that work of art sometime in the future? Does it have the right to lend that work of art to other institutions? What is the proper method of evaluating gifts for tax purposes? What if an institution has purchased a work of art which suddenly starts to disintegrate? Who, then, is responsible? Who owns the copyright of works in the collection? What is the role of trustees? What obligations and responsibilities do they have? What are the obligations and responsibilities of the staff? What is a non-profit corporation? Also, the fiscal responsibility of public institutions has recently come under public scrutiny.

In addition to these problems, new questions arise regarding the commercial exploitation of works of art. For example, is an artist entitled to payment when his work is reproduced on Christmas cards or posters sold by a public art gallery that owns his work of art? There are now a number of print publishers and ateliers that produce original prints and distribute them throughout the country and, in fact, the world. What is their obligation in the sale of such work to the distributor? How do they guarantee authenticity? How does the collector know that it is truly a limited edition and that other copies will not be printed later? How does the artist guarantee that he is properly paid and that there will be no unauthorized editions issued? How does the collector ensure that he is not buying a forgery or a fraud? How does copyright affect the collector?

Another recent phenomenon has been the rise of the auction house as a purveyor of "high art." How does the purchaser ensure that he has purchased an original work of art and not a copy, or that what he has purchased is what was in fact advertised? What protection is there for the auction house that relies upon an expert opinion of a painting which later turns out to be a forgery?

Art is an international commodity and a series of international laws now affect it, such as the UNESCO Convention on the Means of Prohibition and Preventing the Illicit Import, Export, and Transfer of Ownership of Cultural Property, to which Canada is a signatory. What works of art are subject to customs duties by various countries? How many copies of works of art can be forwarded from country to country without attracting entry duties? What are the criteria for a work of art to be considered "an original work of art" for these purposes? What works require an export permit?

The question of internal Canadian taxes has become an important one. The artist must now consider an estate plan and the consequences of leaving a large number of paintings behind. This is important in order to maintain the artist's reputation, to ensure an orderly market for his works after his death, and to maximize the number of dollars available to his beneficiaries while reducing the tax burden. Provincial and federal sales taxes affect the artist in purchasing materials to create a work of art, and these taxes also affect the ultimate sale price of a work.

From the collector's point of view, "capital gains tax" affects the sale of any work of art over $1,000, and it is important for the collector to be familiar with the rules regarding sales by an individual. He is also affected by tax laws regarding gifts to family, museums, or public institutions. He is affected, as well, by heritage legislation which controls the export of works of art from this country and confers special tax benefits, in some instances, for sales or donations to designated public institutions.

From the private dealer's point of view, there are basic corporate and commercial law questions to be answered. Should a dealer incorporate? What are the advantages to incorporation? Can a dealer have a separate personal collection that enjoys tax advantages? Can he get tax benefits from gifts of art?

These are just a few of the ways in which the law affects today's complex art world. As the value of art continues to escalate there will be a greater need for formality and professionalism in the field to avoid potential problems, such as those revealed in the Rothko case, and to solve them when they occur.

This book has been written with the hope that it will be used by artists, professional advisers, private gallery personnel, public gallery officials, government administrators, and collectors, as well as students at art colleges and universities. This book is not intended to be a comprehensive treatise of the field (that may come later), but rather a handbook, written in lay terms, to help those involved in the visual arts.

Since that New York conference of 1973, a number of books on this subject have appeared in the United States. We would like to acknowledge the granddaddy of them all, *Art Works: Law, Policy, Practice,* by Feldman and Weil, which has been a useful source of information.

We thank the Canada Council for awarding Aaron Milrad an Explorations Grant toward the research and travel necessary to develop this book.

The book could not have been put together without the dedicated assistance of our secretaries, Barbara Carvalho and Myra Bates, and the unflagging efforts of our editor and Student-at-law, Linda Davey.

Aaron Milrad

Ella Agnew

CHAPTER 1 COPYRIGHT

THE PRESENT LAW IN CANADA

The Copyright Act is a federal Act and thus applies to the entire country. The present Act came into force in January, 1924. Its terms are those required by an international treaty known as the Berne Convention to which Canada has been a party since 1886. The Berne Convention has been revised from time to time, but Canada is a signatory only to the text of 1928, known as the Rome Text. Works created and published prior to January 1, 1924 are now in the "public domain" and not subject to copyright protection.

In 1962, Canada also joined the Universal Copyright Convention. Canada has not adhered to the 1971 revisions and is bound only by the terms formulated in 1952. The United States does not belong to the Berne Convention, but only to the Universal Copyright Convention. This becomes significant if you wish to protect an artistic work in the United States of America.

What Is Copyright?

Copyright confers the sole right to produce or reproduce a work of art, or any substantial part, in any material form whatever. Copyright applies to literary, dramatic, and musical works as well, but is discussed here only as it relates to visual art works. Once the artist has created a work of art, under the Copyright Act he (or she) has the right to prevent others from producing or reproducing that work or any substantial part of it, provided that the work is "original" in the sense that the artist created it himself and did not copy someone else's product. This does not prevent an artist from using another work as "inspiration," but the artist must have produced or created something which is new (i.e., original) to the artist. There is no copyright in ideas, information, concepts, schemes or thoughts, only in things actually created. Nor is there any copyright in the ideas expressed in a work, or in the methods or style of creating a work. Essentially, what is protected is the form given to the expression of an idea.

Property Rights

Ownership of the physical object (i.e., the painting or sculpture) must be distinguished from ownership of the copyright. A purchaser of a work of art does not obtain copyright by buying the object. There must be a specific transfer, licence, or assignment of the copyright for this right to pass, and such transfer must be in writing. There have been cases where magazines have requested permission for the reproduction of works of art from the *owner* of the work. The permission and payment for the right to reproduce a work of art should in fact be requested from, and made to, the *owner of the copyright;* generally the artist who created it.

Artistic Work

Copyright exists in an original artistic work. "Artistic work" is defined by the Act to include paintings, drawings, sculpture (defined as including casts and models), artistic craftsmanship, and architectural works of art. As well, it includes *engravings* and photographs. *Engraving* is further defined to include etchings, lithographs, woodcuts, prints (original prints), "and other similar works not being photographs."

Copyright in books, cinematographic material, dramatic works, or musical works is discussed here only as it relates to "artistic works."

First Owner

The sole right to reproduce a work of art or any *substantial* part of it resides with the "author" (i.e., creator) of the work as the first owner, with two major exceptions:

1. If an engraving, photograph, or portrait was commissioned by some other person and there is a contract or order for "valuable consideration," then in the absence of any agreement to the contrary, the person who ordered the work is deemed to be the first owner of the copyright.
2. If the artist was in the employ of some other person or company, or under a contract of service, and the work was made in the course of such employment, the employer is the first owner of the copyright.

Term of Copyright

With the few exceptions discussed below, copyright exists for the lifetime of the author and for a period of fifty years after his death. An author can assign his copyright for his lifetime and the first twenty-five years after death. The copyright reverts to the author's estate for the second twenty-five year term after death, unless the artist has assigned the copyright in his will. Since copyright generally survives the author's death for fifty years, proper will planning is very important. The artist may wish to name special executors and trustees, or advisers to the executors, who will give advice regarding the artistic holdings of the estate and deal with the exercise of copyright. If he does not do this, the artist should at least give special authority and perhaps provide instructions to his executors in regard to dealing with his copyright. See Chapter 9 for a discussion of tax planning for the artist's estate.

Photographs

In regard to photographs, the copyright term is fifty years from the making of the original negative. The person who was the owner of the negative when it was made is deemed to be the "author" of the photograph.

Publication of Engravings

As discussed above, engravings include etchings, lithographs, woodcuts, and prints. Although subject to the same term of copyright as other artistic works (the life of the author plus fifty years), engravings are included in the class of works which can be "published." The Act defines publication as "the issue of copies of the work to the public," and states that the public exhibition of an artistic work does not constitute publication.

Because they can be published, copyright treatment of "engravings" differs from that accorded to other artistic works in two respects:

1. Copyright in a work which is unpublished at the author's death exists until first publication and for a period of fifty years thereafter.
2. Twenty-five years after the death of the author of a *published* work, copyright is not infringed by the reproduction of the work, for purposes of sale, if a royalty of 10% of the published price is paid to the owner of the copyright for each copy sold. If the work was not yet published at the time of the artist's death, this provision applies twenty-five years after first publication.

Since mere display of an "engraving" in public does not constitute publication, such a work (as long as it remained unsold i.e., unissued to the public) might well enjoy a perpetual copyright.

Crown Copyright

Where a work is prepared or published by, or under the direction of, the federal or provincial governments, or in any of their departments, the copyright in the work belongs to the Crown in the absence of any contrary agreement with the artist. If a mural or other work of art is created for a public building, it is often possible for the artist to obtain joint copyright with the relevant government department.

Where the Crown holds the copyright in a work, a number of confusions arise with respect to the applicable term of copyright.

The act states that "without prejudice to any rights or privileges of the Crown" copyright in such works exists for fifty years from first publication. For artistic works other than engravings or photographs, publication is, of course, impossible. Copyright in such works may therefore be for the general term of the life of the artist plus fifty years, or it may be that copyright in such works is perpetual because they will never be published. An additional element of uncertainty arises because the provision is stated to be without prejudice to Crown privilege. This may mean that the Crown (i.e., the government) could exercise this prerogative to extend the term of its copyrights at its whim, or indeed

3

make them perpetual. It should also be mentioned that the Crown itself is probably not bound by the Copyright Act, in which case it could use copyright material of others with impunity.

Where the Crown holds the copyright in photographs or "engravings," presumably the copyright would be perpetual if such works remained unpublished.

Corporate Ownership

Corporations, although not specifically mentioned under the Act, are also given protection. Where the corporation is the "first owner" of the copyright, the term of protection is still restricted to the life of the creator (i.e., the artist) plus fifty years. Corporations may also take licences and assignments of copyright.

Who Can Obtain Copyright in Canada?

Under The Copyright Act, the author must be a Canadian, or a British subject, or be a resident in any of Her Majesty's Dominions, or be a citizen of any other country subscribing to the Berne Convention for copyright protection (to which Canada is, of course, a party), or a citizen of a country with which Canada has some reciprocal agreement. These categories include most of the industrialized countries of the world.

How Is Copyright Obtained?

Copyright arises automatically without requiring anything other than to have created the original work of art. As already indicated, the copyright first exists in the creator subject to the exceptions mentioned. It is *not* necessary to register copyright in Canada.

Registration

Although copyright arises automatically, in some cases it may be wise to use the voluntary registration procedures permitted by the Copyright Act. The advantage of such registration is that it creates a presumption that the copyright is valid and it is therefore up to a party attacking the copyright to disprove its validity. It is also evidence of the date of creation where an artist is accused of having copied someone else's work, or where he wishes to establish that another artist has copied his. Copyright can be registered at any time, since there is no requirement of registration within any particular time from the date of creation of the work. The present cost of such registration is $25.00 for each work.

On What Works Can Copyright Be Obtained?

Copyright exists in any *original* work of art, which includes paintings, sculpture, photographs, movies, etchings, engravings, lithographs, woodcuts, and original prints. It is also available for "performance" art.

4

**Protection
of Canadian Artists'
Copyright in Other
Berne Convention
Countries**

Those countries which belong to the Berne Convention give automatic copyright to a work of art created by a Canadian or a resident of Canada. No registration is necessary. Berne Convention countries include most major countries of the world with the exception of the United States of America.

**Protection
of Canadian Artists'
Copyright in
the U.S.A.
and Other
U.C.C. Countries**

Canada and the United States both belong to the Universal Copyright Convention (U.C.C.) as do many South American countries. The United States does not belong to the Berne Convention. As a result, for Canadians to obtain proper protection in the United States (and other U.C.C. countries) it is necessary from the time of first publication to see that all copies of the work are marked with a small "c" inside a circle, the name of the copyright owner, and the year of the first publication, e.g., © Aaron Milrad, 1980. It is therefore recommended that Canadian artists when they sign their works of art also put the "c" in the circle and the year on such works. Instead of a © the word "copyright" or its abbreviation "copr." may appear. The © is recommended since the United States' law requires that the notice be placed where the public can see it, i.e., in a prominent place. This does not have to be in the middle of the canvas, but in a place that would ordinarily be seen and not covered over. It is probably sufficient if done on a painting's stretcher, on the reverse of the canvas, or on the base of a sculpture.

**Protection
of Foreign Artists
in Canada**

If at the time the work was created the artist was resident in, or a citizen of, a country belonging to the Berne Copyright Convention, there is automatic protection for the artist in Canada. As well, there is protection for a published work if it was first published in a Commonwealth country or in a country with which Canada has a separate agreement. Again, no registration is necessary. For example, the work of an English artist created in England would have automatic protection in Canada. The same would be true if the English artist created the work in France, Germany, Switzerland, Sweden, or any other country which was a party to the Berne Convention. For an American artist, protection is automatic in Canada, but the © may be required to ensure protection in other U.C.C. countries.

**Transfer
of Copyright**

The Copyright Act indicates that the artist is the first owner of the copyright (with the two stated exceptions). This copyright can be transferred by way of assignment. The assignment may be either whole or partial and either general or subject to territorial limitations, either for the whole term of the copyright or for any part of it. For instance, there may be an assignment given for Canada, a separate one for England, a separate one for the United States, etc. Different time periods are also possible such as one year, ten years, etc. As well, rather than giving an assign-

5

ment, which is a transfer or sale of the particular right for the time and place given, it is possible to give a licence. This is a lesser right which does not involve an actual transfer of the ownership of copyright. It is a temporary right, usually given for a fee or royalty, allowing the party to use the work for a specified purpose, period, or place. This is the usual arrangement made by artists with publishers who wish to create reproductions of an original work for sale as posters, reproductions, calendars, or in publications.

To be valid, the assignment or grant must be in writing and must be signed by the owner of the copyright or by a duly authorized agent. However, no assignment of copyright is valid for more than the lifetime of the creator and twenty-five years after his death. The last twenty-five years (of the fifty year term after death) is not assignable (unless assigned by will), and the copyright for this period devolves on the legal representatives of the artist as part of the artist's estate.

Infringement of Copyright

Copyright is infringed if the work of art has been reproduced – in two or three dimensions – by copies, photographs, reproductions, or adaptations, without the consent of the owner of the copyright. As well, importation can be prevented of copies made outside of Canada of any work in which copyright subsists, if they would have infringed upon copyright if they had been made in Canada. The owner of the copyright must give notice in writing to the Department of National Revenue to that effect.

The artist should give consideration to copyright when contracting with his dealer, especially in regard to sales to public institutions. The artist will need to consider whether copies of works purchased may be reproduced on posters, greeting cards, jigsaw puzzles, catalogues, and other items commonly sold by purchasing galleries, and if so, the fee to be paid.

Exceptions to Infringement

1. Under the Copyright Act, it is not a breach of copyright to reproduce a work of sculpture, architecture, or artistic craftsmanship if the work is permanently situated in a public place or building. This applies to public monuments which are by their very nature so situated as to invite photographs, drawings, or reproductions. It likely also applies to statues, sculpture, and murals permanently situated or installed in public places such as parks, public buildings, and government buildings. There is some question as to whether it applies to public portions of private buildings, such as lobbies. It is possible to argue that it does not apply to works of art held by a public gallery or museum since their collections are not *permanently* situated or affixed in a public place, and that such a place is not "public" in any event if membership dues are required. However, there have been no cases defining a "public place" under the Copyright Act.

2. It is not a breach of copyright for a newspaper to reproduce a particular work of art in conjunction with a criticism of the artist's work or a review of an exhibition.
3. It is also not an infringement if a work is copied for the purposes of private study or research.
4. As well, an author or artist who has sold or assigned the copyright is not in breach of the copyright if he continues to use any mould, cast, sketch, plan, model, or study made by him for the purpose of the work, if he does not repeat or imitate the main design of that work.

All these exceptions have been termed "fair use." It is also quite common for public institutions or public corporations contracting for the creation or purchase of works of art to require some transfer of copyright. It is important to remember that the ownership and rights to use copyright set out in the Copyright Act can be changed by contract between the parties.

Remedies

Copyright infringement arises when someone does something which the artist has been given the sole right to do under the statute, without obtaining the artist's consent. Infringement usually involves a violation of the right to produce or reproduce the work, and generally is the result of photographic reproduction and resale, in the form of reproductions or prints. A "fake" is also a breach of copyright, as well as constituting fraud. Both civil and criminal remedies for infringement are available under the statute.

Civil Remedies

Where a work has been infringed, the owner of the copyright is entitled to sue within three years from the date of infringement. A number of different remedies are available. The court may issue an injunction to prevent the work from being further distributed. In addition, it may award damages. It can also demand that the infringing party account to the plaintiff for any profits gained from the infringement. As well, it may order up the offending material for destruction and can award legal costs against the infringing party. The courts may also halt the importation of unauthorized copies into the country through the intervention of the customs department. The Copyright Act indicates that in any action where the existence of copyright or the title to it is an issue, the work is presumed to be a work in which copyright exists and the author of the work is presumed to be the owner of the copyright unless the contrary is shown. Also, if the copyright has not been assigned or licenced, the name which is printed or indicated on the work is presumed to be that of the author of the work.

Criminal Remedies – Summary Conviction Offence

Once a judge has determined that there has been an infringement of copyright he may fine the guilty party up to $200.00 for a first offence, or in the case of a second or subsequent offence impose a fine or a jail term of up to two months.

Examples of Copyright Problems

There are numerous examples of breach of copyright and some successful actions which have been taken to prevent the continuing breach. Very few cases, however, ever reach the courts. The money involved is usually insignificant, and the cost of court proceedings too high, to have matters dealt with in this manner.

1. A work of art by Norval Morrisseau was reproduced as a greeting card by a government department. (Does the Copyright Act apply to Her Majesty?)
2. A fabricator attempted to exhibit a defective cast of a sculpture as an original work by someone else. The cast had been rejected by the original artist. Thereafter it was placed on its side, a different base was affixed, and it was signed by a foundry workman as his own creation. It was argued that this was a mutilation of the work and it was stopped.
3. A sculpture by John Nugent placed in front of a government building in Winnipeg was cut and removed without the consent of the artist. Although a work is created for a particular space, the artist does not appear to have any right, under copyright or otherwise, to have the work kept permanently in such a space unless this is done by way of contract provision. In some jurisdictions, the removal of this work would have constituted an infringement of the artist's "moral right." The concept of *droit moral* or moral right is discussed later.
4. There was also an instance where a Jack Bush greeting card, which had been licenced by his estate to the Art Gallery of Ontario, was utilized by a commercial firm. The firm had bought the cards from the gallery and added its own printing to the greeting card as a form of advertisement. Once the copyright problem was pointed out, it ceased doing this and apologized.
5. Some years ago, a drawing appeared in *Maclean's* magazine of Tom Thomson's *West Wind*. This famous painting shows a pine tree growing at the end of a point of land and leaning out over a lake. The work, however, was altered by showing a water skier being towed along in front of the tree. Probably a joke, and probably a breach of moral right. Could this be considered a breach of copyright in the Tom Thomson work?
6. At the time of the 1976 Olympics, various artists hung their works along the streets of Montreal. The city fathers considered a number of the works to be embarrassing because of their political or their sexually explicit content. Shortly before

the beginning of the Olympics the works disappeared overnight and were destroyed. This was a possible violation of the copyright and moral rights of the artists involved.

7. A book about the work of artist Ken Danby contained many full page colour reproductions of Danby works. An Ontario art dealer removed and framed these illustrations and sold them to the public as Danby reproductions. Could this be prevented by either the artist or the publisher as a breach of copyright? If not, was it an alteration which could be considered a breach of the artist's moral right?

8. Whether the destruction of a mural or other work of art would violate copyright is a moot point, as discussed below under the heading Moral Rights. However, altering or revising a work without the consent of the artist does violate copyright. If a work of art is damaged during the artist's lifetime, could it be restored by someone other than the artist? What if the "restoration" was done by someone else, and was so extensive that it amounted to a virtual re-painting of the work? Would this be a violation of the artist's copyright?

9. A serious problem exists today because of the photocopy machine. Often, photocopies of works are of a quality sufficient for resale purposes. Recently, an action was successfully taken to prevent a symphony from photocopying sheet music without obtaining permission or making proper payment. Some artists use photocopying machines as a means of creating art. Would another artist be infringing copyright if he copied such a work?

Moral Rights in Canada and Berne Convention Countries

The Copyright Act provides that independent of the copyright the artist has the right, even after assignment of the copyright, to claim authorship of the work and to restrain any distortion, mutilation, or other modification of the work that would be prejudicial to his honour or reputation.

This would prevent an owner from, for example, drawing a moustache on a work of art or shooting a pistol at it, or advertising that he will hold a painting mutilation party and inviting guests to see him mutilate a particular painting by the artist. There is some question whether the section covers destruction or only distortion or mutilation. To date, there has not been any definitive interpretation of this right in Canada. Various writers on the subject have felt that the right to prevent mutilation did not include the right to prevent total destruction of an art work. It appears that the basis of the moral right relates to preventing someone from putting forward an altered work as having been created by the artist. This is to prevent his reputation from suffering, since he could be subject to criticism and comment for altered works which were really not created by him. In France, a case reported in 1934 held that an artist could not make a claim when murals painted by him on the walls of a church were later destroyed by the church authority.

The question of the destruction of a work of art is not an idle one. It may occur during the destruction or alteration of any major building. There have been cases where murals in apartment buildings, private homes, and public buildings have been destroyed, demolished, or covered over without any thought given to copyright or moral right. There have also been cases where murals on ceilings have been hidden by new lower ceilings.

There have been a number of instances in the U.S. of works of art being mutilated or almost destroyed. For instance, the Arshile Gorky murals in the Newark Airport were covered over, and only recently have two of the twelve or fourteen panels been rescued from behind layers of paint; an Alexander Calder mobile in an American airport had its various parts welded together and its colour changed; a large kinetic sculpture on public display in California has been allowed to sit and rust away without proper care being taken for its preservation.

In France, Bernard Buffet created an interesting work of art from a refrigerator by decorating and painting it, both inside and outside. The work was purchased by a collector who later decided to remove the door and sell it separately. Bernard Buffet went to court and prevented this pursuant to his moral rights under French law. Recently, Jean Dubuffet sued a French motor car company which had purchased an environmental work for its offices. Part way through the commission the buyer refused to continue. Dubuffet was unsuccessful in arguing that the refusal to allow completion of the work constituted a breach of moral right. The court also found that he had not provided for this contingency in his contract with the buyer.

Moral Rights in France

The protection of artists' rights in France has two aspects: a proprietory right consisting of a temporary monopoly over the commercial exploitation of the work, and an intellectual or moral right relating to the creation of the work and its continued existence, for the protection of the reputation of the artist. The first right is dealt with in Canada as copyright. The second, however, appears to relate to the preservation of art and culture for both the artist and community.

Over the years, the French courts and tribunals created a moral right which had no real basis in the Napoleonic Code, the law of France. In 1957, this *droit moral* was codified into statute. The French moral right covers two distinct periods: the period of creativity, followed by the period during which the work of art is available to the public. The first aspect gives the artist the sole right to determine when a work of art is finished and ready to be delivered. The second contains the residual rights of the artist once the work has left his control. One of these residual rights is the right to have the integrity of the work maintained. Others include the right to claim authorship, to modify the work, etc.

The other interesting aspect of this moral right is the duration of its existence. Under the Copyright Act, copyright exists for the life of the author (or artist) plus fifty years. It appears, however, that under French law the moral right is a perpetual one, and cannot be waived or transferred.

Residual Rights or Droit de Suite

In Canada, there is presently no *droit de suite,* a right which allows the artist to share in the proceeds of a resale of the work of art. *Droit de suite* will be discussed more fully in the context of the Keyes/Brunet Report on Canadian copyright revision.

Exhibition Fees

There is no statutory necessity for exhibition fees to be paid to artists. However, it has been the custom of most institutions (with the urging of artist's organizations such as Canadian Artists Representation and the Royal Canadian Academy) to pay exhibition fees. Again, this will be discussed more fully in dealing with the proposed copyright revision.

Rental Fees

Here too, there appears to be no statutory obligation for artists to be paid rental fees by private commercial galleries, by art rental organizations, or by rental sections or departments of public galleries. However, this can be agreed to by contract between the parties, and appears to be fairly common today with most institutions. Again, this will be dealt with in the context of the Keyes/Brunet Report.

AMERICAN LAW OF COPYRIGHT

The Copyright Revision Act now governs copyright in the United States. This new federal Act came into force on the 1st of January, 1978. Prior to this date, a dual system consisting of federal statutory copyright for published works, and common law copyright under state law for unpublished works, was in effect. The new Act substitutes a single system of federal statutory copyright which protects a work from the time of its creation.

Prior to January 1st, 1978, common law copyright protected works as soon as they were created without any necessity for registration or reproducing the © which constitutes copyright notice. The federal copyright protected works only if they were registered or published with the copyright notice. Publication is a confusing concept when applied to the visual arts, but under U.S. law came to include any public exhibition of a work. If a work was exhibited without restrictions on photographing or otherwise reproducing it, copyright could be lost and the work fall into the public domain. Under the pre 1978 law, the common law copyright lasted until either publication or the registration of the

11

statutory copyright, i.e., during the period that the work was in the possession of the artist and not yet shown in public. Thereafter, the federal copyright provided protection for an initial twenty-eight year period and allowed one renewal for a further twenty-eight years. The new Copyright Revision Act almost entirely eliminates the common law copyright. The preemptive effect of the Act applies whether the work was created before or after the effective date of January 1st, 1978, and regardless of whether the work was published or not. State laws still operate, however, in the narrow area of subject matter outside the scope of the federal Act.

How to Obtain Copyright in the U.S.A. – (After January 1, 1978)

In order to obtain copyright in the United States, one of the following has to be done:

1. A copyright notice, consisting of a "c" inside a circle, the name of the artist, and the year of creation, must be placed on the work. Instead of a "c" in a circle, the word "copyright" or an abbreviation may be used. This notice must be placed in a prominent position so as to give "reasonable notice." It is not clear whether placing the notice on the back of a painting will satisfy this requirement.

2. Alternatively, such notice must be registered with the Copyright Office in Washington, D.C. This is *not* necessary to gain protection, but is available if required. Registration is necessary only for bringing an action for an infringement. This registration may occur at any time during the term of copyright. The form and content of the application for copyright are prescribed by the Act. Registration and the obtaining of a certificate of registration constitutes prima facie evidence of the validity of the copyright. Registration is a prerequisite to an infringement suit and therefore before any action can be instituted a certificate of registration must be obtained.

What if the Work Is neither Registered nor the Notice Placed on It?

Prior to the Copyright Revision Act, if a work was presented to the public without either registration or copyright noted on the work, copyright would pass into the public domain and no longer be available. A famous case in the United States, *The Letter Edged in Black Press Inc.* v. *The Public Building Commission of Chicago,* involved such a matter. The Press sought a judgment invalidating the defendant's copyright in the Pablo Picasso sculpture known as *The Chicago Picasso.* The defendant was The Public Building Commissioner of Chicago and the plaintiff was a publisher who wanted to market a copy of the sculpture and who maintained that the defendant's copyright was invalid because the sculpture was in the public domain.

Apparently, in 1963 certain civic centre architects representing the commission approached Picasso with a request to design a monumental sculpture for the plaza in front of the proposed Chicago Civic Centre. By May 1965, Picasso completed the model (maquette). The chief architect, who was in liaison with Picasso, had the maquette brought to the basement of the Art Institute of Chicago and shown without a copyright notice. The design of the maquette was subjected to an engineering analysis to determine the feasibility of constructing the monumental sculpture, and three Chicago charitable foundations undertook to finance the actual construction by contributing $300,000.00 towards the cost. An aluminium model of the design with some revisions was prepared. Picasso approved a picture of this model.

Later, the board members of the commission were given a private viewing of the maquette. It was approved by the commission, and $100,000.00 was sent to Picasso. This money was intended as the purchase price for the entire right, title and interest in the maquette, consisting of Picasso's design for the sculpture, and including the copyright and copyright renewals. Picasso refused to accept the money or to sign away his rights. He stated that he wanted to make a gift of the work. As a result, counsel for the commission prepared a deed of gift to be signed by Picasso, in which he gave the work and the right to reproduce it to The Public Building Commission, gave the maquette to the Art Institute of Chicago, and indicated that these institutions would hold the gifts on behalf of the people of Chicago.

Thereafter, city officials began a campaign to publicize the *Chicago Picasso.* As part of the campaign at least two press showings were conducted where the maquette was placed on public exhibition at the Art Institute. Although no copyright notice was affixed to the work, there was a notice in the Art Institute which read "The rights of reproduction are the property of The Public Building Commission of Chicago © 1966, All rights reserved." Press photographers attended the showing and later published pictures of the maquette and the aluminium model in Chicago newspapers and magazines of national and international circulation. As well, the commission supplied photographs of the maquette and of the uncopyrighted architect's aluminium model to members of the public.

A second showing took place in December of 1966 when U.S. Steel Corporation, with the knowledge of the commission, completed a twelve foot six inch wooden model of the sculpture and invited the press to photograph it. There was no copyright notice on the model, and the pictures were published without copyright notice. U.S. Steel also hired a professional photographer to take pictures of the model, which were used in the publicity drive. Pictures appeared in *Business Week, Holiday* magazine and *Fortune,* as well as in other magazines and newspapers.

Later, the maquette was displayed at the Tate Gallery in London. In conjunction with its exhibition at the Tate, a catalogue was published which included a picture of the maquette. Neither the maquette itself, nor the photograph in the catalogue, had any copyright notice.

On August 15th, 1967, the monumental sculpture was dedicated in the Civic Centre plaza. The sculpture bore the following copyright notice: "© 1967 Public Building Commission of Chicago, All rights reserved." In conjunction with the dedication, the commission distributed a commemorative souvenir booklet, containing drawings and photographs of the maquette and the aluminium model, to the honoured guests. Neither the booklet nor the photographs bore any copyright notice. On the day of dedication, the United States Steel public relations office sent out a press release with a photograph of the monumental sculpture. The photograph bore no copyright notice.

Later, the Art Institute of Chicago sent out its annual report which contained another uncopyrighted picture of the maquette. As well, the Art Institute continued selling a postcard of the maquette. The court was asked to rule whether or not copyright subsisted in the Picasso. The court determined that the copyright in the *Chicago Picasso* was invalid because general publication had occurred without the requisite copyright notice.

The common law protection was lost once the maquette was published, and when the statutory notice was not placed on this work it fell into the "public domain." When the monumental sculpture was finally completed, it could not be copyrighted because it was a mere copy, albeit on a grand scale, of the maquette which was already in the public domain.

In contrast, under Canadian law, copyright is automatic upon creation of the original work and can only be transferred by a "writing." In Canada, even if the copyright had been breached in a particular manner, the artist would not lose the copyright and would retain the right to prevent both a subsequent breach of copyright by the same party and any new infringement.

Under the new U.S. law, the omission of a notice does not invalidate the copyright if *either* of two conditions is met:
1. No more than a relatively small number of copies have been publicly distributed without the notice, or
2. Registration of the work has previously been made, or is made within five years of publication without the notice, and a reasonable effort is made to add the notice to the copies which have been publicly distributed in the United States, after the omission is discovered.

It should be noted, however, that the work will fall into the public domain if no effort is made to correct the error or if the work is not registered within five years of copies being published without the notice.

Another example of this "public domain" problem involved Robert Indiana, the artist who created the "LOVE" image. Since he neglected to protect the copyright, he did not receive a cent from any of the posters, reproductions, three dimensional sculptures, t-shirts, sweat shirts, etc., which came out with the red and green "LOVE" design. On the other hand, the man who created the "Happy Face" did remember to copyright that image and it is rumoured that he made many millions of dollars.

The new U.S. Act also indicates that an innocent infringer, who acts in reliance upon an authorized copy from which the copyright notice has been omitted, and proves that he or she has been misled by the omission, is protected from liability with respect to any infringing act committed before receiving actual notice of the registration.

As well, the Act states that the removal, destruction, or obliteration of the notice, without the authorization of the copyright owner, does not affect the copyright protection in the work.

Term

The term of the copyright under the Revised Act is increased to cover the life of the artist plus fifty years. This brings U.S. Copyright law into accord with the law of the Berne Convention countries. Posthumously published works are protected for fifty years from the author's death, and not for fifty years from first publication. This was done so that all of an individual's works would fall into the public domain on the same date, to avoid the confusion which arises when the term of copyright has run on some works but not on others.

The Act increases the term for statutory copyrights in existence on January 1, 1978, to seventy-five years. However, any pre 1978 copyrights which are still in their first term (the first twenty-eight years) will have to be renewed even if the time for renewal comes after January 1st, 1978.

Public Broadcasting

The Act permits public broadcasting stations to use works of art without the permission of the copyright owner. In the absence of any other agreement, the station has merely to pay a required fee which will be settled by the Copyright Royalty Tribunal.

Fair Use

The Act also continues the doctrine of "fair use." This permits a limited amount of copying for non-commercial purposes such as newspaper and magazine reviews, and educational study and teaching, without the permission of the artist.

Transfers of Copyright

The statutory copyright may be transferred, but only in writing. A sale of a work of art, without a written agreement to the contrary, will not transfer the copyright from the artist. Formerly, copyrights in the United States could be transferred orally. Also, there was a presumption that copyright was transferred on the sale of a work of art unless otherwise agreed. Under the new Act, the maximum period for which an artist may transfer a copyright is thirty-five years, after which time it returns to the artist or the artist's estate. As well, the Act takes into account the fact that different aspects of copyright can be dealt with separately, such as by giving rights in publication to one person, display to another, photographs to a third person, etc.

Commissioned Works

Prior to 1978, the law apparently allowed a person who had commissioned a work of art under contract to automatically obtain the copyright in the work unless the agreement with the artist specified otherwise. The new Act provides that the artist owns the copyright in such commissions unless there is a written agreement to the contrary (subject to the rule that works prepared by full time employees belong to the employer).

Moral Rights in the U.S.A.

As under the old law, the new Act does not provide for a "moral right." A famous case, *Alfred Crimi* v. *Rutgers Presbyterian Church,* exemplifies the problem. In that case, members of the National Society of Mural Painters had been invited to enter a competition to design and execute a mural to be placed at the rear of the church. From the twenty artists who competed, Alfred Crimi was chosen for the fresco mural, a painting 26 feet wide by 35 feet high, for which he was to be paid $6,800.00. A contract was drawn up between the parties, stipulating the terms of the commission, the price, the fact that the artist was to have the work copyrighted, and that the copyright was to be assigned to the ownership of the church. The mural was completed and signed by the artist. Thereafter, it appears that some of the parishioners objected to the mural, feeling that a portrayal of Christ with so much bare chest, placed more emphasis on physical attributes than on his spiritual quality. The number of objections increased for seven or eight years, until the church was redecorated and the mural painted over (without first giving notice to the artist). Once the artist discovered what had happened, he sued the church asking for three alternative remedies:

1. to compel the defendant to remove the obliterating paint from the mural and restore it;
2. in the alternative, to permit the artist to take the mural from the church at the church's cost, or
3. in the event that it could not be removed, a judgment against the church for $50,000.00.

The court held that from a study of other cases, the unconditional sale of the mural carried with it the transfer of the common law copyright and the right to reproduce. The artist took no steps to withhold or control that right, and the sale therefore constituted an abandonment of all of his rights. The court went on to determine that the claim of the plaintiff was without merit because the work had been sold unconditionally. There were no precedents to indicate any residual or moral rights in an artist for the protection of his artistic reputation in such circumstances.

The California Art Preservation Act

This law was enacted in 1979, and became effective on January 1, 1980. Although the U.S. federal government has introduced legislation to establish moral rights for artists anywhere in the country, California is the first U.S. jurisdiction to implement such laws. Unlike its European counterparts, the California Act allows an artist to restrain not only the alteration of his work, but also its destruction. The artist can also sue for damages if one of his works is damaged and his reputation injured. The new law applies to paintings, sculpture, and drawings; but specifically excludes murals or other works which are integral parts of a building and thus cannot be removed without damaging or destroying them. It also excludes works created under a contract for commercial use, and probably excludes prints, photographs, collages, and crafts.

The California Act differs from the classic *droit moral* in providing a finite term of fifty years, and in allowing the right to be waived by the artist.

The most controversial exclusion under the Act is for a work of art which is not of "recognized quality," a concept which the Act specifies must be determined with the aid of expert witnesses. While meant to exclude frivolous actions for the removal of someone's graffiti or for throwing away kindergarten finger-paintings, the exclusion has caused some understandable concern.

The Act applies only to damage or destruction caused intentionally, and to gross negligence in the course of the framing, conservation, or restoration of a work.

PROPOSED CANADIAN COPYRIGHT REVISION (Keyes/Brunet Report)

In April, 1977, the report, *Copyright in Canada: Proposals for a Revision of the Law,* by A.A. Keyes and C. Brunet, was made available by the Department of Consumer and Corporate Affairs. This report has been circulated to groups, associations, and individuals interested in copyright, seeking their views and opinions. Numerous briefs have been received by the federal government in response. The material is now back in the Department of Consumer and Corporate Affairs in Ottawa and will have to be dealt with by them. The earliest the Act will be revised, if at all, is 1984 or 1985.

The excellent Keyes/Brunet study reported on the history of copyright in Canada, the various committees and commissions which have dealt with copyright over the years, and considered the problems of copyright and its revision from both artistic and economic viewpoints. The existing Act was examined section by section, discussed in detail, and a recommendation for change (or no change as the case might be) made at the end of each section. The following are the aspects of the report which most affect the visual artist, gallery, and collector:

Ownership of Copyright

It was agreed that the author should still be the first owner of copyright. In regard to photographs, however, it was recommended that the ownership vest in the person owning the material on which the photograph was taken. This recommendation may be changed, however, since it would appear more equitable for ownership of the photograph to vest in the person who took the photograph than in the person who owned the negative.

As well, it was recommended that ownership of the copyright in a commissioned work should belong to the person commissioning the work *in the absence of an agreement to the contrary.* This obviously presupposes the possibility of contrary agreements. The principle that the employer is the first owner of the copyright in works made by his employees in the course of their employment would be retained. The report also supported the principle that a work commissioned for one purpose should not be used for another, in the absence of an agreement to the contrary. For example, a work of art commissioned for the Toronto subway system could not later be removed and placed in the Transit Commission's head office without a specific agreement by the artist.

Exhibition Rights

The authors of the report also recommended that any new act provide a specific right to exhibit an artistic work in public. They felt that the same arguments which warrant the granting of a "performance right" to playwrights or composers could be used to justify a similar right for artists. This right, which is not included in the present Act, is particularly important in regard to an artist's right to charge a fee for commercial exploitation and exhibition.

Moral Rights

It was recommended that the following expanded moral rights be provided in Canadian copyright law:
1. The author's right to enjoy respect for his authorship, including a right to restrain false attribution of authorship, and a right to restrain the circulation of copies of the work under his real name where he has chosen to use a pseudonym or to remain anonymous.
2. The author's right to restrain any distortion, mutilation, or other modification of his work, or any action in relation to the work which would be prejudicial to his honour or reputation.
3. The author's right to restrain any distortion, mutilation, modification, *or any other action* in relation to the *original* of an

artistic work in the nature of a sculpture, a painting, a drawing, or an engraving.

4. As corollaries to the right to publish:
   (a) That the author have the right to stop publication, i.e., distribution of copies, despite previous authorization, provided that the publisher receives compensation; and a right, after publication, to withdraw the work from circulation by having the first option to buy back copies available for sale;
   (b) That moral rights be attached to the person of an author, but that they may be transmitted on the death of the author to his heirs or, through testamentary disposition, to a third party;
   (c) That the term of protection for moral rights be the same as for pecuniary rights (life plus fifty years) and be accorded to original literary, dramatic, musical, and artistic works;
   (d) That remedies for infringement of moral rights be the same as those granted for the protection of the pecuniary rights, including injunctions and damages.

Under the present Act, it is doubtful whether an author has a remedy against someone falsely identifying him as the author of a work. As well, recommendations 2 and 3 make it clear that an artist should be permitted to prevent any distortion to the work whether prejudicial to his honour or not. Also, the recommendations indicate an intention to give protection to public or private works which have been created for a particular environment or place, in order to prevent them from being moved, altered, repositioned, etc. Recommendation 4 would now expand the remedies for infringement to include damages as well as injunctions. The recommendations, however, do not seem to extend to preventing the *destruction* of an original work of art.

Photographs and Engravings

Under the existing law, photographs and engravings (engravings are defined as including "etchings, lithographs, woodcuts, prints, and other works not being photographs") are not protected for the same period of time as other artistic works. Presently, "engravings" unpublished at the time of the author's death are protected until publication and for fifty years thereafter. Photographs are protected for fifty years from the making of the original negative from which the photograph was made. The report recommended that photographs and engravings enjoy the same term of protection as all other artistic works, i.e., the life of the author plus fifty years.

The Making of Three Dimensional Objects

The British Copyright Act indicates that an object of any description which is in three dimensions does not infringe the copyright in an artistic work in two dimensions, if the object would not appear to persons who are not experts in regard to objects of that description to be a *reproduction* of the artistic work. This provision is inserted to dispel any notion that copyright in a two dimensional work could be infringed by the making of a three dimensional work. The exception stipulates that the reproduction must not resemble the original in a way that would violate the artist's first right to reproduce a work of art in any material form and to convert it from two to three dimensions or vice versa.

Keyes and Brunet recommended that making a three dimensional object of a two dimensional artistic work should not constitute infringement if the object made is *not* a reproduction of the original work.

Droit de Suite

This is a "consequential right" whereby the creator of an artistic work shares in the proceeds of any resale of an original work. This right is limited to original fine art. It was first instituted in France and spread to a few other countries, such as Belgium and West Germany. Generally, it applies to public sales (i.e., at auction), and in some countries extends to sales by public dealers. It does not apply to private sales. Some countries calculate payments for *droit de suite* as a percentage of resale price, while others give a percentage of the increased value on resale. As of January 1, 1977, California has provided a *droit de suite* in the California Royalty Act.

Keyes and Brunet recommended that a *droit de suite* not be provided in any new Copyright Act. International treaty would require Canada to give such rights to foreign artists as well, and would result in a net outflow of funds from Canada. While such a right could be included as a term of the contract between an artist and a buyer, it would be difficult, if not impossible, to bind anyone who was not a party to the original agreement.

Registration of Copyright

The authors felt that there was no advantage in registration, and recommended that it be eliminated entirely.

ARTISTS' RIGHTS SOCIETIES

Various arts groups and organizations in the United States and Canada, including Canadian Artists' Representation, have suggested the establishment of an organization to monitor copyright and ensure the payment of proper fees. This contemplates an organization similar to CAPAC, BMI or ASCAP, which provide such services for composers, musicians, and performers, and would be a non-profit organization with a secretariat. An artist would register with the organization, and copyright fees would be collected by the organization and forwarded to the artist during his lifetime and to his estate thereafter. Organizations, magazines, public institutions, and others who require the use of copyright would be able to contact the organization for information about the artist, or a particular work, and for addresses. This is a possible future development in both Canada and the United States.

PATENTS AND INDUSTRIAL DESIGNS

A work of art may also fall under patent law as being an "invention." The concepts and registration requirements under the patent law are very technical and difficult to deal with in this short space. Special technical publications are available which deal with this topic. A patent may possibly be the applicable protection for a mechanical work of art such as a kinetic sculpture, or a sculpture or assemblage with any moving parts. It may also be applicable to laser art and its extension into holography. Such works should be examined by a competent patent attorney with a view to determining whether they are proper subject matter for a patent.

Another Act which gives protection to property is the Industrial Design and Union Label Act. This, like the Patent Act or Copyright Act, is a federal Act and applies throughout Canada. Unlike copyright, an industrial design must be registered in order to be protected in Canada. The term "originality," when used in copyright, means simply not copying someone else. When used in industrial design, it means something that has the quality of innovation; something new that has never been done before. The design may be a new design for a lamp, radio, television set, lighter, furniture, hanging mobile, etc. The Act applies to items meant to be reproduced in quantity.

An industrial design will be registered if it is found that the design is not identical to one previously registered, or does not so closely resemble any design already registered as to cause confusion. A certificate of registration is issued which gives an exclusive right for an industrial design for a term of five years, and which may be renewed for one additional five year period. The Act indicates that the author of any design is considered to be its proprietor or owner unless the design was created for another person for good or valuable consideration. Designs are assignable under the Act. In order for the design to be protected it must be registered within one year of its first publication in Canada and, after registration, each article must be marked with the name of the proprietor and the letters "Rd." If the articles are difficult to mark, the information can be provided on an accompanying label.

The regulations under the Act indicate that when a design is reproduced, or intended to be reproduced, on more than fifty single articles, unless together they form only a single set, it must be registered under this Act rather than under the Copyright Act. Therefore, where an artistic work is intended to be used as a model for fifty or more separate items created by some form of industrial process, the work is determined to be an industrial design and must be protected under the Industrial Design and Union Label Act rather than the Copyright Act.

A British case in 1925 held that sketches which had been made for "advertisement show cards" (representing a male and a female crowned figure) were designs capable of being registered under the British equivalent of our Industrial Design and Union Label Act. The Copyright Act did not apply to them because they were used or intended to be used as models for items produced by an industrial process. Since the sketches had not been registered as required by the British Act, the plaintiff lost the right to sue for damages when the designs were copied.

It is very difficult to distinguish between a design and an artistic work under these various Acts. For example, is a Christmas card a design or an artistic work? Judges seem to indicate that each case must be determined on its own facts. The question is an important one in regard to editions of graphics and sculpture above fifty in number. Various authors have suggested a definition which would establish that the difference between an artistic work and a design is that a design is intended to be applied to, and become part of, another article, whereas an artistic work exists on its own and is appreciated for its own artistic qualities. For instance, if a print was sold as an "original print," it would be considered an artistic work. If, however, the original print was applied to wall coverings, its nature would change and it would become a "utilitarian item" requiring registration under the Industrial Design and Union Label Act. In this context, it should be noted that for some years Chateau Mouton Rothschild has had artists such as Chagall, Picasso, and Motherwell design labels for wines of a particular vintage. If protection of things such as these is required in Canada, the question arises of whether the artist can rely on the Copyright Act or whether he must register under the Industrial Design and Union Label Act. Lawyers would have a great deal of ammunition to argue the question either way.

CHAPTER 2 THE ARTIST, THE DEALER, AND THE PATRON

SALE THROUGH COMMERCIAL DEALERS

The professional artist will usually have his work handled by a commercial art gallery. This enables the artist to have his work shown to the largest possible audience in the best possible manner. It also frees him from the difficulties and embarrassment of attempting to sell his own works. It leaves him time for doing the thing he does best – creating art.

It is not unusual for art dealers to have commercial relationships with dealers in other cities and countries, nor is it uncommon for a dealer to have more than one branch. Some Toronto dealers have branches in Montreal, others have branches in Calgary; some Toronto, Montreal, and Vancouver galleries have relationships with galleries in New York, London, and elsewhere. The work of the late Jack Bush, for instance, was shown in Toronto, New York, and London, England on a regular basis, and on a less frequent basis in Zurich, Hamburg, and Boston—all through such commercial gallery arrangements. Similar arrangements allow foreign artists to have their work shown in Canada. There are numerous advantages to dealing with commercial galleries in addition to those above. For instance, colour photographs and transparencies which commercial galleries have used for catalogues, frequently are made available for museums and museum catalogues when an artist achieves a show in a public art gallery or museum. The notices and posters prepared by galleries can become collectors' items, and often posters and reproductions can be a new source of revenue for the artist and the gallery, especially in limited or signed editions.

It is usual for a particular art dealer and gallery to have a "stable" of artists. Being added to such a group may be helpful to the image and reputation of a newcomer, and give him credibility earlier than would normally occur. In addition, each private dealer and gallery has its own list of customers. It is common for the gallery to have a party on the opening night of the artist's show and invite its best customers to this private preview. The artist is generally present and has the opportunity to meet collectors and museum personnel.

Contracts

As long as the relationship between the artist and the dealer is harmonious there is really no need for a written contract. However, without such a contract there is no recourse to a document in the event that the harmony ceases to exist, or creditors of the dealer are seizing assets, or perhaps even a

23

bankruptcy occurs. As long as the artist's work is selling well and the dealer is solvent, few problems arise. But if either of these two conditions changes, each of the parties may have a different version of the outstanding agreement between them.

Outright Purchase and Sale

There are many variations to this form of contract. It has been not unusual to see this type of arrangement for Miro, Chagall, Motherwell, Andrew Wyeth, etc., and for Picasso during his lifetime. It is possible for an artist of this calibre to set his own terms and seek the best deal he can get with competing art dealers. If a particular dealer cannot continue to offer a worthwhile arrangement for the artist, the artist can find another who will deal on an acceptable basis.

In this type of contract, the artist may feel that once he has been paid he no longer needs to be concerned with the manner in which the particular dealer sells the work, or the final price that the dealer receives. However, the wise artist will still make certain that there is a written contract. The artist's livelihood is at stake, whereas for the dealer the artist is only one "supplier of a product" to the gallery. Often the contract is less important to the dealer than it is to the artist, yet oddly it is the artist who most frequently fears entering into a contract. A contract of this type should cover at least some of the following items:

1. Discussion of the "end price." This is to ensure a means of consultation between the artist and the dealer to arrive at a sensible end or retail price. It would not do anyone any good to have the paintings inflated out of all proportion to the original sum paid to the artist. Ultimately, there will have to be more shows later on and if the prices are "wrong" the work will not sell. It is unusual for an artist and dealer to agree to reduce the price later on, since this would be considered an embarrassment. Instead, what would happen is that if the price were fixed, and not changed for some years to come, few (if any) sales would occur until the price, through inflation or increased reputation, came back into line. There have been occasions in Canada when artists or dealers have raised the prices of works of art beyond their market potential, to the detriment of all parties. The advice given to Jack Bush by the noted critic, Clement Greenberg, was to let his work be a bargain—get the work out and placed and increase prices on a gradual basis. Clement Greenberg always considered it better to have more work sold at a lower price than to place a very high value on the works and sell only one or two a year, since the latter does not help an artist expand his reputation.

2. Control over the exhibition of the work if it is to be exhibited outside the dealer's gallery. This is especially true in regard to private showings by the dealer at public institutions or through arrangements made with other commercial galleries.

3. Control over the use of any paintings in a "group exhibit." This would ensure that the artist would be shown with artists equal in calibre to himself.
4. The dealer may wish to try to obtain an acknowledgement that he will be the sole and exclusive dealer for the artist in a certain territorial area for a given period of time, and that the artist himself will not market his works in that area except through the particular dealer.
5. The artist may wish to obtain a list of purchasers in order to keep a record for his own purposes.
6. The parties may want to agree on the number of paintings which have to be purchased per year or the number that the artist has to make available.
7. If the artist has extra works available, should the dealer have a first right of refusal to purchase these works, and what would become of the works if they were not purchased by the dealer? Would the artist be free to sell them to someone else in the same territory?

These are but a few of the considerations that would be dealt with by a contract of outright purchase. Needless to say, this type of contract is rare. The more common form of contract or arrangement is one where the dealer acts as the artist's agent in selling the works of art to the public. For this service, the artist pays a certain percentage of the sale price to the art dealer. This is normally called a "consignment contract."

The Consignment Contract

When the dealer acts as the artist's agent for the purposes of sale of the work, the artist retains "ownership" of the work of art until it is sold, and if it is not sold the work is returned to the artist. At no time does the gallery owner actually own the work, but merely receives a commission for his services based on the ultimate sale price of the work.

Legislation

It is important to point out the different kinds of consignment relationships which can exist between an artist and his dealer, because these may have different legal consequences and requirements under provincial law. The province of Ontario has enacted a Personal Property Security Act (P.P.S.A.), and similar legislation exists in Manitoba. Also, at the time of writing, this kind of legislation is being considered in Saskatchewan and British Columbia, and the provinces of Alberta and New Brunswick are also known to be showing interest.

Where such legislation is in effect, in order to preserve the artist's ownership rights against creditors of the art dealer, certain forms of consignment relationships must be documented in writing, and notices filed in the applicable provincial office for P.P.S.A. registration. Whether this is necessary will depend upon whether the agreement between the parties could be described as a security agreement. The most common form of consignment contract, in which the dealer simply agrees to exhibit the artists work, either on an ongoing basis or through shows at the gallery, probably does not fall into this category. However, if the dealer is obligated to *purchase* any works or to accept and sell a particular number of works, or if he is obliged to give monetary advances to the artist, then the agreement could be construed as one of security, and will require registration. In relationships of this kind, a two stage process is required to ensure that the artist retains ownership of the works until they are actually sold. There must first be a written contract between the parties, and then a notice of that contract must be filed in one of the offices established throughout the province for registration under the P.P.S.A.

Therefore, it is usual (or at least prudent) to add a schedule, or schedules, to a consignment contract, listing the works of art as they are received from time to time. The artist should acknowledge his release of any interest in the works as they are sold.

In Ontario, registration is valid for a three year period only, and must be renewed if it is to extend beyond that time.

Although registration of a pure consignment contract may not be necessary to preserve the artist's rights, the existence of a written agreement will be the easiest way to establish that the relationship is one of pure consignment and that the artist is the owner of the works, in the event that creditors of the dealer seek to seize any works for payment.

The States of New York, California, and Connecticut have special legislation dealing with consignment between the artist and his dealer. This legislation will be discussed at the end of this chapter.

Oral Agreements

What if there is neither a written agreement nor registration? As long as there is an oral agreement that title to the works will remain with the painter, then as between the dealer and the artist, the artist will have title to the works of art. A written contract, of course, will spell out the details of the arrangement much more clearly, and can be resorted to in order to determine the actual relationship between the parties. An oral agreement may very well become "fuzzy" over the years. The major problem, however, is third parties. If the contract is not one of pure consignment, and is not in writing and registered in accordance with the Personal Property Security Act, these works may be seized by gallery creditors. This will be inevitable in the event of a bankruptcy of the dealer, where the goods would fall into the estate of the bankrupt rather than be returned to the artist. There was a case in one of the western provinces where a famous Canadian print maker had left many thousands of dollars worth of prints with a particular dealer. The agreement was an oral one, and eventually the dealer went bankrupt. Since there was no written agreement reserving title to the artist, it could not be properly filed. As a result, all the work of the artist passed into the hands of the dealer's trustee in bankruptcy. Not only did the artist lose both the work and the proceeds, he also had his commercial market interfered with by the block sale of these works by the trustee in bankruptcy. The same problem could arise, and the same result occur, with subsequent mortgagees of the dealer who may have been given a chattel mortgage or debenture on the stock-in-trade of the gallery.

Once an artist and dealer decide they would like to do business and a contract is to be drawn, what are the major areas of concern and negotiation?

Written Agreements

With the increase in the value of works of art, and a proliferation of artists and galleries, written contracts are becoming more common. A check list of possible contract terms has been added as Appendix A to this chapter. Some of the more important matters for consideration by the artist and dealer are the following:

EXCLUSIVITY

Is the gallery the exclusive dealer for a particular area and, if so, for what period of time? How many pictures are to be provided to the dealer by the artist? Does the dealer also have access to earlier works?

COMMISSION

What rate of commission will be paid by the artist? Does the dealer have an obligation to sell any particular number of paintings per year?

SALES BY THE ARTIST

Is the artist free to make any kind of sale or gift in the dealer's geographical area without violating the agreement? For example, can he make gifts to family and friends? Is there a limit on the number of gifts and sales which can be made by the artist? This question is particularly important for sales to provincial or federal government agencies. For example, can the artist sell to the *Art Bank* free of commission to the dealer? Can he sell to the Canada Council, the Ontario Arts Council, or the Alberta Heritage Foundation—without paying the full, or a reduced, commission to the dealer? Can the artist *negotiate* with a government agency or a public commission, or is this the exclusive field of the dealer? If the artist has more than one dealer, which dealer would be involved in government sales? Would it depend, for instance, on the location of the agency or commission?

COSTS

The contract will have to specify responsibility for framing, insurance, damage, stretching, or casting sculpture. Who will be responsible for payment for announcement cards, opening night cocktail parties, and photographs to be distributed to various magazines or newspapers? These and other costs should be specifically allocated in the agreement.

CONTROL

Who has control over the date of the show and the time period? Who has control over the hanging of the show? Who has control over whether a painting by the artist can be exhibited in a group show, either within or outside the gallery? Who has control over the use of the painting for various museum or public gallery shows? Ultimately, who has control over the sale prices?

COPYRIGHT

The transfer or licencing of any aspect of copyright, such as the right to photograph a work or make any reproductions of it, must be in writing and would usually be included in the consignment contract. See Chapter 1 for a detailed discussion of copyright.

PAYMENT

When is payment made to the artist and how is it made? When a work of art is sold on a "time" basis by the gallery, payments from the purchase may extend over a period of many months. It is common for a dealer to give a purchaser time to make payment for the picture. Should the artist have to wait for his percentage of the sale price until the dealer has received payment in full? Should he get a portion of each instalment payment based upon his portion of the sale price? Should he be paid first? This is a matter of negotiation. Who should take the risk of the purchaser not completing the contract and defaulting on payment? What if the purchaser goes bankrupt before making payment, and the work now forms part of the bankrupt collector's estate because title to the work was not reserved by the dealer or not registered so as to affect third parties? What if the work is sold to a purchaser who pays in part by the exchange of another work of art with the dealer? On what basis is the artist paid? Should the artist have the right to inspect gallery records and invoices? Can the dealer give discounts? To whom? Institutions only? At whose expense?

PRACTICAL ASPECTS

Each contract will vary with the particular artist and dealer. Rarely are two relationships the same. What is important is to recognize the various areas for consideration and to deal with them before any problem can arise.

In addition to the legal aspects, there are a number of practical aspects to be considered in entering into a contract with a dealer. It is extremely important for the artist to be able to discover the dealer's reputation in the marketplace, as well as his financial integrity. A starting point would be to ask other galleries and artists about their knowledge of, or experiences with, the dealer. Another important source of information is the Professional Art Dealers Association of Canada. This association is a non-profit organization composed of dealers across the country who qualify for membership. Membership is by invitation only, and the prospective member must have been in business a minimum of five years, have made a contribution to the art and cultural scene of the area in which he is located, and be financially responsible. Once a gallery has become a member, it is governed by the code of ethics of the association. As well, the artist may check with organizations such as the Royal Canadian Academy, Canadian Artists' Representation, and the Ontario Society of Painters or other regional artist groups. In the United States, the Art Dealers Association of America Inc. would be appropriate to contact for information on particular galleries. As well, since the dealer is in business, the Better Business Bureau and Chamber of Commerce could be consulted.

Special Consignment Laws in the United States

The States of California, New York, Connecticut, Ohio, and Texas appear to be leaders in legislation related to the visual arts. These states have enacted legislation dealing with consignments of art work by artists to dealers for the purposes of exhibition and sale. These statutes attempt to clarify the fiduciary or "trust" character of the artist/dealer relationship when a consignment contract is involved. They also create potential criminal liability for improper misappropiation of the consigned art or the proceeds of such consigned art. As well, the Acts restrict the artist's rights to voluntarily waive the trust relationship. No such laws are in effect anywhere in Canada.

New York Legislation

This legislation (Article 12-C of the New York General Business Law), was enacted in 1966. It indicates that notwithstanding any custom in trade, whenever an artist delivers a work of fine art of his own creation to an art dealer for exhibition and/or sale on a commission, fee, or other basis of compensation, the delivery is deemed to be "on consignment." As a result, the dealer is deemed to be the agent of the artist and such work of fine art is *trust* property in the hands of the dealer. As well, it makes any proceeds from the sale of the work of art trust funds in the hands of the dealer.

The term "art dealer" means a person engaged in the business of selling works of fine art, but does not include an auctioneer. The term "fine art" means a painting, sculpture, drawing, or work of graphic art. The term "artist" means a creator of a work of fine art or, if deceased, his heirs or personal representatives.

A work of art initially received on consignment is deemed to remain trust property even when the gallery buys the work for its own account, and it remains trust property until the price is paid in full to the artist. If the work is sold to a bona fide purchaser before the artist has been paid in full, the proceeds of the resale are also deemed to be trust funds in the hands of the dealer to the extent necessary to pay the balance owing to the artist.

Any agreement or contract whereby the artist waives the provisions of the legislation is void, except that the section dealing with proceeds which are to be held as trust funds may be waived if the waiver is clear, in writing, and signed by the artist. Such a waiver is not valid for the first $2,500.00 of gross proceeds of sales received in any twelve month period, and is not valid with respect to a work of art received on consignment but subsequently purchased by the dealer for his own account.

California Law

The California law was passed in 1975 and is loosely modelled after that of New York. In New York, however, general commercial law applies to loss or damage, while the California Act has a provision holding the gallery responsible for any loss or damage to the work during the term of consignment. As well, the California legislation does not permit any contractual waiver by the artist, unlike New York which allows a partial waiver.

It is to be noted that by creating the *trust* provisions, not only is the dealer responsible for holding these trust funds separate and apart from other accounts and solely for the artist, but the funds are insulated from the claims of other gallery creditors.

Connecticut Legislation

In 1979, Connecticut passed legislation dealing with consignment of art works to galleries. Now such consignments must be in writing, establish a repayment schedule to the consignor, and set a minimum resale price. (Note, however, that it is not clear whether the minimum price setting provisions conflict with U.S. federal anti-trust laws which prohibit price fixing.) The Connecticut legislation also establishes that the dealer is responsible for the costs of insurance on any works consigned, and for loss or damage to the goods. The works may only be displayed if the consignor has given prior written consent, and if displayed, must attribute authorship to the artist.

The Artist's Agent

A recent phenomenon in the art world is the "artist's agent," who acts as an art "broker" or middleman between the artist and the public. He generally represents a number of painters, sculptors, and printmakers; and sometimes operates in a restricted geographical area, particularly in parts of the country where the artist is not represented by a dealer. The agent or representative normally will have the works on consignment, and will often make them available to the public at less than retail price. Usually, the agent does not have facilities to display the works, but rather makes appointments to show the works elsewhere. He may, in fact, not have the works themselves to show at all, but only have photographs of the works to show prospective purchasers. An agent may attempt to sell to galleries as well as directly to the public, and also will try to obtain public or private commissions for the artist. The agent may also attempt to interest a commercial gallery in representing the artist, in exchange for a fee from the artist or an extra commission on sales.

This field is a recent development, and not yet clearly defined enough to hazard a guess as to the type of contract or other safeguards which should be utilized.

The "Private Dealer"

Another recent phenomenon has been the growth of the private dealer in Canada. Most often, the private dealer operates out of his own residence, which may have been modified for the purposes of displaying the art works in that setting.

Unlike the artist's agent, who represents only the artist, the private dealer often obtains works for resale on consignment from collectors. Such dealers also often purchase at auction or elsewhere for resale at a profit. It is not usual for private dealers to allow works to be returned for credit, or to allow works to be traded in for others.

Some private dealers have commissioned artists to produce fine art prints. Normally, the dealer will purchase the entire edition of the work at a wholesale price and then act as the distributor and/or retailer of the edition.

The Artists' Cooperative

For many younger or newer artists whose reputations have not yet grown to the point where their work interests a commercial dealer, the artists' cooperative is one of the few ways to get a show of their work before the public. Although such cooperatives exist in many different forms, generally such outlets are non-profit organizations run by the artists themselves. They are sometimes also operated as adjuncts to art schools or colleges. Commissions from sales are generally used to maintain and operate the cooperative. Such outlets are, of course, rarely found outside of the major urban centers.

THE PRIVATE PATRON – CONTRACT CONSIDERATIONS

History

Throughout history, many artists existed only through the patronage of a particular church or royal family. Even today, it is not uncommon for artists to have a particular private or corporate patron, especially during the artist's formative years. The patron often makes a stipend available to the artist on an annual basis, in return for all or a portion of the artist's output during a specified period. In this situation, the artist has very little bargaining power and often must deal with the patron on the patron's own terms. There is little room for flexibility other than negotiation of the time period of the contract and the monetary consideration.

Contract Terms

Today, the more usual type of patron is one who requests a particular work of art to be done for his home or office. Often, portraits are requested of retiring chairmen, public officials, judges, and others in public life. If the contract between the dealer and the artist stipulates that the dealer has control of this particular type of contract, most of the problems will be handled by the dealer, and the artist can look to his contract with the dealer to determine his rights. For the dealer, or the artist if he is dealing directly with the patron, it is important to have a written contract between the parties and that its terms be clear. Some of the concerns to be dealt with by such a contract are as follows:

1. Artistic control of the work — i.e., must the work be approved by the patron and if so, what are the criteria for approval?
2. The time for delivery;
3. Approval of the installation site and responsibility of the parties if the space differs from the original size specified to the artist. (In a case in which we were involved, the artist had created a large mechanical and light or neon piece for a specific spot. The dimensions were given to the artist by the builder, and the work created was based on these dimensions. Unfortunately, the final site varied considerably in size from the original dimensions given and the work of art did not fit the space and could not be cut down because of its mechanical and electrical functions.);
4. Whether the work can be moved or resold by the patron;
5. How payment is to be made and at what stages during the commission. It is wise to arrange for payment to occur in different stages, e.g., one-third at the time of execution of the agreement, one-third upon acceptance of the final maquette or drawing, and the balance upon completion of the project;
6. Responsibility for the various arrangements such as insurance, travel, installation, etc., and whether these costs are to be paid in addition to the price of the work of art;
7. What if the work is proceeded with, but the final drawings or maquette are not acceptable to the client? Should there be a cancellation charge? Should the payments made to date under the agreement remain with the artist? Should there be a further fee chargeable? Who has rights to the work, and the preliminary drawings or maquette, in the event of cancellation?
8. Who should own copyright in the final work? Who should own the copyright in the maquette or drawings or preliminary drawings?
9. Should there be an obligation on the patron to maintain the

work, especially if it is a mural or a sculpture with moving parts?

10. Does the artist give a warranty on his work?
11. What if either the artist or the patron dies during the period of the contract? Is the agreement terminated? What if the work is half built? What about payments made on account by the patron? Should insurance on the life of the artist be considered by the patron?

Satisfaction of the Patron

A most difficult problem to deal with is a commission for a portrait. The English common law (there is no reason to expect that Canadian law would be any different) has been extremely unsympathetic to the artist in this situation. The problem that may arise is that the patron is not satisifed with the "likeness" and refuses to pay. Only after the work has been created does the artist receive notice that the work is not satisfactory. The English courts have uniformly held that the contract itself must determine the rights of the parties. Is the contract one which allows the patron to determine whether or not he is satisfied with the work of art? If this is the case, then if for any reason the patron does not find the work satisfactory, he does not have to pay for it. Thus, there is a great risk in accepting this type of commission unless the contract enables the artist to present a portrait or bust that is "reasonably satisfactory." It would be expected in this case that the court would try to determine what was reasonable in the circumstances rather than allow the patron to make the determination unilaterally. For the artist, the answer may be to get as large a percentage of the fee "up front" as possible.

The problem becomes even more difficult when the work of art is in the form of a mural or is somehow affixed to an existing structure or thing. If the contract states that the patron is to be satisfied, and he is not, what can either party do about the result? The patron is not satisfied, yet he now owns a work which cannot be removed. The artist has painted or prepared the work and has not been paid. In these circumstances a court may well decide that the artist should be paid on an "unjust enrichment" basis which would give the artist payment for time and materials but probably not the amount that was provided for under the agreement.

As a result, you can see the difficulties that may be encountered and why an extremely carefully worded contract is necessary in such a relationship, as well as the importance of obtaining prepayment of at least a large portion of the fee for the commission. The famous case of the portrait of Winston Churchill by Graham Sutherland comes to mind. The portrait was not to the satisfaction of the surviving family and was destroyed. Another situation involved a former President of the United States, Mr. Lyndon Johnson, who also was not satisfied with a portrait and refused to approve it.

Recently in Kitchener, Ontario, a patron commissioned an artist to paint his portrait. The artist had various photographs taken of the client and agreed to paint the picture. After painting the facial aspects of the portrait, the artist somehow lost the photographs upon which the painting was based. Nevertheless, he completed the portrait, which appeared to be a very fine example of his work. The portrait was delivered to the patron who upon unwrapping it was shocked to discover that instead of showing his head of white hair the artist had made him bald. Needless to say, the portrait was rejected and the artist received no money. A number of questions arise: Would the artist have the right to sell the work? Would it be an embarrassment to the patron? Could he prevent its sale or exhibition in public? To date, there have been no cases in Canada deciding these points.

THE PUBLIC PATRON

Until very recently it was common for all levels of government, as well as public or educational institutions, to utilize some of their funds for the commissioning of major works of art. Generally, this was associated with a new building or development. Major works of art are often commissioned for new university buildings, city hall squares, subway systems, airports, government buildings, and hospitals. Until recently, the Department of Public Works in Ottawa had 1% of its funds for capital expenditures set aside for works of art for new federal buildings. The minister of the relevant department could decide if funds were to be allocated for this purpose or not. Recently, however, there have been cutbacks in government, and restraints on spending which have given rise to cuts in budgets. Very often, the art work has been the first thing to go. It is hoped, however, that this situation will change in the near future.

Municipal governments have also commissioned or purchased works of art. Not too many years ago, the Henry Moore sculpture entitled *The Archer* which stands outside the Toronto City Hall was a *cause celebre* in that city and one of the reasons for the defeat of its mayor. Toronto has, however, maintained its resolve and gone on to commission a major wall sculpture, made of different kinds of nails, by David Partridge, which is now located inside the main entrance to the City Hall. The Art Gallery of Hamilton recently commissioned a major sculpture by Kosso Eloul which has become the "symbol" of the gallery. The Toronto Transit Commission, when building its new subway line, followed Montreal's lead and arranged for a major work of art to be created for each of the new subway stations.

Expo 67 and the Olympics both led to an outburst of works of art commissioned from Canadian artists for use in conjunction with those events. Artists have also been commissioned to create works for the Canadian pavillions at other World's Fairs.

Contract Considerations

In many of these situations, the commissioning party will have formulated a contract which it will ask the artist to sign. Rarely has the artist considered negotiating changes in the contract or providing his own form of contract to the institution. Often the artist is so pleased to receive the commission that he refuses to "rock the boat." Unfortunately, few organizations have contracts which are tailored for the particular use to which they are being put. In the past, there has been difficulty because of the use of contracts which were created as general subtrade contracts. These contracts would better apply to the work of plumbers or electricians than that of an artist. As well, we have seen a number of contracts which were unfair to the artist and did not recognize the artist's needs — they were one sided contracts for the benefit of the institution. This appears to have occurred without malice, but rather in an attempt to protect the institution or commissioning organization at all costs, and with no perspective into the world of the artist. Such contracts can generally be revised once an explanation is given to the public body.

Some Contractual Concerns in Public Commission Contracts

1. What is the obligation of the artist?
2. How is payment to be made? Is prepayment possible?
3. If the work is to be constructed as part of the building, who is responsible for obtaining a building permit?
4. Are there firm starting and completion dates? Is there a warranty by the patron that the building and the site will be available? If the site is not ready, what are the consequences?
5. What will be the effect of the space being made available in a different size? If the work must be rebuilt, who is responsible for the cost?
6. Is there a cancellation fee?
7. Who has copyright?
8. Who will maintain the work? This is one of the major considerations in providing a work of art to a public institution, i.e., will it survive? Will it have to exist in a damaged state? Questions of "moral right" may also arise. As an example, what if a mural is prepared for a particular government building or site, and later the building is to be demolished or the site totally changed? Can the mural be altered or destroyed? Can the work be moved? Does the contract take into account an alternative? In contracts with the Toronto Transit Commission for its subway art, the enlightened management of the Toronto Transit Commission agreed that if the subway station was ever demolished or not continued in use, the work of art would be offered as a gift to as many as three different public institutions, and if not accepted by any of the institutions would be offered back to the artist or his

estate before it could be destroyed.

9. Arbitration – can disagreements be resolved by arbitration rather than by the courts?
10. Are transportation, insurance, and other disbursements associated with the creation of a work of art paid for separately?
11. What if the work is rejected? Is there a clause dealing with ownership of such a rejected work?
12. Is ownership reserved by the artist until payment is made in full?
13. If it is an electrical or kinetic type work, is there a warranty period required from the artist?

It is suggested that for public commissions, it is of benefit to both parties to have their solicitors tailor a contract to the particular circumstances, rather than use a government or institutional form contract. When the problems of such form contracts are pointed out to government departments or institutions, they are often quite willing to cooperate in obtaining a properly drawn agreement. It is important for the artist to recognize this special need and to make the patron aware of the problem.

PRINT CONTRACTS

Printmaking Contract

The artist, his dealer, or a printmaker may initiate the idea of producing a print or set of prints. If a decision is made to do this, the artist will need to know how to proceed. Artist/dealer contracts often state that the dealer will have the exclusive right to sell such prints, but they do not usually give the dealer exclusive rights to select the manner in which the prints will be produced. Normally, this is within the jurisdiction of the artist.

Some artists prefer to have their own printing equipment and do their printing at home or in their studio. For instance, the American artist, Sam Francis, and the Canadian artist, David Blackwood, prefer to work in this manner. Sometimes the type of prints to be created will determine the method to be used. If, for example, mono or single authographic prints are to be made, such as Harold Town has done, or a small series of etchings like those of David Blackwood, it makes sense to do them in the artist's studio rather than sub-contract the work to a print publisher. The same is true of unique prints such as those done by Paul Fournier. On the other hand, if the usual large series of prints (75 to 200 together with artist's proofs) is planned, then sophisticated printmaking equipment may be required. This will be especially true of work done by a complicated process such as lithography, etching, engraving, or some other form of printmaking which requires the help of a master printer. Often the artist will create the image which will then be translated to a lithographic stone or plate by a master printer under the direction of the artist. The print will then be produced with the help of professional printers, again under the direction of the artist. (The definition of an original print is a difficult one and will be discussed separately in Chapter 3.)

Once the artist determines that he wishes to print the work in consultation and cooperation with a print *atelier,* a contract should be entered into between them. The artist will seek out a printmaker in whom he has confidence, and negotiate with the print studio for the production of the prints. It is common to produce four or five different images at one time, which are normally variations on a theme. This is usually most practical from a marketing and "cost" point of view.

The contract between the parties would normally specify some of the following items:

1. The number of prints.
2. The number of artist's proofs which the artist will receive (generally without charge).
3. The number of prints available to the printmaker without charge.
4. The price to be paid for the printing, and whether this is to be a flat fee or on a percentage basis.
5. Control of the artistic integrity of the work, and the quality of the work (the *bon à tirer*), is usually reserved by the artist.
6. Ownership of copyright.
7. The payment of federal and provincial sales taxes, if applicable.
8. Restrictions as to the time period, and perhaps the manner, in which the print(s) may be sold.

Print Distribution Contract

Usually associated with the printmaking contract is a further contract between the artist and a print distributor. Often, the artist or dealer will enter into a contract with the print distributor who in turn arranges for the printing of the work, preferably on terms specified by the artist. In this case it will be the print distributor who will enter into the contract with the printmaker. The print distribution contract should contain most of the following elements:

1. A provision stating that the artist will create an original print in a particular medium.
2. An agreement by the distributor to enter into a contract with the print workshop. (Normally, a copy of the agreement is attached.)
3. A warranty by the artist as to the originality of the work.
4. A warranty by the artist that he has the right to enter into the agreement (i.e., that he is not bound by a dealer/artist agreement).
5. The time period and geographical area for distribution.
6. The edition size.
7. The number of artist's proofs.

8. The cost of production.
9. The suggested retail price.
10. Artistic control of the print.
11. The length of time for production.
12. Terms of payment to the artist. (Remuneration may be by way of a fixed sum payable to the artist periodically, or may be a percentage of the wholesale or retail price. If the latter, provision is normally made for the inspection of the books of the distributor relating to the print, coupled with accountant's statements provided on a periodic basis.)
13. Amount of coverage and responsibility for insurance on the works.
14. Determination of what is to be done with any unsold prints. (For example, the artist may be given a right to purchase them at cost, they may be wholesaled in bulk, or provision can be made for an extension of the agreement.)
15. Cancellation or obliteration of the master image at the completion of the printing in the presence of both parties.

ART RENTAL AGREEMENT

It is common these days for public art galleries to have art rental departments. Often as an inducement to membership, members of the art gallery have the right to enter into a "members' gallery" or "rental gallery" to view various works which can be rented or purchased. Usually the rental paid is credited against the purchase price. These works are often supplied by the artist directly, and sometimes are supplied by commercial art galleries. The agreement to supply a work for rental takes into account the following matters:

1. The right of the gallery to hold the work for a specific period of time.
2. Matters of insurance, transportation, and crating.
3. How the rental fees should be split.
4. What commission is chargeable by the gallery in the event of the sale of the work.
5. Questions of copyright.
6. Warranty by the artist or dealer that he has the right to enter into the agreement without it being in conflict with any existing artist/dealer arrangement.

A similar type of agreement would be entered into by the artist in regard to any works of art given to a charity auction.

LOAN AGREEMENTS WITH PUBLIC GALLERIES

It is common for art galleries to request various works of art still owned or retained by the artist, for gallery purposes such as a group show, a retrospective of the artist, a travelling show, etc. It is also common for dealers to lend works to such shows, since it enhances the reputation of the artist and at the same time gives publicity to the gallery. Often the institution has a form of contract which it has prepared for such purpose. As well, organizations to which the institution belongs may have prepared a "standard form" agreement to be used by the member gallery. Although it is a standard form, the artist should carefully look at the form to see if it is applicable to the fact situation at hand. Similar contracts will be used when a gallery borrows a work from a private collector.

BOOK PUBLISHING AGREEMENT

Recently, it has become fairly common in Canada to see both a limited edition and a trade edition book published about a particular artist. Often the limited edition will consist of a leather bound copy of the book, together with an original work or works by the artist, usually in the form of a limited edition print or series of prints. An example of this type of book is the volume on Norval Morrisseau by Jack Pollock and Lister Sinclair. Other examples are books on Ken Danby, Alex Colville, and ones soon to be released on André Biéler and Rita Letendre. The limited edition book is often commercially necessary in order to finance the trade edition. Generally, the trade edition will sell less than ten thousand copies. The great exception has been the book by David Silcox and Harold Town on Tom Thomson, which was a complete sell out of 50,000 copies and was probably the largest selling art book ever published in North America.

In such a book contract, the artist will need to consider the following matters:

1. Approval of the author by the artist. (This is a crucial matter, for the right author may make it possible to obtain a greater readership, and will enhance the book by his reputation as well as enhance the reputation of the artist.)
2. Whether payment is to be a percentage of gross sales, net sales, or a flat fee.
3. Territorial jurisdiction of the printer.
4. Subsidiary rights, if any, such as soft cover, serialization, movie, television, and associated rights.
5. Copyright.
6. The publication date.
7. A warranty of copyright by the artist in the works to be reproduced.
8. Artistic control over the book, the title, and the cover and jacket copy.
9. An agreement by the artist to provide (and a description of) the works of art for a limited deluxe edition.
10. An agreement by the artist to sign and number the art works and the books.
11. Any advances to be made to the artist.
12. Provision for certified accountant's statements.

13. The number of books the artist will receive without charge, and the price to be paid for additional deluxe or trade copies.
14. The rights of the publisher in the event that the artist does not perform.
15. Insurance on the manuscript and the works of art.
16. Any rights of first refusal to the publisher on additional book publishing projects.
17. Concepts of arbitration to settle any dispute.
18. Rights of the artist in the event that the book goes out of print (and a definition of what will constitute being out of print).
19. Whether the publisher can assign the contract.
20. Obligations of the publisher for costs associated with production of the prints such as atelier costs, packaging costs, etc.
21. Approval by the artist of the quality of reproduction, colour fidelity, etc., of the art works.
22. Whether the artist's agreement to allow the works to be reproduced for the book extends to reproduction for advertising posters, catalogues, etc.
23. Responsibility for obtaining permission to reproduce works if any copyright is held by third parties.
24. A minimum promotional budget may be specified.

APPENDIX A

ARTIST/DEALER CONTRACT CONSIDERATIONS

1. The exclusiveness of the contract, and the pictures to be provided.
2. The rate of commission.
3. Whether the artist can make gifts or sales himself, and any other sales which can be made without payment of the dealer's commission.
4. The number of shows to be obtained.
5. The time period of the contract.
6. Rights in regard to authorization of any group shows.
7. Responsibility for insurance (fire, theft, and travel risks).
8. Responsibility for damage to the work.
9. Artistic control of the shows.
10. Control of prices.
11. Payment for announcement cards and control over their form.
12. Payment for advertisements and opening night parties.
13. Payment for the cost of photographs for advertising or catalogues, and for the catalogues themselves.
14. Determination of how pictures are sold, and how payment is to be made.
15. Whether the contract is assignable by the gallery.
16. Who has the right to works created prior to the contract.
17. Who has control of storage and where.
18. Whether the artist guarantees the parts of sculptures such as kinetic and light works.
19. Who pays for framing and who owns it at the end of the term of the contract.
20. Who owns copyright.
21. Whether the artist has the right to inspect inventory records and obtain information about the number of pictures that are held in the gallery.
22. If damage or deterioration of works occurs in the gallery, who determines the choice of the restorer, pays the cost, and has rights to inspect?
23. Does the gallery have the right to sell pictures at auctions? Does it have an obligation to protect works of art by that artist sold at auctions by placing a reserve bid? Does it have an obligation to try to buy works being sold by collectors?
24. What commissions will be paid to the dealer for work sold under separate contract to government or private individuals? Who determines the price? What discounts are permitted and to whom?
25. Who takes the risk if a sale involves time-payments?
26. How is the money allocated as it is received?
27. What happens in regard to exchanges of works of art with a customer? What happens in regard to a return?

28. Does the gallery have the right to purchase for its own account? At what price?
29. Does the gallery have the right to rent the picture?
30. Who gets the financial benefit of any prizes received?
31. Does the artist have the right to inspect the gallery's financial records in relation to his work?
32. Should there be any guarantee of sales given to the artist?
33. Should there be liability insurance for electrical and other types of work which go on display? Who should pay for it?
34. Who has the right to negotiate private and public commissions and on what basis?
35. Who has the right to publish original prints, reproductions, or posters?
36. How should disputes be resolved? Should there be a system for mediation established to prevent having to go to court?
37. Is the contract with the gallery subject to some particular person being owner or director of the gallery?
38. Who gets paid for leasing and rental agreements and what percentage?
39. Are inter-gallery transfers permitted?
40. What provincial or state law is applicable to the contract?
41. Will there be advances of funds by the dealer? It is not uncommon for contracts of consignment to be modified by advances made to the artist. This is especially true where there is a proven market for the artist's work. The artist may not have a show more than once every two years, and as a result may not have sufficient funds to live on during the fallow periods in between. If the gallery has confidence in the artist, and is financially able to make advances, this is often done. Generally, the advances are made against future pictures to be given to the dealer for resale. Because of the additional benefit to the artist, and the cost to the gallery, the percentage of commission to the gallery may be increased. As well, the dealer may be given the benefit of purchasing work at a better discount for the dealer's own stock. Any such contract requires very accurate accounting on a periodic basis to determine the state of affairs at any given time, i.e., whether the artist owes the gallery pictures against advances already received, or vice versa.

CHAPTER 3 THE COLLECTOR: PURCHASE OF WORKS OF ART

PURCHASE AT AUCTION

There has always been much romance and folklore surrounding auctions and auction conduct. We have all heard of wonderful bargains obtained at auctions by knowledgeable purchasers when unknown works have turned out to be important masterpieces. The auction has also been thought of as the place to obtain bargains by purchasing in competition with the professionals. You could obtain a work of art at the same price that a dealer would pay, and save one-third to one-half the price of the work on the retail market. So the story goes.

Unfortunately, few masterpieces go unnoticed on the auction floor. As well, you may be bidding against non-professionals who do not necessarily know value, and even where you are certain that you are bidding against a dealer it is difficult to know whether he is bidding for his own stock, or as agent on behalf of a collector from whom he receives a fee. If he is bidding on behalf of a collector, you are not competing with him for a wholesale price, but in fact against another collector for retail price or more. Even if the dealer is bidding for himself, you do not know why. For instance, he may have pre-sold the piece and thus be prepared to pay a "retail price," or it may be a work from a period that he requires for his stock and for which he is prepared to pay a premium. Works are purchased for many reasons other than their quality or their price. They may fit a particular need which has nothing to do with their fair market value at the time. It is, therefore, not unusual to see works sold at auction above retail prices. Dealers are sometimes heard at auctions lamenting that "the successful bidder could have bought a similar work at my gallery for less than he paid for it here." In the past, auctions had more of a "gaming room" than a fine art atmosphere. Trying to identify the "big shooters" and recognize their bidding technique has been a favourite pastime. Knowing who was bidding on a particular work could influence other bidders. Everyone was on the lookout for new "highs" (always greeted with applause), or the great long shot purchased for a pittance and later revealed as a long lost masterpiece worth many thousands of times what was paid for it.

Today there are professional publications which document prices at auctions and categorize the prices of various "schools" or even individual artists. Auctions are now treated like a stock market; quotations are given and future conduct predicted on the basis of analyses of past auction room sales. Special services for this purpose can be subscribed to and reports received on a periodic basis. Books are published which indicate the artists who have been the "hottest" sellers at auction over the past years, what "schools" to avoid purchasing because they have reached new highs, what artists and types of art may be under priced and should be purchased now for future gain. Auction houses and their sales are now looked at under a microscope and publicized as if part of the commodities exchange.

In the 1978/79 auction season, the three largest art auction houses, Sotheby-Parke Bernet, Christie's, and Phillips, all reported the highest net sales totals ever obtained. Sotheby reported $412,000,000 worldwide, Christie's $250,510,000, and Phillips $68,220,000 (all expressed in U.S. dollars). These totals do not include the additional 10% buyer's premium paid or the amounts bid for any lots which were unsold (reported in the Artnewsletter of September 4th, 1979).

Advice to Bidders

What advice, then, can be given to the brave collector who wishes to attend an auction and the even braver collector who is prepared to bid?

Catalogue Terminology

Buy the catalogue and read it very carefully. There are terms and conditions in the catalogue which are peculiar to auction sales. *You may not be buying what you think you are.* The description of each work must be carefully examined and cross referenced to the glossary of terms used in the catalogue. For instance, there is a vast difference between a work described as:
(a) By Tom Thomson;
(b) By T. Thomson, or attributed to Tom Tomson;
(c) School of T. Thomson;
(d) In the manner of Tom Thomson, or "Circle of Tom Thomson";
(e) In the style of Tom Thomson;
(f) Studio of T. Thomson;
(g) Thomson;
(h) After Tom Thomson.

Of all these descriptions, only the first would normally describe a work of art actually by, and warranted to be by, Tom Thomson, and even in regard to item (a) there may be a restricted warranty rather than a warranty or a guarantee as to the actual artist. For instance, following the name of the artist one catalogue indicated that "the work is ascribed to the named artist, either by an outside expert or by our own staff and such ascription is accepted as reliable by the gallery. This is our highest category of authenticity in the present catalogue, and is assigned only upon exercise of our best judgment, no unqualified statement as to authorship is made or intended." Instead of buying a painting, you may be buying a lawsuit.

There is also a difference between the phrases "signed" and "bears signature." The former usually means that, in the opinion of the auction house, it is the signature of the artist, whereas in the second case they are less sure.

The same is true for dates. "Dated" means that it is the opinion of the auction house that the work was executed at the time of the date whereas "bears date" indicates that it may not have been executed at that time.

Know the rules of the game before you play. Each catalogue at each auction sets out the conditions of the auction. The conditions of sale generally also contain information regarding the warranties, the representations, and the obligations of the auction house. They normally also set out the purchaser's rights in regard to the return of a work of art in the event that it is not as represented in the catalogue. Generally, the conditions also set out the obligations of the purchaser and the rights of the auction house in the event of non-payment.

Reserve Bids

The concept of the reserve bid should be clearly understood. A reserve is generally indicated in the catalogue by an asterisk next to the description of the work. However, there may simply be a general statement in the catalogue indicating that each sale is "subject to any reserve bid placed... by the vendor." The reserve bid is normally placed on the work by the consignor, and indicates that there is a minimum amount for which the work may be sold. Generally, a work will start at an opening price and be bid up in various multiples ($500, $1,000, $10,000, etc.) at each bid. When a bid is received from the floor that is below the reserve, the auctioneer will normally bid on behalf of the reserve bidder up to the next multiple and then await a further bid from the floor. This is generally done until just before the reserve price is reached, after which time the action remains with the floor, subject to bids by the auctioneer on behalf of persons who have placed an advance or absentee bid. If the reserve price is not reached, this fact is not generally announced at the auction. Instead, the high bidder will be informed privately that the price offered has not reached the reserve.

An auction catalogue will also often contain a provision stating that any lot may be withdrawn from sale without prior notice. Since the catalogue is often prepared and distributed well in advance of the sale, a lot may have been privately sold beforehand.

Advance Bids

It is customary for auction houses to accept advance bids from persons who are unable, or do not wish, to attend the auction. Arrangements are made in advance, by bidders who have passed the appropriate credit check, to have the auction house bid on their behalf. In this way, the purchaser can both remain anonymous, and avoid the excitement of the auction room which might cause him to bid more than he would normally intend to pay.

Telephone Bids

Arrangements can also be made in advance to bid by telephone. Such an arrangement is sometimes used for transatlantic bids on major works of art.

Presale Estimates

As a convenience to customers, auction house catalogues normally contain presale estimates of the price range anticipated for each work being auctioned. Prospective purchasers can examine these to see what the auctioneer anticipates will be the "spread" within which the work will sell. This will sometimes give a clue as to the reserve bid since the reserve is generally somewhat less than the presale estimate. Presently, the reserve bid is not revealed to the buying public, although there has been agitation (especially in the United States) to have reserve bids made public before the auction. There has been some interest in this matter by the Attorney General's office in the State of New York.

Catalogue Services

The catalogues of each auction house may be purchased on a yearly basis. In this case, the catalogues are automatically sent in advance of the sale, and the ultimate sale prices are forwarded a few weeks later, indicating the successful bid on each work sold. These price lists now generally indicate which works were unsold because they did not reach the reserve price. Often this is done by omitting the lot number of the unsold work from the price list. Earlier lists often failed to indicate works bought back by the consignor. Recently, however, this has changed, particularly in the United States where the fear that some jurisdictions might pass legislation to require this has led to voluntary compliance.

In Canada, auction catalogues often do not contain pre-estimates. As well, the conditions are rarely spelled out as carefully as they would be in an American or British catalogue.

Payment of Auction House

Until very recently, the auctioneer's commission was almost invariably paid by the vendor and, as a result, the auctioneer's obligation was to the vendor. First in Britain, and more recently in the United States, two of the major auction houses (Sotheby Parke Bernet and Christie's) began charging a commission to both the vendor and the purchaser. This commission is generally about 10% of the sale price to each. Where the vendor alone pays the commission, it is usually 20%, but may be less on higher priced items. In Britain, some question has been raised by the commercial dealers as to whether it is proper for the auction houses to charge both the vendor and the purchaser a commission, since this might give rise to "divided loyalties" and conflict with trust or agency laws. This question may yet reach the courts in Britain. Despite such problems, which also exist under Canadian law, Sotheby's has recently announced that it will follow the same practice here, and it is possible that other auction houses will follow suit. The practice is advantageous for the auction house since it is able to attract more consignments when the vendor is charged only 10%. Both the auction house and the vendor are aware, of course, that purchasers will rarely bid a full 10% less than they would have otherwise. Collectors bidding at such auctions should bear in mind that not only will this 10% be added to the price of the work, but any applicable sales tax will be calculated on the price of the work including the commission. In most provinces this will mean that the price paid will be almost 20% higher than the amount of the final bid.

The Preview

The wise bidder will generally not offer on an item unless he has attended the preview and carefully examined the work. Often the work will differ from the catalogue reproduction. The colour may be different, repairs or scratches on the surface may not be revealed by the photograph, or the work may have been repaired or patched on the back.

Especially worrisome at auction is the purchase of framed fine art prints. How carefully have the works been framed? If the work has a mat on it, is the mat non-acidic or is it one of the colourful mats which sits against the work and over the years has "bled" both colour and acid on to the work so that it is now permanently stained or damaged? Mats made from "pulp paper" may cause irreversible damage. As well, prints may have been permanently damaged by being "dry mounted," i.e., cemented down onto a cardboard backing and then framed. Like a postage stamp to a stamp collector, for resale purposes the back of a print is as important to its collector as the front.

As well, the margins on a work may have been cut down for various reasons, such as to fit a particular frame or area in which it can hang. This may also be covered by a mat and not revealed. At a recent auction of Eskimo prints, for example, one of the bidders insisted on having the frames removed. When the auctioneer complied, it was found that the margins on many of the works had been cut, and that some of the prints had been dry mounted as well.

Another problem which arises with prints and other works on paper which have been framed, is the problem of the closeness of the work of art to the glass covering it. If the work is pressed against the glass, when the frame is removed much of the image may be affixed to the inside of the glass rather than to the paper. There was a case recently, involving a Matisse crayon drawing which had been improperly framed. When the frame was removed, much of the crayon drawing remained on the glass rather than on the paper. Fortunately, by qualified restoration it was possible to transfer the image back to the work without permanent damage, and a law suit was avoided. Often permanent damage does occur and cannot be corrected. Therefore, a wise buyer who wishes to purchase a work which is framed under glass will ask the auction house to have the frame and glass removed so that he can inspect the work. A refusal to do so by the auction house could be a warning signal to avoid bidding on that particular work of art.

The Law of Sale at Auction

History

To a great extent, Canadian auction sales are governed by the English common law. Many jurisdictions in the United States are also governed by similar law. In addition, most if not all common law provinces in Canada have a Sale of Goods Act which regulates sales by auction. For instance, in Ontario, the Sale of Goods Act indicates the following:

(a) Where the goods are put up for sale in lots, each lot is prima facie the subject of a separate contract (i.e., a separate sale);

(b) The sale is complete when the auctioneer announces it is complete by the fall of the hammer or in any other customary manner and until such announcement is made any bidder may *retract* his bid. (This is rarely known by bidders, who feel that once they have made the bid they are automatically bound by it. The Sale of Goods Act states otherwise);

(c) Where a sale is not notified to be subject to a right to bid on behalf of the seller (i.e., a reserve bid), it is not lawful for the seller to bid himself or to employ a person to bid at such sale or for the auctioneer knowingly to take any bid from the seller or any other person acting for him. Any sale contravening this rule may be treated as fraudulent by the buyer. This would lead to the right of the buyer to the return of his money;

(d) A sale may be notified to be subject to a "reserved or upset price" and a right to bid may also be reserved expressly by or on behalf of the seller. This implies that such information would have to be noted in the catalogue or announced by the auctioneer prior to the particular work being auctioned;

(e) Where a right to bid is expressly reserved, but not otherwise, the seller or any one on his behalf may bid at the auction.

The rules of the common law, as long as they are not inconsistent with the Act, apply. Therefore, rules relating to the law of principal and agent (that the auctioneer acts as agent for the owner and has the right to sell), fraud, misrepresentation, duress or coercion, mistake or other invalidating cause, continue to apply to contracts for the sale of goods.

Law Reform in Ontario

The Ontario Law Reform Commission report on the Sale of Goods, which appeared in the middle part of 1979, specifically covered sales by auction. The commissioners felt that certain changes in the existing Sale of Goods Act should be made, and recommended the adoption of the following provisions in place of the existing Section 56 of the Sale of Goods Act:

(a) Where goods are put up for sale by auction in lots, each lot is the subject of a separate sale;

(b) A sale by auction is complete when the auctioneer so announces by the fall of the hammer or in any other customary manner;

(c) A sale by auction is *with reserve* unless the goods are put up without reserve (this was subject to the dissent of two commissioners);

(d) In an auction with reserve, the auctioneer may withdraw the goods at any time until he announces completion of the sale;

(e) In an auction *without reserve,* after the auctioneer calls for bids on the article or lot, that article or lot cannot be withdrawn unless no bid is made within a reasonable time;

(f) In an auction *with or without* reserve, the bidder may retract his bid until the auctioneer's announcement of completion of the sale, but a bidder's retraction does not revive any previous bid;

(g) A right to bid may be reserved expressly by, or on behalf of, the seller;

(h) Where a seller has not reserved the right to bid, *it is not lawful,* except in the case of a forced sale, for the seller to bid or to employ a person to bid at the sale, or for the auctioneer knowingly to take any bid from the seller or his agent. (A forced sale would be one by a mortgagee or a creditor.);

(i) Where subsection (h) is contravened, the buyer may treat the sale as fraudulent and may avoid the sale and recover damages, *or* may affirm the sale and recover damages, *or* claim an abatement in the price.

Catalogue Representations

It is clear that in Canada, the terms of the sale at auction are governed not only by the material in the catalogue, but by the announcements and representations made immediately preceding the commencement of the sale. Before the sale, the seller may make a deviation from the terms stated in the catalogue, and even if the buyer did not hear, or was not present at the commencement of the sale, such deviation would form part of the terms of sale (it would, however, be a possible defence to an auctioneer's suit for payment if the buyer was not aware of such change). Nor does it appear that the standard of care in making catalogue descriptions is very high. Where the description of property is inadequate, but not misleading, the courts have held that they would not interfere with the sale.

There have also been cases indicating that the *owner* of a work is not responsible for any warranties which the auctioneer made without authority. Whether the misrepresentation will allow the purchaser to rescind the agreement depends on the relevance of the representation and how material it was to the purchaser making the bid.

Catalogues may, however, be very important in containing disclaimers of liability which may or may not be effective in enabling the auction house to avoid liability. The whole concept of disclaimers made to consumers is now undergoing vast changes of interpretation by the courts. In some cases there is consumer legislation being passed to prevent exculpatory type warranties by vendors or manufacturers, and to hold the manufacturer or seller responsible regardless of the disclaimer, especially if it is unreasonable or unfair.

Warranties

It would appear that there are generally no specific warranties applicable to sale at auction, apart from sale of goods legislation and general contract law. It is respectfully suggested that there is room for specific legislation dealing with auctions, both as to warranties of authenticity and as to conduct. The question of express and implied warranty is a difficult one to deal with. As mentioned above, catalogues usually contain exculpatory clauses negating warranties. An example of such a condition in a major Canadian auction house catalogue in 1979 appeared as follows:

Each and every lot is sold by the vendor with all faults and defects and with all errors of description and is to be taken and paid for whether genuine and authentic or not and no compensation shall be paid for same.

The next paragraph, however, softens the stand of the auction house for it continues:

Notwithstanding the previous conditions of sale, if within 14 days after the sale of the lot, the purchaser gives notice in writing to [the auction house] that the lot sold is a deliberate forgery and within 7 days after such notification the buyer returns the same to [the auction house] in the same condition as at the time of sale and satisfies [the auction house] that considered in the light of the entry in the catalogue the lot is a deliberate forgery, then the sale of the lot will be rescinded and the purchase price of the same refunded.

It is clear, however, that this qualification to the general disclaimer of warranty is a very limited one indeed. Firstly, it applies only to "deliberate forgery," and this phrase is left totally undefined. Would it be possible to have an "undeliberate forgery?'' We can assume that the warranty would extend to a "Krieghoff" painted by Tom Keating, but would not apply to a work which had merely been wrongfully attributed to Krieghoff. Would it apply to a work which was not created in order to pass it off as the work of another, but later had a signature forged to it? Secondly, the purchaser must "satisfy" the auction house that the work is a "deliberate forgery." We may be able to assume that the auction house could not profess to be unsatisfied in the face of convincing evidence, but what kind of evidence would be required to establish the necessary facts? Inevitably, such proof would require obtaining expert opinions, probably in writing. Is it reasonable to expect that a purchaser could obtain such information within 14 days? Even if it were possible to make an appointment to have a work examined within such a short period, the very nature of the kind of forgery to which the warranty is limited suggests that it might only be discernable through the use of sophisticated and time consuming (not to mention expensive) chemical analyses and x-ray examination. Presumably, a purchaser is not going to bid on a work if he already suspects its authenticity. Should he be put to the expense of seeking expert opinion on every purchase in order to insure himself against the possibility that he has, in fact, not received what he has paid for?

This type of condition must give purchasers a great deal of concern. As well, it will surely give lawyers a great deal of concern, especially in light of the Sale of Goods Act in Ontario and similar acts in other provinces. Generally, under such acts there are these implied conditions and warranties:

(a) That the seller has the right to sell the goods;
(b) That the buyer will have and enjoy quiet possession of the goods;
(c) That the goods will be free from any mortgage or encumbrance in favour of a third party not known to the buyer before or at the time the contract is made;
(d) Where the sale of goods is by description (as described in the catalogue, for instance) there is an implied condition that the goods will correspond with the description.

The Act generally gives the purchaser the right, in circumstances where the goods are in fact different from those advertised, to rescind the sale and reject the goods or, if the goods have been accepted and title has passed to the buyer, to sue for damages though not to rescind the transaction. As well, statutes dealing with limitations of action become important, for even where the work differs from the work as described, if sufficient time has passed from the date of sale (six years in Ontario), any action is at an end. This applies not only in regard to misattributions and wrongful descriptions of works sold at auction, but also in some instances to a work purchased in good faith from a vendor who does not have title to the work.

TITLE

The one warranty which is clearly available to the purchaser is the warranty that the vendor has good title to the picture. If this is not the case, the purchaser is generally entitled to rescind the contract and obtain a refund. Again, this must be looked at in the light of limitation statutes.

STOLEN WORKS OF ART

Generally, a thief does not have any right, title, or interest in a work of art, and as a result, a purchser buying from a thief has no higher right to the work than the thief himself. This, however, is not an absolute. A case is currently about to be heard by the courts involving a painting by a famous Canadian artist, which was "owned" by a succession of purchasers, some of whom apparently displayed it publicly, who were unaware of the fact that it was stolen from an institution. If an innocent purchaser buys at fair market value from a thief, and keeps the work on open display, the original owner would generally lose the right to sue for the return of the work after the appropriate limitation period has passed. In Ontario the limitation period is six years. In the case above, the vendor will certainly use this argument. The last purchaser, who had the painting confiscated by the police, will argue that the vendor did not obtain good title to the work himself, and thus did not give good title to the purchaser and must, therefore, refund the purchase price.

Express Warranties

Any of the warranties expressly made by the auctioneer, if given negligently or falsely and proved to be untrue, would give rise to rescission and the return of the funds to the purchaser.

Where there is any doubt as to the proper party to be sued, the auctioneer, the auction house, and the vendor, (if he is known) should all be joined as party defendants.

It is interesting to know that the classic definition of *caveat emptor* comes from the English case of *Wallis* v. *Russell* reported in 1902. The judge in the case, Lord Justice Fitzgibbon, stated that the doctrine applies "to the purchase of specific things, e.g. to a horse or a picture upon which the buyer can and usually does exercise his own judgment." In addition to pointing out the care that must be taken by someone who is choosing a specific object, the judge, by choosing horses and pictures to illustrate his point, is suggesting that the risk is equally high for the purchaser of either.

With the vast amounts of money being spent today at auction, it seems odd that, contrasted with something like the stock exchange, the auction market is almost completely unregulated. As mentioned earlier, there appears to be great opportunity for the applicable governments to regulate auction procedures and auctioneers, and ensure that they operate in a legitimate and proper manner. There are numerous auction houses throughout the country, many of which are "store front" operations with the potential for a great deal of possible abuse. The very reputable auctioneers most certainly would want regulation of the industry, at least by a self-regulating body if not by government.

Advertisements for Auctions

The auctioneer is a fiduciary (i.e., in a trust position). He is a fiduciary for the vendor and is obliged to notify the public of the time, place and the manner of sale. The advertisement itself, however, is no more than an *invitation* to attend and bid if you so desire. It has no contractual value. If in fact a sale does not take place, the prospective purchaser has no remedy for things such as loss of time, travel expenses, etc. Cases to this effect have occurred in Canada and in Britain, and this also appears to be the law of most, if not all, of the states of the United States of America. One such case occurred in New York in 1936, when a collector travelled from overseas to attend an auction, only to discover that the sale had been cancelled while he was en route. In response to a suit by the would-be purchaser, the court ruled that he had no cause of action.

Puffing

It is noted in the Sale of Goods Act that unless there is a notification by the vendor that the vendor or his agents will be bidding on the work, such bids may not be accepted. Even if there is such notice, this does not entitle the owner to engage in "trap bidding" to artificially inflate the price. When an unauthorized bid from the owner is accepted, the Sale of Goods Act permits the buyer to rescind.

Mock Auctions, Chill Bidding, Damp Bidding, The Ring and Private Auctions

Anything constituting a mock auction is illegal by statute in both New York State and California. A mock auction is one where the seller alone, or in collusion with a buyer or buyers, pretends to consummate a sale but no real sale takes place. Such "auctions" could be used to artificially inflate the value of a particular work, or the work of a particular artist or school, by establishing a false precedent as to market value. In Canada, such an auction may be illegal under the Criminal Code.

The Criminal Code may also apply where a purchaser deprecates the quality of goods in order to obtain them at a better price for himself. This is usually called *chill bidding* or sometimes *damp bidding.* This type of chill bidding may also give rise to an action for slander of goods or title. A famous case of defamation involved the art dealer Lord Duveen, who was sued for defamation after claiming that a painting owned by a Mr. Hahn, and which was being auctioned, was not an original Leonardo Da Vinci. In fact, Duveen had never seen the picture. At trial, the jury could not agree on a result and before retrial the matter was settled out of court by Lord Duveen for $60,000.00 (a great deal of money in 1929).

Another illegal tactic is for a group of bidders to agree in advance not to bid against each other on particular pieces which they all have some interest in acquiring. In England, this was known as "the ring." An English Act of 1927 makes this type of bidding illegal. Again in Canada this may be prohibited by provisions in the Criminal Code dealing with conspiracy. Policing such conduct, however, is almost impossible. The ring generally operates by the dealers agreeing not to compete against each other for certain works. Once these works are acquired as cheaply as possible, a second auction known as a "private" or "knock out" auction is held among the dealers involved. Any profits or losses resulting from this knock out auction are divided among the participants. The reserve bid was developed in England to neutralize this type of ring control over prices.

Other Laws Relevant to Auction Practices in Canada

In various common law provinces, there are also Acts, such as the Business Practices Act in Ontario, which deal with unfair trade practices. The Ontario Act deals with false, misleading, or deceptive consumer representations, especially as they relate to a particular standard, quality, grade or style of goods. It also deals with misleading statements of opinion on which a consumer relies to his detriment. The Act indicates that no person shall engage in any unfair practice, which includes the actions noted above, and states that a contract induced by such conduct may be rescinded. The Act also indicates that it is not possible to contract out of the terms of the statute. There do not appear to have been any cases under the statute concerning auctions or auction sales.

The Criminal Code

The Criminal Code of Canada, as well as civil legislation, affects auction sales in Canada. The federal Criminal Code is applicable to deliberate, false, or misleading statements or conduct, under the heading of false pretences or fraud. Exaggerated commendation or deprecation of the quality of anything is not a false pretence under the Act unless it is carried to such an extent that it amounts to a fraudulent misrepresentation of fact. Whether this is so, of course, depends on the facts of each situation. The Code also contains provisions making it illegal to enter into an agreement, whether oral or written, for the purchase or sale of goods without a bona fide intention of actually buying or selling them, where this is done to profit from rising or falling prices.

PURCHASE FROM COMMERCIAL GALLERIES

In most countries there is a network of private commercial galleries which are in the business of buying and selling works of art. Commercial galleries have been in existence since the demise of the church or state patron. In Canada, many leading galleries belong to the Professional Art Dealers Association of Canada, a non-profit trade organization. The association sets standards for membership, establishes a code of ethics for its members, and attempts to establish and regulate proper business practices. In the United States, the Art Dealers Association of America fills a comparable role. There are also dealer associations in Britain, France, and Germany, as well as in other countries.

In addition to the galleries which belong to these associations, there are numerous art galleries, private art dealers operating from their homes, and furniture and interior design stores which carry works of art or ornamentation as part of their inventory. Works may be purchased from any of these sources. A survey some years ago indicated that most "art" was purchased from furniture stores and interior designers and not through fine art galleries.

The best advice that can be given in regard to all such purchases of works of art is the following:

1. Deal with a reputable art dealer; one who has been in business for a number of years, is held in high regard by local public institutions, is a member of trade and business associations, and who generally is a good "corporate citizen";
2. Since it is usual for galleries to have "stables" of artists and even to deal with a particular area or style of art, it is important for the collector to see what works are available from the reputable dealers in the community;
3. When considering the purchase of a work of art, it is quite proper to find out the purchase price, the terms of repayment, whether time payments are possible, what interest, if any, is charged, and whether any discounts are available for cash. Often galleries will allow a number of months for payment of works without an interest charge. This can be of real benefit to collectors;
4. When purchasing a work of art, a proper bill of sale should be obtained from the vendor. The bill of sale should indicate and warrant that the work of art is by the particular artist, and indicate the medium of the work (oil, acrylic, watercolour, etc.), the year of the work (or if unknown, note that fact), and its provenance. Provenance deals with the prior history of the work, such as indicating a collection in which it was held prior to entering the hands of the dealer. This may be very important for the collector when the time comes for resale. It gives "pedigree" to the work;
5. If the work is an unframed image on paper (a drawing, fine art print, watercolour, etc.), it is important to make certain that the work is framed using only non-acidic or "museum" mat and board in order to prevent possible future injury to the work. A good dealer will generally ask whether the purchaser wishes to spend the additional money for this type of matting

and framing. What may be an inexpensive print when purchased could be an extremely expensive work in the future. This has been the case, for instance, with the early Eskimo prints of Canada which will be discussed in the section dealing with original prints;

6. The price of the work should also be indicated in the bill of sale as should the terms of payment. Not only is this important to show that title has passed to you, but will also be important in regard to any resale and consequent tax which may become payable. (See Chapters 7 and 8 for a more complete discussion of taxes.) Records of purchases and sales are important to retain;

7. Warranties and implied warranties on purchases from commercial dealers are similar to those mentioned in the context of auction sales. As discussed there, there is a warranty of title under most provincial Sale of Goods Acts as well as a number of other implied warranties. Wherever possible, obtain written warranties from the vendor as to authorship, medium, and date;

8. If there is a disclaimer in the bill of sale, this should be a warning to the purchaser about the nature and quality of both the dealer and the work being purchased;

9. Generally, reputable galleries will, as a matter of practice, carefully outline what is being purchased and stand behind the sale. It is not unusual for galleries to have an informal policy of either accepting back the work within a particular time limit (and sometimes without time limit) at the price originally paid for the work, or agreeing to act as agent on any resale of the work by the purchaser, on a reduced commission (generally 15% to 25% of the sale price). If the work is returned for credit, it is not unusual to allow the purchaser to choose any other artist's work which is carried by the particular gallery;

10. When a collector purchases privately from another collector, there must be a very clear understanding that risks are involved. Generally, the vendor should be well known to the purchaser. A bill of sale containing all possible particulars should be prepared, including a warranty as to title. If possible, the original bill of sale to the vendor should be inspected.

11. The purchase from private sources of such things as pre-Columbian works from Mexico or South America, special tribal art from Africa, antiquities from Europe, or other "heritage" works, requires special care. The question which must be answered is whether the work of art is one which falls under the UNESCO Treaty, or bilateral treaties to which Canada is a party, so that it would require an export permit. If the work he wishes to buy falls into this category, the purchaser should make certain that the work has been legally

imported into this country. If it has not, the work can be seized and returned to its country of origin.

In the private sale, therefore, questions of title, authenticity, and heritage are particularly important. Since the vendor is not a dealer, mercantile laws regarding the passing of title by a retailer are not applicable. Consequently, a search under any Personal Property Security registry in the province would be essential, in the same manner and for basically the same reasons as when buying a used car. Such a search would reveal any liens or charges against the property which have been filed in the province. As well, the wise purchaser would search executions (judgments filed with the sheriff) against the vendor. As well as uncovering any liens of this nature, such a search also would be an interesting credit check;

12. In any province with a Retail Sales Tax Act, the purchaser is responsible for payment of such tax (even in a private sale). In the event that the tax has not been paid, the vendor may be ultimately responsible for the tax. It is therefore important for a vendor to make certain that the retail sales tax is paid and transmitted to the provincial authorities.

THE ART ADVISER

A relatively new development in the area of private art collection is the individual or organization whose function is to give advice regarding purchases. The services of such a consultant are most commonly utilized by corporate collectors, who will often retain the adviser to search for suitable works to recommend to the corporation, or to its art purchase committee.

Any relationship between such a consultant and a corporation should be clearly documented in writing. The most important aspect of such a contract would be to clearly establish who is to receive the benefit of any commissions or discounts available to the consultant. It is common for the art adviser to be able to obtain a discount of at least 10% from commercial dealers. Since the consultant will be acting as agent for the corporation, full disclosure of any such benefits is essential. If the agent were to retain the amount of the discount without the approval of the corporation, this could be construed as a "secret profit" for which the consultant could be forced to account. In fact, since even the most honest agent may find it tempting to recommend more expensive or more heavily discounted works when this provides his source of income for his services, it is recommended that such relationships are best handled by having the consultant receive a fee for his services paid by the corporation for the time expended by the consultant. In this way, the corporation will receive the benefit of any discounts or commissions available to the agent, who will recommend purchases and purchase at the best possible price.

It is also obviously important that the consultant not have any financial interest in the works of art nor in any commercial gallery from which he is recommending purchases.

ORIGINAL PRINTS

History

Prints were not commonly collected or traded in North America until the last fifteen or twenty years. However, during the early part of the twentieth-century, prints were often created for use as illustrations in limited edition books of original writing or poetry. This was often done by Picasso, Matisse, Bonnard, and other European artists. The recent resurgence of printmaking in North America has led to the opening of print galleries; created numerous "print collectors"; and resulted in much trading in prints. Canada has a very special place in twentieth-century printmaking, particularly because of the work of the Innuit in Northern Canada and the print industry this has generated. In past years, collectors have lined up to purchase newly released prints from Baker Lake or Cape Dorset available each year through approved sales outlets. Each edition consists of approximately fifty impressions. These prints, which often sold for less than $100 in the early 60's are now selling for many times their original cost. Recently, the early print entitled *Enchanted Owl* sold for over $14,000. There are numerous other examples of older Innuit prints which sell today for many thousands of dollars.

As well, prints by Miro, Chagall, Dali, Dubuffet, Johns, Motherwell, and other internationally famous artists, may cost many thousands of dollars. It is extremely important, therefore, for the purchaser to understand the concept of the "original print" and to know what is being purchased. Because of the large amount of money now involved in the print market, abuses have arisen which must be watched carefully. Forgeries, unsigned prints which have been "signed" and "numbered," posters which have been made into limited editions by trimming and adding signatures and numbers, reproductions from catalogues or books passed off as originals, and damaged works camouflaged to appear as if they were in perfect condition, all appear in the marketplace.

Definition

The definition of original print is extremely fuzzy and difficult to pin down. This is primarily because there are new means and methods of print production constantly being developed. One might normally think that an original print is a print which is original (i.e., a new image) and created and printed by the artist in a strictly limited edition. Unfortunately, this is not necessarily true. The image is generally created by the artist, but increasingly the work is printed by a master printer. One would expect, therefore, that the printer would be in consultation with the artist for approval of the image; but while this should be the case, it sometimes is not. As well, the image may be reproduced by mechanical means or by photomechanical means, such as commercial lithography. The work may in fact be a commercial photolithograph of an existing painting by the artist. Sometimes the work is created by a printmaker based on an existing mural, image, stained glass window, or other work of art. The artist then approves the particular image and signs and numbers it. Is this an original print? The answer is not clear. At best, such a print would appear to be a less important work of the artist and somewhat suspect. There are even stories of an internationally famous artist who, for the right money, will sign 50 or 75 blank pages for a publisher to imprint with any image it selects.

At the moment, the best definition of an original print is: an image that has been made specifically for the purposes of creating the print, which is printed in a limited number under the artistic control of the artist. As well, the term "original print" is now generally being displaced by the term "fine art print" since a print by its very nature is a multiple and cannot be any more original than the other prints in the series.

Some artists prefer to create their own work from beginning to end in their own studio and with their own presses. The vast majority, however, deal with master printers and print ateliers. Others deal with their particular commercial gallery representatives who arrange for the works to be printed. See Chapter 2 at page 36, for a discussion of printmaking contracts.

The Difference between an Original Print and a Reproduction

A reproduction is generally an exact duplicate of a work that has been created earlier in another form, such as a print made of a painting or work on paper, or a mechanical reproduction of an existing painting. In France these are known as *estampes*. Examples are found in every art book which is published. It is when such a reproduction is held out to be an original, sometimes with the consent of the artist who is prepared to sign and number the works, that it becomes a problem for the collector. Often, although not actually specifying originality, advertisements for such works are disguised to lead the customer to believe that what is being purchased is in fact an original. Advertisements have appeared in this country indicating that a work is "signed and numbered in a limited edition by the artist." Such a statement can apply to reproductions of existing works, as well as to freshly created images for the print medium. These works would have little, if any, resale value.

The concept of "limited editions" has also been extended. Some print organizations have used "limited" as meaning limited to the number of purchasers by a given date, rather than to a pre-determined size of the edition. That is, the size of the edition will be "limited" to the 100 or 1000 or 10,000 people who send in their application by a certain date. It is therefore important to read such promotional material carefully.

Restrikes

Great care and caution must be exercised in purchasing fine art prints. There have been cases where "restrikes" have been passed off as proper originals. A restrike is a print which has been published from a cancelled plate, block, or master. For instance, when an etching or engraving is completed and the series fully printed, the blocks or plates may fall into the hands of entrepreneurs who reprint the cancelled image. This is very easy, of course, when the artist has neglected to cancel the plate at all. In other cases, a block or plate which has been cancelled by scoring lines across it will have these lines filled in so that the image can be produced again. Generally these "restrikes" are sold after the death of the artist, and are thus done without his consent, direction, or artistic control. Such abuses can be prevented by making it a term of the printmaking contract that any masters or plates must be *destroyed* in the presence of the artist, or gifted to a public institution upon proper terms. This does not, however, prevent abuses by the artist himself.

In Canada, one of the few protections available when purchasing fine art prints is to purchase from well recognized and legitimate galleries and outlets. This is true not only for old master prints, but also for contemporary prints by North American and European printmakers. There are even instances in the marketplace of reproductions of Innuit prints being made in the Far East and passed off as originals here in Canada.

Multiple Copy Sculpture

Similar problems to those concerning the "originality" or authenticity of prints, arise in regard to works of sculpture. It is not unusual for sculpture to be cast after the death of the artist. For example, none of Degas' sculpture was cast during his lifetime, and pieces by Rodin, who is long deceased, are still being cast today. Also, because of the high cost of casting, it is usual for sculpture to be cast in editions. Should the fact that a work has been cast after the artist's death be indicated by the seller? Should the edition size be stated? Consider the situation for an institution like the Rodin Museum, for example, which has many of the plaster casts created by Rodin. Should the museum be involved in casting copies of Rodin's work after his death? What information should be supplied if it does so? What happens to the market value of a sculpture purchased during the artist's lifetime when other copies are produced after the artist's death? What if a second posthumous series of castings is made or a third? Would such additional copies also be considered originals?

There are two views regarding the originality and propriety of such works:

1. One view is that it is sufficient if the casting is done under the

authority of the executor of the estate.
2. The second view is that the casting, no matter how good, does not have the ultimate control or approval of the living artist, and is not, therefore, an original.

The states of California, New York, and Illinois have felt it necessary to pass legislation dealing with original prints.

California Legislation

The California legislation came into effect on the 1st of July, 1971. The definition section states that "fine print" includes engravings, etchings, woodcuts, lithographs, and serigraphs. The legislation does not apply to any works which sell unframed for less than $25.00 or framed for less than $40.00. For all other works, no catalogue, prospectus, or circular offering the prints for sale in the state is to be distributed unless it clearly discloses the following relevant information (and this information must also accompany the print):

1. The name of the artist and the year when the image was printed.
2. Exclusive of trial prints, whether the edition is a limited edition and if so the maximum authorized number of signed and/or numbered impressions in the edition.
3. The authorized maximum number of unsigned and/or unnumbered impressions.
4. The authorized maximum number of artist's, publisher's, printer's, or other proofs, over and above the regular edition.
5. The total size of the edition.
6. Whether the plate has been destroyed, altered, defaced, or cancelled after the edition.
7. Where the master for a multiple copy work has been used to produce an edition, and is then modified in order to produce a new or altered image, each new form of impression is referred to as a "state." Where a print is offered for sale which has existed in prior states, the total number of states must be given and a designation made of the state to which the subject print relates.
8. If there were any prior or later editions from the same plate, the series number of the edition and the total size of *all* other editions.
9. Whether the edition is a posthumous one or a restrike, and if so, whether the plate has been reworked.
10. The name of the workshop where the print was created.

If the legislation is violated, there are both civil and criminal remedies. Civilly, the purchaser may receive back his money together with interest, or if the vendor has wilfully (knowingly) offered or sold the print in violation of the legislation the purchaser may recover an amount equal to three times the amount of the purchase price together with interest. There is a limitation period of one year after discovery of the violation.

Illinois Statute

Illinois' Statute Relating to Sale of Fine Prints is similar to California's legislation, and came into effect July 1st, 1972. This statute exempts sales by the artist directly to the public. It requires the vendor to disclose whether the print is an etching, engraving, lithograph, or woodcut, and contains more stringent penalties than the California legislation.

New York Legislation

In 1975 New York passed legislation dealing with certain deceptive practices in regard to the sale of fine art prints and posters. The legislation indicates that whenever the word "signed" is used it must in fact mean hand signed by the artist. As well, it is illegal to sell, or offer for sale, a print that has been altered, or to remove any lettering (i.e., try to turn a poster into a fine art print), unless the fact of alteration is clearly disclosed. Any purchaser who has purchased a work in violation of the legislation is entitled to rescind the purchase and obtain a refund.

New York City has also regulated deceptive advertising and labelling of "limited edition" products under its consumer protection laws. These laws indicate that it is a deceptive practice and contrary to the law for any person to advertise, label, or otherwise claim any product as a limited edition, if in fact the product is not limited either to a pre-determined maximum quantity or to the actual quantity ordered within a specified short period of time. This law applies to fine art prints as well as other "collectables" such as books, stamps, coins, etc.

Canadian Developments

Since three of the major commercial states in the United States have felt it necessary to pass legislation of this type, Canadian provinces should also consider the status of fine art prints and whether they should be covered by special legislation. If some of the practices associated with fine art prints occurred in the stock market they would undoubtedly lead to prosecution under various securities legislation. It would appear appropriate for consumer legislation to apply not only to fine art prints, but also to any other "multiples" such as sculpture, photographs, limited edition books, etc.

The Professional Art Dealers Association has presently constituted a committee of member dealers, augmented by representatives of various artists' organizations, print workshops, ateliers, and artists to deal with definitions for, and the future direction of, the fine art print in Canada. It is hoped that this may lead to positive steps by the industry to help the situation and possibly lead to government legislation in the consumer field. The preliminary report of the committee indicates the following:

1. Correct labelling is the prime necessity. No definition of

original print can ever achieve what correct labelling can do. A clear differentiation should be made between an original etching, lithograph, silk screen, woodcut, offset lithograph, etc., and a photomechanical reproduction of a work originally conceived by the artist in another medium. Fuzzy or vague terminology such as lithoprint, original print, etc., must be eliminated, as such practices are misleading and cause great confusion in the print market. *A reproduction must be labelled and advertised as a reproduction.* It is important that the buying public know that a work is a reproduction, especially if it is a signed, limited edition reproduction, and not an original print.

2. The report also recommends to artists that they make sure their works are properly labelled. The question of the artist's proof is also dealt with. It is generally accepted that 10% to 12% in additional copies of the edition may be struck as artist's proofs and labelled as such. The Art Dealers' report suggests that artists number the artist's proofs so that the purchaser can determine not only that the work is an artist's proof, but the size of the edition of artist's proofs. It is recommended as well that this be done in roman numerals, e.g., number II/XV. It was also suggested that the size of the regular edition should also be noted on the artist's proof so that the edition size would appear after the artist's proof's numbers (e.g., II/XV (edition 150)).

3. The report also makes recommendations to print workshops, printers and publishers. It recommends that the print workshops have complete documentation available regarding the medium, number of proofs, edition size, and any other material relevant to the print edition.

The report is aimed at galleries which mislabel, either through ignorance or design; artists who are either careless or take advantage of the public; and workshops which are less than careful and professional about production. If the recommendations are followed, this will be of major benefit to the art buying public.

CHAPTER 4 NON-PROFIT STRUCTURES AND THEIR USES FOR THE VISUAL ARTS

INTRODUCTION

On first survey, a person may be impressed with the vast number of different structures that appear to be employed in the visual arts field.

In the business or profit sector there are three principal ways of organizing activities:
1. a sole proprietorship (a self-employed artist or dealer),
2. a partnership of two or more persons (basically an unincorporated business association), and
3. a corporation (identified by the words "Incorporated" "Corporation" "Limited" or an abbreviation).

There are also trusts, which do not generally carry on active business but instead have their trust assets invested to obtain the best return for the beneficiaries.

In the non-profit sector, however, there appear to be a bewildering array of associations, councils, charities, societies, foundations, organizations, systems, corporations, companies, etc. Nevertheless, the carrying on of non-profit activities can also be reduced to three basic ways of organizing activities:
1. the individual volunteer,
2. the unincorporated group, and
3. the non-profit corporation.

Trusts also exist in the non-profit sector.

This chapter examines the non-profit corporation and touches briefly on the trust.

Unincorporated groups are not governed by statute law, but rather by the common law. It is hoped that in most cases the common law principles reduce to common sense rules dictating that you have to deal fairly with fellow members and the funds of the group. However, many unincorporated groups do model their organizational structure on that set down for corporations both in the business and non-profit spheres.

Charities will also be dealt with in this chapter. It should be made clear at the outset that a charity is not a special type of structure, but rather a structure, be it a trust, an unincorporated association, or a non-profit corporation, whose objects are charitable and which fulfils certain other criteria required by the government in order to obtain registered charity status.

NON-PROFIT CORPORATIONS

Corporations are generally seen by the public as vehicles for commercial activities, but there is another kind of corporation, known generically as the non-profit corporation. There are in excess of 15,000 non-profit corporations carrying on their activities in Canada. These corporations are structures in much the same way as business corporations, with one essential difference: a business corporation's function is to carry on business with a view to making a profit and to distribute any profit in excess of the corporation's needs to its shareholders, while a non-profit corporation's function, despite the fact that the corporation may carry on an ancillary business that generates profits, is to further its charitable or membership purposes and consequently to expend its revenues only for those purposes.

Many non-profit corporations are not immediately recognizable as corporations. Business corporations are readily identifiable because they include the words Corporation, Limited, or Incorporated. Non-profit corporations can be camouflaged by tags such as Society, Association, Foundation, Council, or Organization, the same terms used by unincorporated groups. Some, but not all non-profit corporations, include the terms Corporation, Limited, or Incorporated in their name.

A corporation, whether profit or non-profit, is regarded in law as a person separate and apart from its shareholders, members, employees, directors, and other people associated with the corporation. A corporation can be sued, it can be fined, it can contract, it can go bankrupt, it can receive grants, and its existence can be terminated. It survives its individual members, and its members are not liable for its debts unless they have contracted otherwise with the corporation's creditors.

Non-profit corporations in the visual arts can provide financial assistance to artists, promote their individual member's efforts and achievements through shows and publicity, and can provide a base and support for lobbying a particular point of view. A non-profit corporation may also allow members to achieve economies of scale.

Examples of non-profit corporations in the Canadian art world are The Nightingale Arts Council (A Space, an alternate gallery), The Professional Art Dealers Association of Canada (P.A.D.A.C), The Royal Ontario Museum, The National Ballet of Canada, and The Art Gallery of Ontario Foundation.

Each of the ten provinces provides for the incorporation of non-profit corporations and about 12,000 are incorporated provincially; approximately 3,000 more are incorporated at the federal level. A provincially incorporated corporation may carry on business within its province as a matter of right, but it cannot do so outside the province without the grant of appropriate rights and powers by the extra-provincial jurisdiction concerned. This is not usually difficult to obtain.

Federally incorporated corporations have the right to carry on business in all the provinces. The fact that a federal corporation is incorporated with power to carry on business in all the provinces, but in fact carries on business in only one province, does not affect its status as a federally incorporated corporation. A federal non-profit corporation is subject to those provincial laws which are of general application, such as laws relating to taxation, mortmain (holding land), and licencing for certain purposes. However, the status or powers of a federally incorporated corporation cannot be interfered with by the provinces in any manner which would be discriminatory or which would prevent the exercise of powers granted on incorporation by the federal government.

Provincial incorporations will not be discussed as they all vary in detail, but not greatly in substance, from federal incorporation.

Although in many cases a non-profit corporation may be incorporated either federally or provincially, in some cases federal incorporation is not possible. Our constitution gives certain authority to the Parliament of Canada and other authority to the provincial legislatures. Consequently, the federal government may not incorporate a corporation which has objects over which the provincial legislatures have authority, e.g., a non-profit corporation which limits the scope of its activities to a particular province.

A federally incorporated non-profit corporation is, at the time of writing, incorporated pursuant to Part II of the Canada Corporations Act. Business corporations were formerly incorporated under Part I of this Act (which has now been supplanted by the Canada Business Corporations Act). The Canada Corporations Act refers to non-profit corporations as "corporations without share capital."

Federal Incorporation

The Minister of Consumer and Corporate Affairs incorporates a federal non-profit corporation by granting a charter by way of letters patent to the persons who submit the necessary application. Upon incorporation, the applicants automatically become members of the corporation. The corporation is incorporated, without share capital, for the purpose of carrying on, without pecuniary gain to its members, objects to which the legislative authority of the Parliament of Canada extends, which are of a national, patriotic, religious, philanthropic, charitable, scientific, artistic, social, professional, or sporting character, or of similar objects.

To obtain letters patent, a minimum of three adult individuals must submit an application (in duplicate) stating the proposed name of the corporation, the purposes for which its incorporation is sought (otherwise known as the company's objects), the place within Canada where the head office of the corporation is to be situated, the names in full and the address and occupation of each of the applicants, and the names of at least three applicants who are to be the first directors of the corporation. It is also necessary to submit by-laws (in duplicate) of the proposed corporation which must include the following:

(a) conditions of membership, including whether societies or companies may become members of the corporation;

(b) mode of holding meetings, provision for quorum, rights of voting and of enacting by-laws;

(c) mode of repealing or amending by-laws with a special provision that the repeal or amendment of by-laws not embodied in the letters patent shall not be enforced or acted upon until the approval of the Minister has been obtained;

(d) appointment and removal of directors, trustees, committees, and officers; their respective powers and their remuneration;

(e) audit of accounts and appointment of auditors;

(f) whether, and if so how, members may withdraw from the corporation; and

(g) custody of the corporate seal and certification of documents issued by the corporation.

The Department of Consumer and Corporate Affairs then returns one of the applications to which it has attached an official looking certificate and seal. Upon incorporation, the corporation exists as an independant person for all legal purposes, separate and apart from its members. Any of the matters set out in the letters patent can subsequently be changed only by obtaining supplementary letters patent.

Letters patent, supplementary letters patent and the by-laws can be collectively referred to as the "constating documents" and are the constitution of the corporation.

Corporate Name

The corporation's name can consist of a separate or combined French and English form and it may be legally designated by either the French or English form of its name or by both forms. A non-profit corporation cannot have a name which is similar to that of any other organization whether profit or non-profit, except where it is related to a business, society, or association which has consented to the use of the name in writing. A corporation also cannot have a name which is thought objectionable on public policy grounds. The name of a corporation can be changed by supplementary letters patent.

Powers and Objects

Corporations do have powers beyond those set out in the objects of their letters patent and their supplementary letters patent. These are set out in the Act and provide a very large scope for incidental activity. However, some powers are limited by the objects. For example, the final two power clauses enumerated in the Canada Corporations Act say that a corporation has the power "to carry out all or any of the objects of the company and do all or any of the things set out in this subsection as principal, agent, contractor, or otherwise, and either alone or in conjunction with others; and to do all such things as are incidental or conducive to the attainment of the objects and the exercise of the powers of the company."

Another reason that the objects of a corporation are important is that the Canada Corporations Act provides for the winding-up of a corporation where it operates outside the scope of its objects or tries to exercise any powers which are not truly ancillary or reasonable to its objects. The corporation may be wound-up and dissolved under The Winding-Up Act, upon the application of the Attorney General of Canada to the proper court. When considering the winding-up application, the court can determine whether the cost of winding-up should be borne by the company or personally by any or all of the directors who participated or acquiesced in the carrying on of the unauthorized activity or the exercise of the non-incidental powers. This means that if a non-profit corporation attempts to earn money for distribution among its members, the corporation can be wound up at the personal expense of the directors. It also illustrates that the objects of the non-profit corporation should generally be drafted very broadly in order to allow a corporation involved in the arts field to participate in a variety of activities as times change, without the need to constantly seek supplementary letters patent to amend the objects. It may, of course, be desirable to incorporate for a very narrowly defined purpose in some cases.

The stated objects of a corporation can also be of assistance in determining whether or not a non-profit corporation is eligible for registered charity status.

As a footnote, the Canada Corporations Act uses the word company and not the more modern term of corporation. The word "company" is used in the old sense of limited company or company whose liability is limited to its own assets and not those of its members. The word "company" is sometimes used by unincorporated groups but in these cases it means company in an informal sense, whose liabilities will be met by its members.

Membership and Members' Meetings

Introduction

There can be any number of classes of membership in a non-profit corporation. These classes may be set out in the by-laws, or may be contained in the letters patent or supplementary letters patent. Differing privileges and conditions for each class of membership should be specified in the by-laws. Some of the conditions and privileges could relate to voting rights, duration of membership, ability to transfer membership, fees which can be levied, preconditions to membership such as ethnic origin (where this is for a legitimate reason), attendance at certain institutions, or cultural interests.

The draft by-laws submitted with the application for letters patent must spell out provisions relating to the holding of meetings of members. Some guidelines and essential formalities for the calling and conducting of members' meetings are set out in the Canada Corporations Act and frequently the by-laws repeat the statutory requirements. There are two kinds of members' meetings — annual meetings (held annually, of course) and general meetings, which are meetings other than annual meetings. The corporation must hold an annual meeting of members not less than eighteen months after its incorporation and subsequently at least once every calendar year and not more than fifteen months after the holding of the last preceding annual meeting.

Members and Auditors

At the first annual meeting, the voting members must appoint auditors for the corporation to hold office until the next annual meeting of the corporation or until a successor is chosen. (If they fail to do so, the directors must appoint the auditor.) At subsequent annual meetings, the membership should have placed before it the audited financial statements for examination and approval. If the members wish an opportunity to question the auditor, he can be required to attend the meeting. The auditor acts as the membership's watchdog in overseeing the activities of the directors and the staff, to ensure that money is being properly disbursed and accounted for.

ACCOUNTANTS AND AUDITORS

Not everyone is aware that an accountant may not necessarily be an auditor, although an auditor is necessarily an accountant. An auditor is required by law to do behind-the-scene investigations to ensure that the figures compiled for the statements are accurate, and present as true a picture as possible of what is actually happening in the financial area. The Auditor's Report in the front of the financial statements will qualify the extent of the investigation that has been carried out, if necessary. One common qualification involves the fact that the auditor has no way of knowing whether or not anyone is stealing from loose coin collections because there are no receipts against which he can double-check.

On the other hand, a person acting as an accountant rather than an auditor would provide Notes to the Reader, or Accountant's Comments, which usually state something to the effect that the information given to him is not inconsistent and consequently appears accurate.

A chartered accountant (C.A.) may act as an auditor in any province, but in 1980, a certified general accountant (C.G.A.) was allowed to act as an auditor only in British Columbia.

Because an auditor is required to do more investigation, the fees for his services are usually greater than those required for the services of an accountant.

For their own protection, non-profit organizations, whether unincorporated or incorporated, need to have a competent accountant or auditor act for them; preferably one who is interested in the arts and in that organization. A federal non-profit corporation requires the services of an auditor. As a matter of practice, it is usually better to pay the professional for his advice in order to be able to demand and obtain the same quality of service as regular business clients. Nothing prevents the organization from subsequently asking for a donation which may be in the same range.

If the membership is not satisfied with the performance of the auditor he may be replaced, at either the annual meeting by a majority of votes (unless the by-laws provide otherwise), or during the term of his appointment if two-thirds of the meeting so vote. Auditors have rights and the auditor must be given notice of any motion to be brought before the meeting so that he has an opportunity to defend the work done and bring matters to the attention of the membership.

The remuneration of the auditor is set by the membership, since the auditor is working for it, unless the membership specifically delegates the task to the directors. Delegation frequently occurs, as many members do not have the necessary commercial knowledge to determine appropriate remuneration.

Members and Directors

The members must also elect directors from time to time. If the letters patent or supplementary letters patent do not provide otherwise, the directors must be elected yearly. However, the charter can provide that the directors hold office for two years so elections are only required biennially. The directors can also be elected by varying constituencies. In this way, different classes of members can be assured of representation. The corporation may also obtain the benefit of having continuing directors on the board because a class of directors may hold office for up to five years. The only limitation is that one class must retire from office each year.

Directors are responsible to the membership. Some of the basic rules as to the calling and conduct of directors' meetings are set out in the Canada Corporations Act and these are usually supplemented by additional provisions in the by-laws of the corporation.

Typical Agenda of a Members' Meeting

A typical agenda for an annual membership meeting for a non-profit corporation (as well as for other non-profit organizations) will include the following:

1. The chairperson (frequently the president has this task allot-

ted to him by the by-laws) determines whether a quorum of the membership is present.

2. New members are accepted (if this is required by the by-laws).

3. The minutes of the previous meeting are read (or the reading of the minutes is dispensed with if the membership has had previous opportunity to read them), amendments are entertained, and the minutes or the amended minutes are adopted.

4. The financial report is placed before the membership for discussion and acceptance.

5. The auditor is appointed for the forthcoming year and his remuneration is set (or the task is delegated to the directors).

6. Any by-laws passed by the directors during the year are placed before the membership for confirmation.

7. The prior acts of the directors are approved.

8. Directors are elected.

9. New business.

10. Termination of meeting.

Functions of Directors

The first directors of a federal non-profit corporation are named in the application which later becomes the letters patent. They hold office until they resign or until the first annual members' meeting is held. The first directors are responsible for much of the standard paperwork that is associated with setting up any organization. First directors would usually attend to at least the following matters:

1. approving the form of membership cards;

2. approving the form of the corporate seal. (The legal fiction is that a corporation signs with its seal and this "signature" is witnessed by the signatures of its officers.) A corporate seal is not used as frequently as in the past because, in most cases, the signature of an officer or officers on behalf of the corporation is now considered binding on the corporation;

3. opening a bank account in the corporate name after passing the appropriate by-law and resolutions;

4. appointing an auditor if the members have not done so.

First directors and continuing directors should also be aware of the following:

1. They may be empowered by the by-laws to accept membership applications.

2. Every corporation needs a president and a secretary. The by-laws may provide for more officers. The by-laws also set out the duties of the officers. The president must be a member of the board of directors of a federal corporation, but it is not necessary for the other officers to be directors. This allows for an advantageous sharing of the work load by volunteers.

3. The directors are responsible for seeing that proper accounting records are kept with respect to all financial and other transactions of the corporation. More particularly, the Canada Corporations Act requires that the corporation must keep records of:
   (a) all sums of money received and disbursed by the corporation and the matters in respect of which receipts and disbursements take place;
   (b) all sales and purchases by the corporation;
   (c) all assets and liabilities of the corporation; and
   (d) all other transactions affecting the financial position of the corporation.
4. The corporation is required to keep certain other records which include:
   (a) a copy of the letters patent, all the by-laws of the corporation, and any supplementary letters patent;
   (b) the names (alphabetically arranged) and the addresses of all the present and past members;
   (c) the names and addresses of all past and present directors, together with the dates for the periods they were the directors.

   These records can be inspected by members and creditors.
5. The corporation must also keep minutes of all proceedings of members' meetings and directors' meetings and of any executive committee. These minutes should be signed by the chairman of the meeting, and are evidence of what took place at the meeting.

The directors of a corporation are required to monitor the functions of the corporation, set policy and programmes, and see that policy is followed and programmes are implemented. Very often, of course, in small non-profit corporations directors are required to wear two hats and not only set policy but also implement it.

It can readily be seen that being a director of a non-profit corporation is not merely an honour, but also a responsibility. This responsibility is not only moral, but is governed by legal rules based on ethical responsibility.

Directors and the General Manager

Directors of non-profit corporations are not always termed directors. They may be called trustees, or may have some other title which sounds unusual to outsiders. In large organizations, however, directors are usually designated as such, or as trustees. It is not infrequent in art galleries and other non-profit organizations to have one person called the Director. This Director is usually an employee, and reports to the board of trustees. In private industry the Director would probably hold the position and office of General Manager. References to directors will not include a person holding this position.

Director's and Trustees' Duties

FIDUCIARY DUTY

Trustees were first associated with a concept early recognized in old English law called the trust. A trust demands of its trustees a high standard of conduct, known as the fiduciary duty, which embodies concepts of integrity, fidelity, confidence, fairness, and good faith. A trustee of a trust must always put first the interests of the persons for whom he holds in trust, and he is entrusted with the obligation of preserving property.

When a person is a trustee of a non-profit association, which is not technically a trust in law, the same general ideas of integrity, fidelity, confidence, fairness, and good faith still operate. However, a trustee of a trust knows exactly who the beneficiaries of the trust are, to whom he stands in a fiduciary capacity; but the directors or trustees of an arts organization have a more difficult task in knowing for whom the property is held in trust, and whose interests (among what can be a widely divergent membership and public) are entitled to priority. These directors have the job not merely of preserving property, as trustees of a trust would, but also of deciding among alternative risks and priorities.

When corporate law was developing, it adopted the fiduciary duty test from the common law governing trusts, to determine whether a director had acted properly. Some of the common law rules which then evolved for corporations have now been codified by the various Acts governing corporations, so that directors have some clear guidelines for conduct when they believe there may be a conflict between their personal interest (usually pecuniary) and the interest of the corporation (be it profit or non-profit). The Canada Corporations Act also sets out what to do in such circumstances.

CONFLICTS OF INTEREST

A director is obliged to declare to fellow directors any conflict of interest. If a director is interested in a contract or proposed contract with the corporation, he must declare his interest to the directors of the corporation at the meeting where it first arises or comes to his attention. For instance, if the director is a shareholder of a corporation with which the corporation wishes to contract, the director is required to declare his conflict of interest. By way of example, a director of a gallery, who is the holder of shares in an art trucking company which is bidding for the shipping and crating business of the gallery, would have a conflict of interest. A director would also have this conflict if his spouse, or another member of the immediate family, is the holder of the same type of shares.

A director cannot vote on any matter concerning a contract in which he has such a conflict of interest. The director is well advised to leave the room when the matter is under discussion and being voted on, even though this is not a statutory requirement, so that no charge of subtle pressure can be levied later.

If a director does not make a declaration of his interest in a contract, or proposed contract, he is accountable to the corporation and is liable for any profit realized by such a contract, unless the contract is confirmed by a vote of the members.

CARE AND SKILL

Business corporation law has evolved a higher standard for directors of a business corporation than simple honesty and integrity. The courts are beginning to ask whether the director has acted with the standard of care and skill that one would expect of a reasonably prudent person in similar circumstances. Ignorance and stupidity will not be accepted as a defence. These standards will be applied to the directors of non-profit corporations as well, particularly where public funds are being handled.

Lawsuits against directors for malfeasance or misfeasance are anticipated in present times. The Canada Corporations Act provides that the director of a non-profit corporation may be exonerated by the corporation for all his costs sustained in any action or proceeding brought against him, in respect of any acts done by him in the execution of the duties of his office, except such costs as arise by reason of the director's own wilful neglect or default. Today, director's liability insurance is available to cover cases other than those incurred by reason of wilful neglect or default. This coverage should be considered by all directors.

Another provision which emphasizes the responsibility demanded of directors today, is that they can be personally liable for up to six months' wages of all employees of the corporation if the employees are not paid. This provision also illustrates that ignorance of commercial matters will not excuse a director from responsibility.

People should not be discouraged from accepting directorships in non-profit corporations by provisions such as these, but they must be aware of their responsibility to become knowledgeable. It is most important to ask questions. In many cases, simple questions can be of more benefit to the corporation than very sophisticated analyses. Directors of a non-profit corporation must not just passively accept reports, but be actively involved in scrutinizing what passes before them and happens around them.

This has been a very brief sketch of the obligations and liabilities of directors. A full discussion of the particular problems of directors of public art galleries is included in Chapter 5, which should be consulted for a more comprehensive look at directors' responsibilities. Most of the concepts discussed there apply to all non-profit organizations.

CHARITIES

Introduction

Many arts groups are curious about, or wish to obtain, charitable status. A charity can be an unincorporated organization, a non-profit corporation, or a trust. It is possible for a legal charity to exist, but not be recognized for tax purposes as a "registered charity." Two obvious advantages to being a registered charity are that registered charities do not generally pay tax, and persons can be encouraged to donate to a registered charity because the donation is usually "income tax deductible." However, there are disadvantages to being a registered charity and these must be examined also.

Until December 31, 1976, a charity recognized by the Revenue authorities was known as a Registered Canadian Charitable Organization. A charity did not have to be a Registered Canadian Charitable Organization in order to be exempt from tax, but needed this designation in order to be able to issue receipts for use by donors. A Registered Canadian Charitable Organization was a body to which the Minister of National Revenue, in his discretion, had granted registration. This exercise of discretion required the Minister to investigate the activities of the organization before certifying and granting charitable status. However, since January 1, 1977, the exercise of ministerial discretion has been abolished. All organizations that had been previously granted Registered Canadian Charitable Organization status continued automatically to be registered charities, and can remain so unless their registration is revoked.

Obtaining Registered Charity Status

An organization wishing to become a registered charity now completes an application for registration form (a copy of which is Appendix A to this chapter) and forwards it to the Minister of National Revenue together with a copy of its financial statements for the fiscal year prior to the date of the application, and certified copies of the governing documents under which it operates such as letters patent, memorandum of association, articles of association, charter, trust deed or constitution as well as the by-laws or their equivalent. As well, a complete statement must be given containing full details of the aims and objectives as well as the structure of the charity. If it can be determined that the sole purpose and objects of the group is the relief of poverty, the advancement of religion, the advancement of education, or other purposes of a charitable nature beneficial to the community as a whole, registered charity status is automatically granted if all necessary information has been supplied.

It is a precondition for being a registered charity that no income of the organization is payable or otherwise available for the personal benefit of any proprietor, member, shareholder, trustee, or settlor of the organization. It should be noted that while it is provided that no *income* may be payable to certain persons, this does not preclude the legitimate employment of persons who may be otherwise involved in the charity. It does mean, however, that a bank account cannot be used as a source of funds for personal purposes by persons associated with the charity. It is also important to know that a charity set up to provide services to only one part of the community will not be eligible for registration. For example, if a wealthy man sets up a foundation for the education only of his lineal descendants, the Minister will not register it as a charity.

Types of Registered Charity

Prior to 1977

Prior to 1977, charities were divided for tax purposes into three basic groups, charitable organizations, non-profit corporations, and charitable trusts. (The term "non-profit corporation" was not used in the sense examined above; that type of non-profit corporation might or might not have been classified as a charity for tax purposes.) Charitable organizations carried on their own charitable work. Non-profit corporations and charitable trusts sometimes carried on their own charitable works, but in general merely supplied funds to other charities. Different taxation rules were applicable to each of these three basic groups.

1977 and Thereafter

For 1977, and subsequent taxation years, the old classifications of non-profit corporations and charitable trusts have been grouped together as charitable foundations. Although the previous classification of charitable organizations remains unchanged, different rules now apply to charitable organizations.

The portion of annual income which is donated to other registered charities is the key factor in determining whether a particular charity is a charitable organization or a charitable foundation. A charitable organization may not donate more than 50% of its annual income to other charities unless they are related to it. A charitable foundation may carry on charitable activities of its own, but its principal activity is to make donations to other charities.

The definition of a charitable organization in the Income Tax Act, provides that it is an organization, whether or not incorporated, all the resources of which are devoted to the charitable activities carried on by the organization itself. On the other hand, a charitable foundation is a corporation or trust, constituted and operated exclusively for charitable purposes, which is not a charitable organization.

Consequently, a charitable organization can be an unincorporated body, a corporation, or a trust, which uses at least 50% of its income for its own activities or the activities of a related organization. A charitable foundation cannot be an unincorporated body, but must be a trust or a corporation, and must donate at least 50% of its money to other charities.

Rules of General Application

Because the rules which determine whether an organization is a charitable organization or a charitable foundation are based on an annual determination of how income is spent, the rules for determining income are very important. The income of a registered charity does not include capital gains or capital losses. Nor does it include gifts, if the donor has stipulated that the property given (or property substituted for it) be held for at least ten years. This is why charities often run two campaigns; one for operating funds, and another for endowment or building purposes. Registered charities can also accumulate property (frequently money) with the approval of the Ministry of National Revenue, and are deemed for tax purposes to have expended the property, and any interest earned, on their own charitable activities.

Registered charities have to make both private information returns and public information returns, or risk losing their registered charity status. Examples of these forms are attached as Appendices B and C to this chapter. Charities are also obliged to keep proper records.

Rules for Charitable Organizations

It has been outlined above that charitable organizations can make donations of up to 50% of their income to other charities, and unlimited donations to associated charities. Another restriction placed on charitable organizations is that they are required to keep their fund raising costs to a reasonable percentage of the amount raised. Commencing in 1980, the Income Tax Act obliges charitable organizations to expend on their own charitable activities, or donate to other charities, 80% of receipted donations from the previous year, or risk losing their charitable status registration. The 80% requirement is waived in certain situations if more than the required percentage has been expended in previous years. These rules force a charitable organization to keep its costs to 20% or less of its receipted donations. It should be noted that business revenue and donations from other charities are not *receipted* donations and consequently are not factored into this calculation.

A charitable organization may carry on a related business. For instance, a public art gallery could run a bookstore on its premises, because this would be ancillary to the gallery's objectives of educating the public about art. Such a bookstore might also be related by virtue of the fact that it sells posters and reproductions of the art exhibited in the gallery. An art rental service may be similarly related, because it makes original art available to the public. The Act also states that a related business includes an unrelated business if substantially all the people involved in operating it are volunteers. In cases where there is doubt as to whether or not a business is related, this provision may be of assistance.

Charitable Foundations

A charitable foundation is classed as a public foundation if more than 50% of its trustees or directors deal at arm's length, and not more than 75% of its capital was derived from the donations of a single person or group of persons not dealing at arm's length with one another. If fewer than 50% of a foundation's trustees or directors deal at arm's length, or more than 75% of its capital was derived from the donations of a single person or group of persons not dealing at arm's length with one another, it is classed as a private foundation. Private foundations may apply to become classed as public foundations in order to take advantage of the less stringent rules which are applicable to public foundations.

Prior to 1977, when what are now referred to as charitable foundations were described as non-profit corporations or charitable trusts, the Act stated that a charitable foundation could not carry on any business. In practice, however, Revenue Canada did not ordinarily revoke registration if a business was conducted that was incidental to the charitable aims of the corporation or trust. For 1977 and subsequent taxation years, the prohibition against carrying on business applies only to private foundations. The Minister may revoke the registration of a private foundation which carries on any business. A public foundation may carry on a related business.

No charitable foundation, whether public or private, is allowed to acquire control of a corporation by commercial means. A charitable foundation can, however, acquire control by gift. If a charitable foundation did acquire control of a corporation by commercial means its registration as a registered charity would be revoked.

There are other refinements in calculating the income of a charitable foundation in addition to the fact that capital gains and capital losses are not included in or deducted from income. A charitable foundation is allowed a deduction (called a "reserve") in calculating its income, of up to the amount of the foundation's total income for the immediately preceding year. This reserve must be included in calculating the next year's income. This allows the charitable foundation time to plan its financing programmes and still comply with the requirements of the Income Tax Act, and also allows them to build a reserve limited to one year's income.

Rules for Public Foundations

As stated earlier, a charitable foundation, whether public or private, donates at least 50% of its income to other charities. An additional requirement is that a public foundation must spend on its own charitable activities, or donate to other charities, an amount equal to at least the greater of (a) 80% of the donations for which the foundation issued receipts received in the previous year and (b) 90% of the foundation's income for that year. Thus, the 80% of donations rule applicable to all registered charities may have to be exceeded in the case of a public foundation. However, the figure of 90% of the foundation's income is not unduly onerous because of the reserve which is allowed.

Public foundations, like charitable organizations, can apply to the Minister for permission to accumulate monies, and also benefit from the averaging rules which oblige the Minister to look at past performance, and refrain from revoking registered charity status if amounts disbursed in a year are less than required, but in past years have been greater than required.

Rules for Private Foundations

Private foundations have more stringent rules because, in the past, a few taxpayers were abusing the ability to establish private charities. They were having the charity invest in the donor's business, or lend money to the donor's family at a low rate of return; they were renting premises to the charity at high rent, and in some cases hiring family members at high salaries for relatively little work.

Consequently, the capital of the private foundation is now divided notionally into two groups. The first consists of prescribed investments (e.g., blue chip stocks and bonds), assets employed in the work of the foundation, and property held with the consent of the Minister. The private foundation must expend 90% of the income earned from this capital on its charitable activities. The second group consists of all other capital property, and the private foundation must expend the greater of 90% of the income earned from this capital, or 5% of the fair market value of the property, on charitable activities. Therefore, if the capital is invested at little or no return, or if expenses are artificially high, the foundation may be obliged to distribute capital to make up the shortfall.

Summary

To summarize, a charitable organization can lose its registered charity status if it:
1. fails to keep proper records,
2. fails to report,
3. carries on a business not related to its charitable activities, or
4. fails to maintain its fund raising costs at a reasonable percentage of the funds raised.

A charitable organization can become a charitable foundation if it does not expend at least 50% of its resources on its own charitable activities or those of related charities, but donates them to outside charities.

A charitable foundation can lose its registered charity status if it:

1. fails to keep proper records,
2. fails to report,
3. acquires control of a business corporation through commercial means.
4. incurs any debts, other than its current operating expenses, in connection with the purchase or sale of its investments or in the course of administering its charitable activities,
5. fails to maintain its fund raising costs at a reasonable percentage of funds raised, or
6. fails to expend minimum percentages on charitable activities.

Revocation of Registered Charity Status

It is much easier to become a registered charity than it was to obtain status as a Registered Canadian Charitable Organization prior to 1977. A charity merely has to fulfil certain preconditions. However, it is much more difficult to retain charitable status, as the above summary shows. What are the consequences of having registered charity status revoked? A registered charity must, within one year of revocation, pay off its existing debts, pay its expenses of winding-up, and distribute the balance of its property to other registered charities. Failure to do this within the year makes the charity subject to a tax of 100% of the value of the assets which it owns on the day that the Minister's intention to revoke its registration is mailed, less the amounts which have been paid or distributed for expenses, or to other charities. If the charity distributes property to a person who is not a registered charity or otherwise a qualified donee, that person is jointly and severally liable with the charity for the 100% tax on this amount.

NEW DIRECTIONS – THE CANADA NON-PROFIT CORPORATIONS ACT

There is presently (1980) before the Canadian parliament, a Bill providing for an Act to regulate Canadian non-profit corporations. The present Canada Corporations Act is recognized as archaic, and this view has been emphasized by the enactment of the Canada Business Corporations Act to replace Part I of the Canada Corporations Act. The proposed Canada Non-profit Corporations Act would replace Part II of the Canada Corporations Act, which is applicable to corporations without share capital. A review of Part II of the Canada Corporations Act shows that it merely contains a few extra rules, and a cross reference to the sections formerly applicable to all business corporations, with a direction to substitute the word "member" for the word "shareholder."

The proposed Act was initiated by the Senate, and has been studied by the Standing Senate Committee on Banking, Trade and Commerce. This proposed legislation has yet to be passed by Parliament and was last reported to be expected in force sometime in 1981.

Non-profit corporations which have been governed under the Canada Corporations Act will be governed in future by the Canada Non-profit Corporations Act, once they have applied to be continued under the new Act. The Boards of Trade Act will also be repealed, so that non-profit corporations, chambers of commerce, and boards of trade will be governed by the same Act.

Member and Charitable Corporations

The proposed Canada Non-profit Corporations Act (CNCA) recognizes that non-profit corporation law should parallel business corporation law in many instances. However, the CNCA also recognizes that non-profit corporations have a different function from business corporations in that they do not earn money for their shareholders. Different rules have to be formulated to deal with the varying functions of non-profit corporations. Consequently, the proposed CNCA does not deal with all non-profit corporations in the same fashion. It distinguishes between membership corporations, which are incorporated to carry on activities that are primarily for the benefit of their members, and charitable corporations, which are incorporated to carry on activities primarily for the benefit of the public. It is possible to be both a membership corporation and a charitable corporation, in which case the corporation is deemed to be a charitable corporation. One major innovation in the proposed CNCA is that on the liquidation of a membership corporation, the remaining property of the corporation is to be distributed in accordance with its articles of incorporation or, if the articles do not contain such provisions, then to each person having a membership interest. On the liquidation of a charitable corporation, the remaining property is distributed in accordance with its articles or, with court approval, to other charitable organizations which carry on the same or similar activities. No explicit provision is made in the present Canada Corporations Act.

Only membership corporations are contemplated under the Canada Corporations Act. The question of whether a corporation is a charitable corporation is left to common law, and this determination is given a seal of approval by the granting of registered charity status, together with a charitable number, by the Department of National Revenue.

Incorporation

The basic philosophical change behind the proposed CNCA is that the scope of governmental discretion is minimized, and as long as there is conformity with the statutory formalities, incorporation will be as of right and not as an act of ministerial prerogative. A consequence of this philosophical change is that matters will be more standardized and streamlined, and meaningless formalities will be dropped.

Incorporation under the CNCA will require the submission in duplicate of articles of incorporation, a Notice of Registered Office and Notice of Head Office (these will be standardized forms), together with a petition signed by the number of persons stipulated by the Act or by regulation.

Objects and Powers

One major amendment is that the CNCA will dispense with the requirement of having objects and powers. This parallels the provisions of the Canada Business Corporations Act. The Bill states that a corporation has the capacity, and also the rights and powers and privileges, of a natural person (i.e., an individual). Consequently, the corporation may pursue any lawful object unless there are restrictions in its articles of incorporation (articles of incorporation replace letters patent). The corporation under the CNCA will be required to have a registered or head office in Canada, and to keep records containing the articles of incorporation, together with any articles of amendment or articles of amalgamation, the by-laws, minutes of all meetings, resolutions of the members and directors, a security register, a register of its members, and a copy of all notices of directors. The Act will allow the corporation to take advantage of modern electronic methods of storage of information (presently not provided for). Members may examine the records, and if the corporation is a charity, a member of the public may do so upon payment of a reasonable fee. Because of the possibility that business organizations might use these lists for commercial purposes, it is provided that lists of members can only be used in connection with an effort to influence the voting of its members or any other matter relating to the affairs of the corporation. A person who contravened this section would be guilty of an offence, and be liable on summary conviction to a fine not exceeding $5,000.00, or to imprisonment for a term not exceeding 6 months, or both.

Innovations

Another new idea which parallels developments in the business world, is that a resolution in writing signed by all members will be as valid as if a meeting of its members had been held, so that physical gatherings will no longer be necessary. Proxy and mail ballots are also expressly provided for in the proposed Act. There are also special new provisions relating to "members' associational interests," which includes such matters as classes of members, rights of members, termination of members, discipline of members, etc. A member has also been given the statutory right to go to court if he is aggrieved by discipline or expulsion proceedings.

Members' Meetings

The CNCA will require members' meetings to be held annually, unless the articles provide for meetings every second or third year. However, the financial report will have to be sent to the members annually, whether or not a meeting is held. In lieu of forwarding financial documents to all of the members, a large non-profit corporation could publish these, as well as notices of meetings, in a local newspaper.

Accountants and Auditors

One welcome amendment which conforms with widespread practice is a provision allowing members of a membership corporation to dispense with having an auditor and appoint an accountant instead. A charitable corporation, however, will still require an auditor, and it will still be a statutory requirement for all non-profit corporations to keep adequate accounting records.

Directors

A membership corporation will require only one director. This is a reduction from the current federal requirement that a non-profit corporation must have three directors. This will be of possible interest to small foundations. However, where a charitable corporation has issued debt securities to the public, it will continue to need a minimum of three directors, with the added proviso that at least two of these directors must not be officers or employees of the corporation or its affiliates. A director need not be a member of the corporation. Directors cannot hold office for a term which exceeds three years, although they may be re-elected. This is a reduction from the present rule allowing five years under certain circumstances.

The proposed CNCA has expressly legitimized cumulative voting, which allows minorities the chance to have their candidate sit on the board of directors. In cumulative voting, if five directors are to be elected, all five votes held by a member can go to one nominee for director.

A further requirement is that directors of a charitable corporation may not transact business at a meeting of the directors unless the majority of the directors are resident Canadians. However, a Canadian director can approve in writing, or by telephone or other communication, the business transacted at the meeting, which has the effect of ratifying that business. Directors can also conduct business by way of resolutions signed by all of them. These provisions are all similar to requirements in the new business corporation law.

Directors will continue to be liable to employees of the corporation for up to 6 months' wages owing to each employee, for services performed for the corporation while they were directors.

Directors under the CNCA will still have a duty to disclose that they are a party to a "material contract" with the corporation. Unfortunately, "material" has not been defined, although one may assume that because a director owns a few shares in a monopoly telephone company he does not have to refrain from discussion of the acquisition of a sophisticated and expensive telephone system.

Directors will be able to register their dissent to business, and this will be important in view of the increased liability provisions applicable to directors. Directors who are absent from a meeting are deemed to consent to the business approved at the meeting, unless their dissents are registered forthwith.

Directors can be sued, although they continue to have the right to indemnity from the corporation if they meet with substantial success in their defence. A corporation may also purchase and maintain insurance for directors. The insurance, however, cannot cover any failure to act honestly and in good faith with a view to the best interests of the corporation.

Unanimous Members' Agreements

One significant innovation for the non-profit corporation is that members may have agreements which restrict the powers of the directors. A member who is a party to a unanimous members' agreement also has all the rights, powers, and duties of a director, to the extent that the agreement has restricted the director's powers to manage the activities and affairs of the corporation, and transferred these to the members. Conversely, the directors are relieved of their duties and liabilities to the extent that they are restricted by the provision of the members' agreement. This legislation will minimize formalities connected with the administration of a membership corporation or foundation which has few members.

The above outline is only a sketch of some of the proposed new legislation. Whether the CNCA achieves all of its aims remains to be seen. Despite the streamlining of formalities and clarification of certain matters, it remains evident that incorporating and running a non-profit corporation (and dealing with the mass of regulations and sophisticated provisions) is not for well meaning amateurs, but rather for people who wish to execute their non-profit activities in a professional manner. This is not to say that persons inexperienced in business management cannot be successfully involved in a non-profit corporation, be it a membership corporation or a charitable corporation, but they must be prepared to spend time and effort in developing in-depth knowledge and expertise.

Appendix A

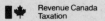

Revenue Canada
Taxation
Revenu Canada
Impôt

T2050
Rev. 77

**CANADIAN CHARITIES AND
CANADIAN AMATEUR ATHLETIC ASSOCIATIONS
APPLICATION FOR REGISTRATION**

REGISTRATION NUMBER

| | | | | | | | –| | –| | |

DATE

- For use by charities and associations when applying for registration for the purpose of the Income Tax Act.

- A separate application must be filed by each branch, section, parish, congregation or other division of a charity that receives donations or has income, on its own behalf, and wishes to be exempt from taxation under Part I of the Income Tax Act.

- One completed application, with full particulars as listed below, is to be forwarded to the Deputy Minister of National Revenue for Taxation, 400 Cumberland Street, Ottawa, Ontario, K1A 0X5, Attention: Charitable and Non-Profit Organizations Section.

- If space is insufficient, attach additional sheets with the information required.

NAME OF CHARITY OR ASSOCIATION

ADDRESS

| | FISCAL PERIOD ENDS | DAY | MONTH |

DENOMINATION *(If a religious charity)*

─────────── **PARTICULARS** ───────────

1. Attach a copy of the governing documents under which the charity or association operates, such as: Letters Patent, Charter, Constitution or Trust Deed, and the by-laws. These documents must be accompanied by a statement which will reveal full details of the activities to be carried on by the charity or association.

2. Attach a copy of a Statement of Receipts and Disbursements and of a Statement of Assets and Liabilities for the last completed year or fiscal period of operation prior to date of application.

3. State name in which the property or assets of the charity or association will be registered.

4. Given name, address and occupation of the executive or directing officers of the charity or association including, in the case of a parish or congregation, the name of the priest, pastor or minister in charge.

ADDITIONAL PARTICULARS to be given by a charity which intends to distribute more than 50% of its annual income to other charities or qualified donees as permitted by the Income Tax Act. Such a charity will be treated as a Foundation and subject to the requirements of either a Public Foundation or Private Foundation depending upon the information given.

5. Attach a list of those directors or trustees who are related by blood, marriage or adoption. If no such relationship exists, check ☐.

6. Are more than 50% of the directors or trustees related to each other by blood, marriage or adoption? ☐ YES ☐ NO
   If "YES", you may disregard Question 7.

7. To the best of your knowledge, did 75% or less of the total donations received to the date of this application come from one person or a group of persons who do not deal with each other at arm's length? ☐ YES ☐ NO
   If "YES", attach an analysis of such total contributions in support of your allegations.

─────────── **CERTIFICATION** ───────────

I,_____ of_____
  Name (Print)   Address

HEREBY CERTIFY that the information given in this application and in any documents attached is true, correct and complete in every respect.

Signature of Authorized Officer	Position or Office
Home Telephone Number	Business Telephone Number	Date

(Français au verso)

Form authorized and prescribed by the Minister of National Revenue

Appendix B

T2052
Rev. 79

REGISTERED CHARITIES AND REGISTERED
CANADIAN AMATEUR ATHLETIC ASSOCIATIONS
RETURN OF INFORMATION (FORM/FORMULE T2052)

ORGANISMES DE CHARITÉ ENREGISTRÉS ET ASSOCIATIONS
CANADIENNES ENREGISTRÉES D'ATHLÉTISME AMATEUR
DÉCLARATION DE RENSEIGNEMENTS

Full Name and Address of Charity or Association
Nom et adresse au complet de l'organisme de charité ou de l'association

REGISTRATION NO. - *Nº D'ENREGISTREMENT*

Return for Fiscal Period
Ended—
*Déclaration pour l'exercice
financier se terminant le—*

| Day Jour | Month Mois | Year Année | 9 | 10 |

41

Total Revenue Received from All
Sources including Bequests,
Income, Grants, etc. (**Omit cents**)
*Revenu total reçu de toutes prove-
nances, y compris legs, revenus,
subventions, etc.* (**Omettre les cents**)

$ | | | | | | | |
12   20

If the name or address has changed within the past twelve months or is incorrect
as shown, print the changes below. (See Instruction 1)
*Si le nom ou l'adresse ont été modifiés au cours des douze derniers mois, ou,
s'ils sont inexacts, faire les corrections ci-dessous (voir l'indication 1.)*

Change of Name/Address only – Changement de nom ou d'adresse seulement

New/Corrected Name of Charity or Association—*Nouveau nom ou nom corrigé de l'organisme de charité ou de l'association*

New/Corrected Mailing Address—*Nouvelle adresse postale ou adresse corrigée*

(Street and No.—*Nº et rue*)

(City/Town – *Ville ou village*)   (Province)   (Postal Code—*Code postal*)

- To be completed by a registered charity or a registered Canadian amateur athletic association.
- A registered charity must also file one copy of the Public Information Return—form T3010 (blue form).
- This document and attachments will form part of the Federal Information Bank B15635.

INSTRUCTIONS

1. Ensure that the registration number, name and address are correct. To correct pre-printed information on this form, please use the area provided. Any changes (except address) must be explained in an attachment to this return.
2. Complete the boxes (above right) to indicate the end of fiscal period and total revenue for that period.
3. Registered charities must answer questions 1 to 11 and, if the answer to question 11 is "YES", must also answer questions 12 to 14.
4. Registered Canadian amateur athletic associations must answer questions 1 to 10 and 15.
5. ATTACH FINANCIAL STATEMENTS for the fiscal period covered by this return (the financial information on form T3010 is not sufficient). These should include a Statement of Revenue and Expenditures for the fiscal period and a Statement of Assets and Liabilities as at the end of the fiscal period. The statements should show the different sources of revenue and sufficient details of the disbursements to show how the funds were spent or invested.
6. The "Certification" block is to be completed and signed by an officer of the charity or association.
7. Mail or deliver one completed return, within three months from the end of the fiscal period of the charity or association, TOGETHER WITH THE REQUIRED FINANCIAL STATEMENTS to:
   Charitable and Non-Profit Organizations Section.
   Department of National Revenue, Taxation
   400 Cumberland Street
   Ottawa, Ontario   K1A 0X5

- A remplir par un organisme de charité enregistré ou une association canadienne enregistrée d'athlétisme amateur.
- Un organisme de charité enregistré doit aussi produire un exemplaire de la Déclaration publique de renseignements—formule T3010 (formule bleu).
- Le présent document et les pièces jointes feront partie de la banque de données B15635.

INDICATIONS

1. Vérifier si le numéro d'enregistrement, le nom et l'adresse sont exacts. Pour corriger les renseignements déjà imprimés sur la présente formule, utiliser l'espace fourni. Tout changement (sauf un changement d'adresse) doit être expliqué sur une pièce jointe à la présente déclaration.
2. Remplir les cases (ci-dessus droite) afin d'indiquer la date de fin d'exercice financier et les recettes totales pour cet exercice.
3. Les organismes de charité enregistrés doivent répondre à toutes les questions 1 à 11 et, si la réponse à la question 11 est «OUI», ils doivent aussi répondre aux questions 12 à 14.
4. Les associations canadiennes enregistrées d'athlétisme amateur doivent répondre aux questions 1 à 10 et 15.
5. JOINDRE LES ETATS FINANCIERS de l'exercice financier visé par la présente déclaration (les renseignements financiers donnés dans la formule T3010 ne suffisent pas). Ces états doivent comprendre entre autres un état des recettes et dépenses de l'organisme de charité ou de l'association pour l'exercice financier et un état de l'actif et du passif de l'organisme de charité ou de l'association à la fin de l'exercice financier. Les états doivent indiquer les différentes sources de revenu et contenir suffisamment de détails concernant les déboursés pour indiquer comment les fonds ont été dépensés ou placés.
6. La case «Attestation» doit être remplie et signée par un agent de l'organisme de charité ou de l'association.
7. Remettre ou expédier dans les trois mois qui suivent la fin de l'exercice financier de l'organisme de charité ou de l'association, une déclaration remplie. AINSI QUE LES ETATS FINANCIERS REQUIS, au:
   Section des Oeuvres de charité et des
   Organisations sans but lucratif
   Ministère du Revenu national, Impôt
   400 rue Cumberland
   Ottawa (Ontario)   K1A 0X5

INFORMATION REQUIRED

1. (i) Have there been any changes in the aims and objectives or in the organizational structure of the charity or association since the date of "Application for Registration" that have not been previously reported? If "YES", attach full particulars.   ☐ YES/OUI   ☐ NO/NON

   (ii) Has the charity or association had a change of name or address within the past 12 months? If "YES", ensure that the "change of name/address" block above has been completed.   ☐ YES/OUI   ☐ NO/NON

2. (i) Have complete books and records been kept (including duplicate copies of receipts) which fully substantiate all financial transactions during the fiscal period? If "NO", attach explanation.   ☐ YES/OUI   ☐ NO/NON

   (ii) Are such records maintained at the address shown on this form? If "NO", attach explanation.   ☐ YES/OUI   ☐ NO/NON

3. Did the official Registration Number and the full name of the charity or association, as shown above, appear on all receipts issued to support donation claims? If "NO", attach explanation.   ☐ YES/OUI   ☐ NO/NON

4. Are records left open at end of the calendar year to permit contributors to increase their year's contribution by making a payment after year-end?   ☐ YES/OUI   ☐ NO/NON

RENSEIGNEMENTS REQUIS

1. (i) S'est-il produit quelque changement dans les buts et les objectifs ou dans la structure organisationnelle de l'organisme de charité ou de l'association depuis la date de la «Demande d'enregistrement» qui n'a jamais été déclaré? Si «OUI», annexer des détails complets.

   (ii) L'organisme de charité ou l'association a-t-il changé de nom ou d'adresse au cours des 12 derniers mois? Si «OUI», s'assurer que la case «Changement de nom ou d'adresse» été remplie.

2. (i) Des livres et des registres complet ont-ils été tenus (y compris les doubles des reçus) pour justifier toutes les transactions financières effectuées au cours de l'exercice financier? Si «NON», annexer une explication.

   (ii) Ces registres sont-ils tenus à l'adresse indiquée sur la présente formule? Si «NON», annexer une explication.

3. Le numéro d'enregistrement officiel et le nom en toutes lettres de l'organisme de charité ou de l'association indiqués ci-dessus figuraient-ils sur tous les reçus délivrés pour appuyer les réclamations au titre des dons de charité? Si «NON», annexer une explication.

4. Les registres restent-ils ouverts à la fin de l'année civile afin de permettre aux contributeurs d'augmenter leur contribution de l'année en faisant un paiement après la fin de l'année?

Continued on reverse   **Suite au verso**

87

5. Have receipts bearing the Registration Number been issued to acknowledge donations in a form other than cash or cheque—e.g. goods, services rendered, etc.? If "YES", attach full particulars.	☐ YES / OUI ☐ NO / NON	5. Des reçus portant le numéro d'enregistrement ont-ils été délivrés pour des dons autres qu'en espèces ou par chèques, c.-à-d. en biens, en services rendus, etc.? Si «OUI», annexer des détails complets.

6. Have donation receipts been issued which include an amount for "loose collections"? (i.e. where a particular donor cannot be identified with a particular donation)? If "YES", attach full particulars.

☐ YES / OUI   ☐ NO / NON   ☐ NOT APPLICABLE / NE S'APPLIQUE PAS

6. Y a-t-il eu délivrance de reçus pour dons comprenant un montant pour «perceptions diverses» (c.-à-d. lorsqu'on ne peut pas identifier un donateur comme ayant fait un don déterminé)? Si «OUI», annexer des détails complets.

7. Are the receipt forms used to acknowledge payments that are NOT donations (e.g. tuition, hall rentals, etc.) clearly distinguishable from official donation receipts which bear the Registration Number? If "NO", attach full particulars.

☐ YES / OUI   ☐ NO / NON   ☐ NOT APPLICABLE / NE S'APPLIQUE PAS

7. Les reçus utilisés à l'égard de paiements qui ne sont PAS des dons (p.e. frais de scolarité, location de salle, etc.) ces reçus se distinguent-ils clairement des reçus officiels pour dons portant le numéro d'enregistrement? Si «NON», annexer des détails complets.

8. Has any amount donated to the organization been returned to the donor during the year? If "YES", please explain in detail.

☐ YES / OUI   ☐ NO / NON

8. Est-ce qu'une ou plusieurs des sommes données à l'organisme ont été remises au donateur pendant l'année? Si «OUI», veuillez expliquer en détail.

9. What replacement procedure is followed in the event of lost or spoiled receipts? Attach full particulars.

9. Quelle procédure de remplacement est prévue dans le cas des reçus perdus ou abîmés?

10. Who are the people authorized to issue official receipts for the charity or association? Attach list of names with official positions.

10. Qui a l'autorisation de délivrer des reçus officiels au nom de l'organisme de charité ou de l'association? Annexer une liste de noms donnant les titres officiels.

11. During the fiscal period, did the charity expend (other than to approved Associated Charities) in excess of 50% of its income by way of gifts to qualified donees e.g. other registered charities, Canadian municipalities, etc.?

☐ YES / OUI   ☐ NO / NON

11. Au cours de l'exercice financier, l'organisme de charité a-t-il dépensé plus de 50% de son revenu sous forme de dons à des donataires reconnus (autres que des organismes de charité associés), par ex. à d'autres organismes de charité enregistrés, à des municipalités canadiennes, etc.

Questions 12 to 14 to be completed only if the answer to question 11 is "YES".

Ne répondre aux questions 12 à 14 que si la réponse à la question 11 est «OUI».

12. During the fiscal period has the foundation:

(i) acquired control of any corporation? If "YES", attach full particulars.   ☐ YES / OUI   ☐ NO / NON

(ii) carried on any business? If "YES", attach full particulars.   ☐ YES / OUI   ☐ NO / NON

(iii) incurred debts, other than debts for current operating expenses, debts incurred in connection with the purchase and sale of investments and debts incurred in the course of administering charitable activities? If "YES", attach full particulars.   ☐ YES / OUI   ☐ NO / NON

12. Au cours de l'exercice financier, la fondation a-t-elle:

(i) acquis le contrôle d'une corporation? Si «OUI», annexer des détails complets.

(ii) exercé une activité commerciale? Si «OUI», annexer des détails complets.

(iii) contracté des dettes autres que pour les frais d'administration courants, l'achat ou la vente de placements et l'administration d'activités de bienfaisance? Si «OUI», annexer des détails complets.

13. (i) How many directors (or trustees) governed the foundation during the fiscal period?   Number / Nombre _____

(ii) How many are related by blood, marriage or adoption? Attach a list providing names and relationships.   Number / Nombre _____

13. (i) Combien d'administrateurs (ou de fiduciaires) géraient la fondation au cours de la l'exercice financier?

(ii) Combien sont unis par les liens du sang, du mariage ou de l'adoption? Annexer une liste des noms et des liens de parenté.

14. Has the foundation made expenditures (including amounts deemed by subsection 149.1(8) of the Income Tax Act to have been expended and amounts permitted by subsection 149.1(20) of the Income Tax Act to be included in amounts expended) on charitable activities carried on by it and/or by way of gifts to qualified donees that in the aggregate are at least equal to:

(i) its disbursement quota as a private foundation, **or**   ☐ YES / OUI   ☐ NO / NON   ☐ NOT APPLICABLE / NE S'APPLIQUE PAS

(ii) the greater of

(a) 80% (50% if this return is filed for a 1977 fiscal period, 60% if for a 1978 fiscal period and 70% if for a 1979 fiscal period) of amounts for which it issued official donation receipts in its immediately preceding taxation year, **and**   ☐ YES / OUI   ☐ NO / NON   ☐ NOT APPLICABLE / NE S'APPLIQUE PAS

(b) 90% of its income for the year.

If "YES" is not applicable to either (i) or (ii), attach full particulars.

14. La fondation a-t-elle dépensé des montants (y compris les montants réputés avoir été dépensés, en vertu du paragraphe 149.1(8) de la Loi de l'impôt sur le revenu, et les montants pouvant être inclus dans les montants dépensés, en vertu du paragraphe 149.1(20) de la Loi de l'impôt sur le revenu) pour des activités de bienfaisance qu'elle a menées et (ou) pour des dons à des donataires reconnus dont le total est au moins égal à:

(i) son «montant des paiements à effectuer» à titre de fondation privée, **ou**

(ii) le plus élevé de

(a) 80% (50% si la présente déclaration est remplie pour l'exercice financier 1977, 60% pour l'exercice financier 1978 et 70% pour l'exercice financier 1979) des montants pour lesquels elle a délivré des reçus officielles au cours de l'année d'imposition précédente, **et**

(b) 90% de son revenu pour l'année.

Si «OUI» ne s'applique pas à (i) ni à (ii), annexer des détails complets.

To be completed by Registered Canadian Amateur Athletic Associations.

À remplir par les associations canadiennes enregistrées d'athlétisme amateur.

15. During the fiscal period has the association accepted a gift or donation the granting of which was expressly or impliedly conditional on the association making a gift or donation to another person, club, society or association? If "YES", attach full particulars.

☐ YES / OUI   ☐ NO / NON

15. Au cours de l'exercice financier, l'association a-t-elle accepté quelque donation ou don fait, de façon tacite ou implicite, sous réserve que l'association fasse un don ou une donation à une autre personne, un autre club, une autre société ou une autre association? Si «OUI», fournir des détails complets.

═══ CERTIFICATION ═══ ATTESTATION ═══

I, / Je, _____ of / de _____

Name (Print) — Nom (en capitales)   Address — Adresse

HEREBY CERTIFY that the information given in this return and in all schedules and statements attached is true, correct and complete in every respect.

CERTIFIE PAR LES PRÉSENTES que les renseignements fournis dans cette déclaration et dans tous états et annexes ci-joints sont vrais, exacts et complets sous tous les rapports.

Signature of Authorized Officer — Signature d'un dirigeant autorisé   Position or Office — Poste ou fonction

Home Tel. No. — Téléphone (Résidence)   Business Tel. No. — Téléphone (Bureau)   Date

Form authorized and prescribed by the Minister of National Revenue   Formule autorisée et prescrite par le ministre du Revenu national

Appendix C

Revenue Canada **Revenu Canada**
Taxation Impôt

T3010
Rev. 79

REGISTERED CHARITIES
PUBLIC INFORMATION RETURN (FORM/FORMULE T3010)

ORGANISMES DE CHARITÉ ENREGISTRÉS
DÉCLARATION PUBLIQUE DE RENSEIGNEMENTS

Full Name and Address of Charity
Nom et adresse au complet de l'organisme de charité ou de l'association

REGISTRATION NO. - *Nº D'ENREGISTREMENT*

Return for Fiscal Period
Ended—
*Déclaration pour l'exercice
financier se terminant le—*

| | | 1 | 9 | | |

Day / Jour   Month / Mois   Year / Année   9   10

If the name or address has changed within the past twelve months or is incorrect as shown, print the changes below. (See instruction 1)
Si le nom ou l'adresse ont été modifiés au cours des douze derniers mois, ou s'ils sont inexacts, faire les corrections ci-dessous (voir l'indication 1.)

Change of Name/Address only – *Changement de nom ou d'adresse seulement*

New/Corrected Name of Charity – *Nouveau nom ou nom corrigé de l'organisme de charité*

New/Corrected Mailing Address – *Nouvelle adresse postale ou adresse corrigée*

(Street and No. – *No et rue*)

(City/Town – *Ville ou village*)   (Province)   (Postal Code – *Code postal*)

- To be completed by a registered charity.
- A copy of this return will be made available for public viewing at the Revenue Canada, Taxation, District Offices and Head Office.
- One copy of the Return of Information—form T2052 (yellow form) must also be filed.
- This document and attachments will form part of the Federal Information Bank B15636.

INSTRUCTIONS

1. Ensure that the registration number and name and address are correct. To correct pre-printed information on this form please use the area provided above. Any changes (except address) must be explained in an attachment to the Return of Information—form T2052 (yellow form).

2. Complete the boxes (above right) to indicate the end of the fiscal period of the charity.
3. This return is divided into five parts. Part II is to be completed only if the charity is a religious organization eligible to claim exemption from completion of Parts III to V. Otherwise all information must be given, if applicable.
4. The "Certification" block is to be completed and signed by an officer of the charity.
5. Mail or deliver one completed return, within three months from the end of the fiscal period of the charity, together with attachments

   to: Charitable and Non-Profit Organizations Section,
   Department of National Revenue, Taxation
   400 Cumberland Street, Ottawa, Ontario K1A 0X5

6. Certain technical terms used in this return appear in *italics* and are explained in the enclosed Appendix B.

PART I – GENERAL INFORMATION

Prepare and attach a statement giving the following information:
(Appendix A is provided for convenience and may be used for this purpose)
1. The name, address and occupation of each executive or directing officer of the charity including, in the case of a parish or congregation, the name of the priest or minister in charge.

2. A brief statement of the primary purpose of the charity.
3. A brief description of the activities of the charity during the fiscal period covered by this return.

PART II – EXEMPTION CLAIM
(See instruction 3 above)
1. Was the charity in existence on 31st December, 1977?
   Yes ☐ No ☐
2. In the fiscal period was the charity a religious organization or, pursuant to subsection 149.1(7) of the Income Tax Act, was it associated with a registered charity that was a religious organization? Yes ☐ No ☐

   If "Yes", state name of *associated charity*, if applicable.

3. Since 31st December, 1977, has the charity received an amount for which an official donation receipt has been or will be issued by it?
   Yes ☐ No ☐
4. Has the charity, directly or indirectly, received as a gift an amount from another registered charity, including an *associated charity*, that, since 31st December, 1977, has issued any official donation receipts?
   Yes ☐ No ☐
Note—To be eligible for exemption from completion of Parts III to V, the answers to 1 and 2 above must be "Yes" AND the answers to 3 and 4 above must be "No"

Continued on reverse

- À remplir par un organisme de charité enregistré.
- Le public pourra consulter un exemplaire de la présente déclaration dans les bureaux de district et au Bureau principal de Revenu Canada, Impôt.
- Il faut également produire un exemplaire de la formule T2052, Déclaration de renseignements (formule jaune).
- Le présent document et les pièces jointes feront partie de la banque de données B15636.

INDICATIONS

1. S'assurer que le numéro d'enregistrement, le nom et l'adresse sont exacts. Apporter les corrections nécessaires aux renseignements préimprimés, dans la section prévue à cette fin ci-dessus. Tous les changements (sauf les changements d'adresse) doivent être expliqués sur une pièce jointe à la Déclaration de renseignements—formule T2052 (formule jaune).

2. Remplir les cases (ci-dessus droite) pour indiquer la date de fin d'exercice financier de l'organisme de charité.
3. Cette déclaration est divisée en cinq parties. La partie II doit être remplie seulement si l'organisme est un organisme religieux admissible à la demande relative à l'exemption de fournir les renseignements des parties III à V. Autrement tous les renseignements voulus doivent être fournis.
4. La case «Attestation» doit être remplie et signée par un agent de l'organisme de charité.
5. Remettre ou expédier par la poste, dans les trois mois suivant la fin de l'exercice financier de l'organisme de charité, une déclaration remplie ainsi que les pièces jointes
   au: Section des Oeuvres de charité et des
   Organisations sans but lucratif.
   Ministère du Revenu national, Impôt
   400, rue Cumberland, Ottawa (Ontario) K1A 0X5

6. Certaines termes techniques utilisés dans la présente déclaration sont indiqués en *italiques* et sont expliqués à l'Appendice B ci-joint.

PARTIE I – RENSEIGNEMENTS GÉNÉRAUX

Préparer et annexer un état fournissant les renseignements suivants:
(L'Appendice A ci-joint peut servir à cette fin)
1. Le nom, l'adresse et l'occupation de chacun des membres de l'exécutif ou de la direction de l'organisme de charité, y compris, dans le cas d'une paroisse ou d'une congrégation, le nom du prêtre ou du ministre responsable.

2. Un bref exposé du but principal de l'organisme de charité.
3. Une brève description des activités de l'organisme de charité au cours de l'exercice financier visé par la présente déclaration.

PARTIE II – DEMANDE D'EXEMPTION
(nº 3 ci-dessus)
1. L'organisme de charité existait il le 31 décembre 1977?
   Oui ☐ Non ☐
2. Au cours de l'exercice financier, l'organisme de charité était-il un organisme religieux ou, conformément au paragraphe 149.1(7) de la Loi de l'impôt sur le revenu, était-il associé à un organisme de charité enregistré qui était un organisme religieux? Oui ☐ Non ☐
   Si «Oui», donner le nom de *l'organisme de charité associé*, s'il y a lieu.

3. L'organisme de charité a-t-il reçu depuis le 31 décembre 1977 un montant pour lequel il a émis ou émettra un reçu officiel pour un don?
   Oui ☐ Non ☐
4. L'organisme de charité a-t-il reçu en don, directement ou indirectement, un montant provenant d'un autre organisme de charité, y compris un *organisme de charité associé*, qui a émis, depuis le 31 décembre 1977, des reçus officiels pour des dons? Oui ☐ Non ☐
Remarque—Pour être admissible à la demande relative à l'exemption de remplir les Parties III à V, la réponse à 1 et 2 ci-dessus doit être «Oui» ET la réponse à 3 et 4 ci-dessus doit être «Non».

Suite au verso

89

PART III
A. Revenue for the Fiscal Period

1. Gifts received for which official receipts for income tax purposes have been or will be issued. ▶ $_____ ◀

2. Gifts received, excluding grants from federal, provincial or municipal governments, for which official receipts for income tax purposes have not been and will not be issued. ▶ _____ ◀

3. Other amounts received
   (a) Grants (specify sources)

   _____ ▶ _____ ◀
   _____ ▶ _____ ◀

   (b) Investment income ▶ _____ ◀
   (c) Net Realized Capital Gains (Losses) ▶ _____ ◀
   (d) Other income (specify)_____ ▶ _____ ◀
   _____ ▶ _____ ◀
   _____ ▶ _____ ◀

   Total Revenue ▶ $_____ ◀

B. Expenditures for the Fiscal Period

1. Remuneration:
   (a) Total amount of remuneration (including benefits) paid to officers or employees on account of the direct performance of charitable activities ▶ $_____ ◀

   (b) Other remuneration paid ▶ _____ ◀
   Total remuneration paid ▶ $_____ ◀

2. Total administration costs other than remuneration ▶ _____ ◀

3. Total amount of gifts to charities designated as *associated charities* by the Minister of National Revenue ▶ _____ ◀

4. Total amount of gifts to *qualified donees* (excluding gifts to designated *associated charities*) ▶ _____ ◀

5. Total amount, other than administration costs and remuneration, expended directly on charitable activities ▶ _____ ◀

6. Total amount expended to purchase assets used directly in the carrying on of charitable activities. (Do not include expenditures to acquire property for investment purposes.) ▶ _____ ◀

7. Other expenditures (excluding investments) ▶ _____ ◀

   Total Expenditures ▶ $_____ ◀

C. Deemed Expenditures for the Fiscal Period

Property accumulated during the fiscal period for specific purposes in accordance with written approval of the Minister of National Revenue ▶ $_____ ◀

PART IV

To be completed by charities whose combined
   (i) capital and surplus, and
   (ii) *property accumulated* for specific purposes in accordance with the written approval of the Minister of National Revenue
exceeds $100,000 as at the end of the fiscal period.

Current Assets ▶ $_____ ◀
Long term and Fixed Assets ▶ _____ ◀

   Total Assets ▶ $_____ ◀

Current Liabilities ▶ $_____ ◀
Long term Liabilities ▶ $_____ ◀
Property accumulated for specific purposes in accordance with written approval of the Minister of National Revenue ▶ _____ ◀
Capital and Surplus ▶ _____ ◀

   Total Liabilities and Equity ▶ $_____ ◀

PART V – ADDITIONAL INFORMATION

1. Number of officers and employees of the charity whose annual gross remuneration (including benefits) exceeded $25,000 ▶ _____ ◀

2. Gross remuneration (including benefits) paid in the year to employees who, during that year, were executive officers, directors or trustees of the charity ▶ _____ ◀

Note: Additional material explaining or amplifying the information provided in this return may, if the charity wishes, be attached. Such material should be labelled "Attachment to form T3010"

PARTIE III
A. Revenus pour l'exercice financier

1. Dons reçus pour lesquels des reçus officiels ont été ou seront émis aux fins de l'impôt.

2. Dons reçus sauf les subventions accordées par les gouvernements municipaux, provinciaux ou fédéral, pour lesquels aucun reçu n'a été ni ne sera émis aux fins de l'impôt.

3. Autres sommes reçues
   a) Subventions (préciser l'origine)

   b) Revenus de placements
   c) Gains (pertes) nets en capital réalisés
   d) Autres revenus (préciser)

   Total des revenus

B. Dépenses pour l'exercice financier

1. Rémunération:
   a) Montant total de la rémunération (y compris les avantages) versée aux dirigeants ou aux employés relativement au travail accompli directement dans le cadre d'activités de bienfaisance

   b) Autre rémunération versée
   Total de la rémunération versée

2. Total des frais d'administration autres que la rémunération

3. Montant total des dons faits à des organismes de charité désignés comme étant des *organismes de charité associés* par le ministre du Revenu national

4. Montant total des dons faits à des *donataires reconnus* (sauf les dons faits à des *organismes de charité associés*)

5. Montant total des sommes, autres que les frais d'administration et la rémunération, dépensées directement dans le cadre d'activités de bienfaisance

6. Montant total dépensé pour l'achat de biens utilisés directement dans la poursuite d'activités de bienfaisance. (Ne pas inclure les dépenses faites dans le cadre de l'acquisition de bien pour fins de placement)

7. Autres dépenses (sauf les placements)

   Total des dépenses

C. Dépenses présumées pour l'exercice financier

Biens accumulés durant l'exercice financier à des fins précises selon l'approbation écrite du ministre du Revenu national

PARTIE IV

À remplir par les organismes de charité dont le total
   (i) du capital et du surplus, de même que
   (ii) de la valeur des *biens accumulés* pour des fins précises selon l'approbation écrite du ministre du Revenu national
est supérieur à $100,000 à la fin de l'exercice financier.

Actif à court terme
Actif à long terme et immobilisations

   Total de l'actif

Passif à court terme
Passif à long terme
Biens accumulés à des fins précises avec l'approbation écrite du ministre du Revenu national
Capital et surplus

   Total du passif et de l'avoir propre

PARTIE V – RENSEIGNEMENTS SUPPLÉMENTAIRES

1. Nombre de cadres et d'employés de l'organisme dont la rémunération annuelle brute (y compris les avantages) dépasse $25,000

2. Rémunération brute (y compris les avantages) versée durant l'année aux employés, qui durant cette année, étaient cadres supérieurs de l'organisme de charité

Remarque: L'organisme de charité peut, s'il le désire, ajouter d'autres documents expliquant plus clairement les renseignements fournis. Ces documents doivent être identifiés par la mention «Pièce jointe à la T3010».

─── CERTIFICATION ─── ATTESTATION ───

I,
Je,_____ of
        Name (Print) — Nom (en capitales) de _____
                                          Address — Adresse

HEREBY CERTIFY that the information given in this return and in all schedules and statements attached is true, correct and complete in every respect.

CERTIFIE PAR LES PRÉSENTES que les renseignements fournis dans cette déclaration et dans tous états et annexes ci-joints sont vrais, exacts et complets sous tous les rapports.

_____
Signature of Authorized Officer — Signature d'un dirigeant autorisé

_____
Position or Office — Poste ou fonction

_____
Charity's Tel. No. — Téléphone (Organisme de charité)

_____
Date

Form authorized and prescribed by the Minister of National Revenue

Formule autorisée et prescrite par le Ministre du Revenu national

CHAPTER 5 THE PUBLIC GALLERY AND MUSEUM IN CANADA

INTRODUCTION

In contrast to the United States, with its private museums created by wealthy families such as Guggenheim, Rockefeller, Barnes, or Mellon, Canada has had a history of public museums and galleries rather than private, or at least privately endowed, galleries. Almost all of our institutions are publicly funded non-profit organizations, created as adjuncts to the cultural policy of a city, a province, or the federal government. This chapter will therefore deal with the public, non-profit, charitable institution since this is by far the most common kind of institution in Canada.

Public museums or galleries are increasingly under the microscope of the media, governments, special interest groups, and the public generally. The age of cultural "democratization" has come. Statistics indicate that more people visit museums and art galleries in Canada each year than attend all the professional sporting events in the country. Museums have increased dramatically in both number and in size. In the early and middle 1970's, a new museum was being opened somewhere in North America every day of the year.

Museums are now in the "numbers game." They are concerned with the number of visitors, shows, donations, and other matters that can be dealt with quantitatively. Major shows such as *Treasures of Tutankhamun,* the show of treasures from Russian museums, and the Chinese show, have drawn huge crowds. They also have resulted in the creation of a special "hype" for the public museum and gallery. Museums today are big business. They have big budgets, big staffs, and big buildings. Some Canadian museums have budgets equal in size to major commercial trading corporations.

This "culture business" has spawned various cultural offspring such as arts magazines, arts and artists' associations, private dealers and dealer associations, government art departments (both federal and provincial), museum organizations, and staff associations. The culture business is a major employer in Canada.

In turn, these cultural organizations have given rise to special funding and funding projects: Loto Canada, Wintario, special provisions of the Cultural Property Export and Import Act, the federal Art Bank, Canada Council, Ontario Arts Council, Alberta Heritage, and various other provincial councils and heritage organizations across Canada.

The museums have come of age. There are multi-million dollar buildings to be maintained, expensive collections to be preserved, and the public to be served. In many cases the small municipal gallery has had to grow up. The Art Gallery of Toronto became the Art Gallery of Ontario and attracted notice through its large collection of Henry Moore sculptures; the National Gallery of Canada stopped serving just Ottawa and became a focal point for important national and international exhibitions; the Alberta-Glenbow Institute became famous for its early Canadian and Western Canadian museum objects; the Edmonton Art Gallery became known for its "colour field" shows; the Winnipeg Museum gained international recognition for its Eskimo collection. There are numerous other examples of the growth of these and similar institutions.

In the aftermath of this growth, we have gigantic institutions and budgets, requiring gigantic responsibilities. These responsibilities rest with both the boards of trustees and with the staff. The responsibilities are financial and legal as well as professional. At times, however, it appears that only the cultural or professional aspects of the institution are being attended to, and little attention is given to the financial and legal responsibilities of boards of trustees and staff. The last thing museums need today is a legal scandal and investigation. All museums and galleries can learn from the headlines raised during 1979 by the financial problems which have beset the Royal Ontario Museum. No president of an institution, or board of trustees, wants to be placed in the position of having to make explanations in public to government investigators.

Museum personnel should be familiar with the structure of the institution and the roles of the executive committee and board of trustees. They must also know their obligations in law and finance. This raises questions about the training of museum personnel. Various museum organizations over the years have discussed the need for professional staff to be exposed to courses on administration, finance, law and other "worldly" matters which affect the gallery. Having regard to the substantial financial and public duties of museum staff, these areas cannot be neglected. As well, the institution may require professional help from lawyers and accountants on an ongoing basis. Often, funding bodies require special financial and legal safeguards, and will demand particular commitments from the recipient institution.

In order to better understand some of the basic legal concepts affecting museums, it is necessary to analyze the structure of each institution to discover what kind of a legal entity it is.

CREATION OF A PUBLIC GALLERY OR MUSEUM

Is it incorporated? If so, has the incorporation come about by way of a special Act of the federal parliament or the provincial legislature? For example, the Art Gallery of Ontario is specifically dealt with by special legislation in the Province of Ontario, the Art

Gallery of Ontario Act. Another example is a private Bill which has been introduced in the Province of Ontario putting forward an Act to incorporate the MacDonald Stewart Community Art Centre. Or is it perhaps incorporated under provincial or federal corporations laws as a non-profit corporation? If so, the institution will probably have applied for registered charity status and received a charitable number from Ottawa. This enables the gallery or museum to receive donations from the public and issue tax receipts for them, making such donations tax deductible to the donor. As well, such an institution is itself exempt from payment of income tax. The taxation aspects of such institutions are considered in Chapter 4 dealing with Non-Profit Structures. Unless the museum is an "arm of the Crown," like the National Gallery, the Museum of Man, etc., it will generally be this kind of non-profit corporation.

The mechanics of incorporating a public gallery or museum are also discussed in Chapter 4. For the purpose of this discussion, it is sufficient to point out that the museum or gallery's incorporating document is its "bible," defining its powers, and governing its conduct, in accordance with its "objects" as specified in the incorporating document, and through internally passed by-laws.

GOVERNMENT OF A PUBLIC GALLERY OR MUSEUM

The museum is generally run by a board of directors, usually called the board of trustees, which sometimes appoints an executive committee from among its most senior members to act as an ultimate authority. The composition of the board of trustees is often set out in the incorporating document, and may be very rigid because of government policy in regard to funding the particular institution and the need for government control of the institution. For instance, the Art Gallery of Ontario Act specifically indicates that the affairs of the gallery shall be managed and controlled by a board of trustees consisting of 27 trustees. Of these 27 trustees, 5 are appointed by the College of Founders, 10 from the general membership of the gallery, 2 from the municipality, and 10 others are appointed by the provincial government.

The board sets *policy,* which must be within the powers of the given institution as set out in its incorporating document. The powers of the corporation must be considered carefully when the policy of the institution is being set or expanded. These policies are then implemented by the professional staff and the director (not to be confused with the board of directors and board of trustees). Generally, this implementation takes place through by-laws and resolutions passed by the board, pursuant to the incorporating document. The curators, controllers, registrars, and staff are the permanent "secretariat" of the institution who carry out these policies.

Boards of Directors

In the January, 1979 issue of *En Route* magazine, an article entitled "Behind Closed Doors," dealing with boards of directors of business corporations, indicated that are some 13,000 people holding directorships in the top 2,500 companies in the country. If you include all the public and privately owned companies in the country, there are more than 100,000 directorships that have to be filled. According to a Conference Board survey, the average board has 10 to 12 members, and meets 5 to 6 times a year. The article points out that, over the years, the role of the board of directors has changed considerably and, naturally, this has altered the kind of qualifications needed in a potential director. Over the last 10 years there have been a lot of changes brought to the board room:

Directors today are legally liable to the shareholders for the performance of the company, and that has made two basic differences. First, it has increased the work load considerably because you have to take enough time to monitor operations in some detail. You can't vote on the proposals without doing the necessary research and that means hours and hours of reading to prepare for each meeting, as well as some time spent evaluating everything afterwards.

The second change is in the kind of people who are being chosen. The trend now is towards more independent directors who have no prior connection with the company and yet are sufficiently knowledgeable to make a contribution to it.

The article indicated that more and more people who are qualified to be directors are turning down directorships:

The work load has increased sharply, as has the legal liability of the director to the shareholder. Also the rules of conflict of interest have tightened up considerably so that many corporation presidents are starting to decline directorships. All of these factors are reducing the supply of suitable board members at a time when, particularly now that a majority of members of the audit committee must be from outside the company, the demand for independent directors is increasing.

Boards of Trustees (or Boards of Directors)

To be asked to become a trustee of an art gallery or museum is more than an honour, it is an obligation and responsibility to the applicant. What are the trustee's duties?

Trustees' Duties

The members of boards of directors or trustees of a corporation, be it business or not-for-profit, are agents and trustees in their relationship to the corporation. Their responsibilities have been developed over the years by various provincial and federal statutes and through common law decisions. In reality, the board of trustees is the mind of the non-profit corporation, and its heart. The whole subject of directors' duties is a developing area, with more and more responsibility being placed on directors as time passes.

The custom of appointing influential or socially prominent and wealthy people in the community as trustees is often advantageous for the institution. It is suggested that the institution owes a duty to such persons as well; a duty to make them aware of the responsibility being placed upon them and of their fiduciary relationship to the institution. Specifically, the duties of a director are as follows:

1. To be informed. It is a fundamental necessity to know what is going on in the institution.
2. To act in good faith towards, and in the interest of, all the members and the institution.
3. To avoid or declare a conflict of interest. There are bound to be some conflicts of interest since boards generally contain people who are involved in the field within which the organization functions because, of course, these are the people who have knowledge of that field. In most jurisdictions, statutes deal with conflict of interest situations. Rules provide, for example, that the party declare the conflict, leave the meeting, and thus not participate in the decision. The by-laws of the institution may specifically permit the trustee to have an interest in companies which deal with the institution if this fact is disclosed and if the contract under consideration is advantageous to the institution.
4. The trustee must acquaint himself with the trust property. This involves becoming familiar with both the physical plant and the art objects within it.
5. There is a duty on the part of the trustee to deal honestly and in the best interests of the institution and, conversely, the institution must deal evenhandedly with the trustee. There have been instances where trustees of an institution have been allowed to take home art, store their collections within the institution free of charge, obtain free advice from the curators, or buy in competition with the gallery and with the advice of the curator. All such dealings are suspect, and contrary to the trust relationship.
6. Both the institution and the trustees must obey the law. This is obviously true in regard to such matters as purchasing works which are known to have been stolen, or which may have been imported in violation of the UNESCO Treaty dealing with national treasures. Questions may also arise concerning obscenity laws and exhibitions which may violate such laws or any other laws of the land. It is important to keep trustees

informed of any potential violation of the law so that they can decide intelligently whether to take the risk or not.

TRUSTEES' MANUAL

The more information a trustee has, the less risk of problems there will be and the better the trustee will perform. For example, institutions should consider the preparation of a *trustees' manual,* like that recently prepared at the Art Gallery of Ontario. This institution, in an attempt to make certain that the trustee is fully informed, provides a number of services for both new and old trustees. For instance, when new trustees are added to the board, arrangements are made to take them on a tour of the institution so that it, and its various departments, are explained. As well, the trustees' manual is handed out to all trustees well in advance of the first meeting each year so that they have an opportunity to study it. Also, each meeting of the board will have in attendance the head of a particular department, such as curatorial, security, education, library, administration, extension, art rental, photography, public relations, etc., who will outline the operation of that department to the trustees.

If a trustees' manual is to be used, these are some of the areas that might be considered for inclusion:

1. The history of the institution.
2. A breakdown of information about funding, to indicate how the institution operates financially.
3. Information about the role of the board of trustees and its legal responsibility.
4. A copy of the incorporating statute or at least the portions relevant to trustees.
5. A copy, or relevant portions, of the by-laws.
6. An outline of any committee system which exists.
7. An outline of the staff departments and the various persons in charge.
8. A summary by the solicitor for the institution of the various legal responsibilities of the board to the institution, the staff, and the public.

Directors (trustees) generally have a duty of skill and care. A director must exercise ordinary judgment and prudence. If, however, a director possesses specific skills (for example, if he is a lawyer, architect, etc.), these skills must be used in the interest of the corporation above and beyond the ordinary skills of directors generally.

Directors, in regard to their obligation to be informed, have a duty to attend regularly the general meetings and the meetings of any committees on which they sit.

SPECIAL INTEREST TRUSTEES

A person who accepts a position as a director or trustee, although he may be the specific representative or nominee of a special interest group such as artists, the municipality, the provincial government, etc., has nonetheless the same responsibilities and duties to the institution and its members as does every other trustee. His duty lies to the institution and not to the special interest group.

As well, because of conflict of interest, the trustee or director may not use special information for his own benefit. The trust or good faith relationship requires that this information be kept confidential wherever required in the best interests of the institution. This is especially true for the "special interest" trustee, who must remember his trust relationship to the institution.

The trustee can be held accountable, both morally and financially, to the institution for any profit or gain realized through dealing with the institution's assets, or for any other advantage he gains because of the nature of his office.

Many laws contain provisions which place direct statutory liabilities upon directors. For instance, the Business Corporations Act of Ontario states, "every director and officer of a corporation shall exercise the powers and discharge the duties of his office honestly, in good faith, and in the best interests of the corporation, and in connection therewith shall exercise the degree of care, diligence and skill that a reasonably prudent person would exercise in comparable circumstances."

Directors may be responsible in various other ways. For instance, if a member of the general public suffers loss or injury as a result of negligence on the part of the corporation or its officers or directors, in some circumstances it is possible to impose liability on each director. Under statutes such as the Income Tax Act, the various corporations acts, etc., there are many forms and returns which must be filed by corporations. In default of filing, directors can be held individually responsible, and may be fined or imprisoned. The same is true if they fail to file proper documentation with income tax returns. Where the corporation becomes insolvent, directors may be held responsible for wages of employees owing or unpaid, for income tax deductions, workmen's compensation deductions, pension or medical deductions, and other deductions which should have been made and remitted to the appropriate department. Generally, however, a director is not held responsible for general contracts made by the corporation.

The director must concern himself with fulfilling his duty and responsibility towards the institution and the trust property, for if he does not, an action may be brought against him for any damages suffered by the institution. The director may also have responsibilities to the public and to third party outsiders.

Indemnification of Trustees

Various jurisdictions allow by-laws to be passed indemnifying directors from loss or damage arising in the course of their activities as a director or trustee. This would, of course, be restricted to those acts done *bona fide* by the trustee on behalf of the institution. For example, the by-laws of the Art Gallery of Ontario provide that:

> No trustee, officer or member of any committee of the board shall be liable for the acts, receipts, neglects, or defaults of any other trustee, officer or member, or for joining in any receipt or other act for conformity, or for any loss or expense happening to the gallery through the insufficiency or deficiency of title to any property acquired by order of the trustee, officer or member for or on behalf of the gallery, or for the insufficiency or deficiency of any security in or upon which any of the monies of the gallery shall be invested, or for any loss or damage arising from the bankruptcy, insolvency or tortious act of any person with whom any of the monies, securities or effects of the gallery shall be deposited, or for any loss occasioned by any error of judgment or oversight on his part, or for any other loss, damage or misfortune whatever which shall happen in the execution of the duties of his office or in relation thereto unless the same shall happen through his own dishonesty.

> As well, the trustee is indemnified and saved harmless out of the funds of the gallery from all costs or charges and expenses associated with any suit brought against him in respect of any deed or act made, done or permitted by him in or about the execution of his duties of his office in relation to the affairs of the gallery, except for such costs occasioned by his own wilful neglect or default.

INSURANCE

An indemnification clause such as the one cited above, assumes the existence of sufficient funds to indemnify the trustee. Some jurisdictions also permit insurance coverage against such liability. This may be purchased by the institution and is becoming more common in various parts of the United States. This can be especially important to smaller institutions which would not have sufficient funds to indemnify their trustees.

CONTRACTS WITH PROFESSIONAL STAFF

Some employees of public institutions are union members, and their contracts will therefore be dealt with as part of a collective agreement. In some institutions, however, there may be either no collective agreement, or one which excludes certain professional staff. Where this is the case, a special contract between the institution and the art executive may need to be negotiated.

A number of institutions have developed their own form of contract to be used when hiring professional staff. As well, the newly created Association of Cultural Executives has developed a contract which they have made available to their members. While it is impossible to provide a model contract which would serve in all circumstances, the following list will indicate the areas of consideration in such a contract:

1. Who are the parties to the contract? (It is amazing how often improper names or designations are given.)
2. The term of the contract and any right to renew the contract by either party.
3. If for a limited term, whether this term is based on the calendar year, school year, the exhibition season, etc.
4. If for an indefinite term, the reasons for which notice could be given, and the amount of notice which must be given.
5. A proper job description, including any information as to whom the employee will report, and how often.
6. The salary payable, and any fringe benefits such as automobile expenses, charge accounts, conference fees, etc., together with any maximum amounts which can be claimed as fringe benefits.
7. Other benefits such as pension plans, medical or dental plans, life or accident insurance, etc., and the amounts to be paid by each party.
8. Sick leave benefits, and whether an employee can be dismissed for physical or mental illness lasting more than a specified length of time.
9. How disputes are to be handled. If by arbitration, how arbitrators will be chosen.
10. Whether employment is conditional upon receipt of funding from a given source or sources.
11. Who will hold copyright in any material which the employee is required to write.
12. Whether the employee may accept additional employment or remuneration outside the institution. Who is to receive any honoraria or fees for permitted outside consultation or services.
13. Information and regulations regarding ethics and responsibilities, as outlined in the next section, must be provided. This can be done by reference in the contract to available handbooks.

PROFESSIONAL PRACTICES IN MUSEUMS AND ART GALLERIES

This area is the subject of a book by the Association of Art Museum Directors of the United States. As well, the Canadian Art Museum Directors Association has ratified an outline of professional practices for art museums. The basis of all professional practices are principles of common sense and disclosure. Making the staff aware of potential conflicts of interest or breaches of good faith is crucial. Failure to provide proper information can result in errors and wrong decisions. Various museum organizations have set standards of care for their professional staff to follow. The staff should, of course, be made aware of these standards. Generally, the rules for staff are similar to those applicable to directors, i.e., good faith, disclosure, non-competition, and a knowledge of the institution. For instance, the "Professional Practices in Art Museums" regulations ratified by the Canadian Art Museum Directors Organization, indicates that a member of the professional staff shall not:

1. Take advantage of his or her professional status by engaging directly or indirectly in art trade, or exhibiting, within his or her institution, works of art for personal gain.
2. Recommend for purchase, whether to his or her own museum or to other persons, any work of art in which he or she has an undisclosed financial interest.
3. Accept any commission or gift from a vendor.
4. Give any certificate or written statement for a fee with respect to authenticity or authorship or monetary value of works of art.
5. Give financial evaluation of works of art which have no connection with the museum program.

The regulations also indicate that any work of art to be purchased or sold by a member of the professional staff for his or her personal purposes must first be offered to the institution. It also indicates that each institution should establish a policy regarding fees for staff engaged in extracurricular teaching and lectures.

LOANS TO INSTITUTIONS

The regulations referred to above also deal with the obligation of an institution borrowing works. They indicate that the borrower must treat borrowed objects with at least the same care and security as is provided for its own collection. As well, the institution must not undertake any repairs, including reframing or rematting, of works on loan without the full knowledge and consent in writing of the lender. The borrower is also to advise the owner of any significant change in the condition of any objects lent, and keep the written records necessary to meet that obligation. The borrower must make itself aware of any restrictions on the loan, including restrictions as to exhibition, reproduction, and insurance.

Immunity from Seizure

Before lending works of art for a touring show, various countries will ask the recipient jurisdiction to pass legislation dealing with immunity from seizure. This was requested, for example, by the Government of the Soviet Union before Russian works were allowed to be shown in North America. This is done in order to make certain that while the works are on display, no one could have them held in the jurisdiction pending trial to determine legal ownership. This could have been a real concern in the example above because of potential claims by descendants of the Czar. Similar legislation was demanded and received by the Government of Egypt in regard to the Tutankhamun exhibition. Such legislation is provincial in nature. At least three provinces (Ontario, Manitoba, and Quebec) have passed laws to deal with this problem on an ongoing basis. The Ontario Act has the unwieldy title, An Act to Render Immune from Seizure Certain Objects of Cultural Significance according to Ontario for Temporary Display or Exhibition. This Act applies only to works of art or objects of cultural significance which are brought in from a foreign country pursuant to an agreement between their foreign owner or custodian (a museum, for instance) and the Government of Ontario or a cultural or educational institution in Ontario. The importation must be for a *temporary* exhibition or display which is non-profit and administered by the Government of Ontario or the cultural or educational institution. In this case, it is guaranteed that no proceeding will be taken in any court, and no judgment will be decreed or enforced in Ontario, which would have the effect of causing a work to be seized. Before the work or object is brought into Ontario, the Lieutenant Governor in Council must determine by an Order in Council that it is of cultural significance and that its temporary exhibition or display is in the interest of the people of Ontario. The Act does not preclude any judicial action to enforce the terms of any agreement regarding the exhibition or transportation of the work or the fulfilment of any obligation assumed by the Government of Ontario under such an agreement.

Loans for Museum Shows (Short Term Loans)

It is common for an institution to borrow works of art for various shows it has organized. The works may be borrowed from collectors, artists, or other institutions. It is recommended that the borrowing institution have a proper form of contract or agreement with the lender, which clearly sets out the relationship between the parties. The agreement should deal with the following:

1. The right of the lender to lend the work.
2. Insurance.
3. The right to reproduce for catalogues, and other copyright matters.
4. The term of the loan.
5. The places where the work will travel.
6. The risk of travel.
7. Particulars of the work, including the title, the medium, the size, and the date of creation.
8. The insurance value (this should be specified by the owner).
9. Rights to photograph and the ownership of any such photographs.
10. Any exclusions in the policy of insurance, such as damage

due to war, hostilities, insurrection, acts of God, etc.
11. The manner of identification of the work in the exhibition and any acknowledgment of ownership.
12. If the work is for sale, any commission payable to the institution.

The institution should also make certain that copyright permission for reproduction of the work is obtained from the owner of the copyright. In most cases, for contemporary art at least, the owner of the copyright is the artist or his estate.

Long Term Loans

Often, long term loans are made to institutions by private collectors. This can occur for a number of reasons, such as to provide better security for a valuable work or to remove a work of art from a country where it is situate, in order to avoid possible political or economic problems. If an institution accepts such a long term loan it is imperative that the terms of the loan be set out in an agreement in writing.

Some of the items that should be covered are as follows:
1. That the lender has ownership of the works and the authority to lend them.
2. That the lending does not violate any laws of the jurisdiction of either the lender or the institution.
3. A complete description of the works being loaned.
4. Responsibility for crating, transportation, and insurance. This includes designating who will be present at the time of the crating and make condition reports on the works.
5. The making of condition reports upon receipt by the institution.
6. The obligations of the institution to care for the work in the same manner as they would their own works.
7. Obligations in regard to display, and any restrictions such as that the name of the lender not be revealed on any of the information cards.
8. Notifying the owner if damage occurs, and whether the museum may make repairs or restoration.
9. Any obligation to create a catalogue, and whether approval of catalogue entries must be obtained.
10. Any right to inspect by the lender.
11. Any right to extend the period of the loan at the request of either the borrower or the lender.
12. Crating, shipping, and insurance when the work is to be returned, and making condition reports.
13. Representations in regard to copyright for publication purposes.

LOANS BY INSTITUTIONS

The institution will have to consider a number of questions before it approves the loan of its own work. Firstly, whether the work will be exposed to undue risk having regard to the type of work, its condition, and where the show will take place; secondly, whether the risk is justified. This second question may depend upon consideration of a number of factors, such as the quality of the institution receiving the work, including its history of professionalism and security and curatorial arrangements, as well as any future benefits which may be received from the borrowing institution in exchange. Generally, the board delegates the obligation of making this decision to the director and the staff; but in law, the board may deny any loan, whether or not it has the recommendation of the staff, if in the view of the board the loan is not in the best interest of the institution. The board must look at any restrictions placed on the work which is being requested for the loan. If the work was received as a gift, or is on a long term loan, there may be restrictions attached which prevent the work from being sent out of the museum.

VALUATIONS

Since the institution can give receipts for income tax deduction purposes, it is imperative for the work of art to be valued properly and in accordance with law. The fair market value of the work must be determined. Should the institution make such a valuation or should it be done by an outsider or outside organization? This question was carefully considered in an article published in *Museum News* in April of 1975. Although dealing with donations in the United States, the underlying philosophy is valid in Canada as well. The article indicates that while it is not illegal for museums to provide appraisals or valuations, since the donee institution has a financial interest in the transaction it is considered an "interested party" by the taxing authority. The article indicates that although the American tax authorities will not dismiss such an application, it is clear that "an appraisal will be given less weight if the appraiser is associated with the donor or the charitable organization." This will also be true under Canadian law. The American experience has indicated that appraisers who are associated with either of the parties to the contribution have often rendered appraisals that were essentially nothing more than shams devised to give colour or legitimacy to grossly inflated valuation figures.

The article states that in considering museum appraisals, administrators must ask themselves whether they can afford the staff, time, and money required to do the appraisals in accordance with the requirements of the taxing authority. As well, a museum appraisal may actually be a disservice both to the donor and to the museum, since obtaining it from an independent third party would mean less possibility of a challenge by the tax department. Such a rejection, if it occurs, could be a serious blow to the institution in regard to receiving further gifts from that particular donor.

An interesting policy is that of the Alberta-Glenbow Institute, which has established a method of allowing the heads of curatorial departments to make minor purchases or to accept minor gifts for the institution at their own discretion. The suggested maximum is $500.00 and may not exceed a total of $5,000.00 for all such gifts in any one year. The institution effects this policy by accepting such gifts for "the study collection," and then formally acquiring the gift by acquisition after the ratification of the transaction by the board on the recommendation of the committee involved. Generally, the institution will provide internal appraisals for the donor up to the $500.00 limit.

GIFTS

Art museums and art galleries may receive gifts of money or of art objects. In regard to gifts of works of art, there are a number of factors to be considered. Consideration must be given to more than just whether the work is of a quality suitable for the institution to accept. The institution must also decide whether it should accept gifts with conditions attached and must consider the potential liability if such conditions are breached. For instance, a work may be gifted with the condition that it must be shown on a particular day every year, or must always be on display, or may *never* be deaccessioned. Never is a very long time. Conditions should be looked at carefully and brought to the notice of the board in circumstances where there is concern.

Generally, gifts should be approved by the committee which deals with the subject area of the gift. If the donor is a member of that committee he must indicate this fact and not participate in the decision making process.

Deed of Gift

It is best for a gift received by an institution to be accompanied by a proper written deed of gift. This will make certain that all the facts are clearly enumerated and available even after the death of the parties who negotiated the gift. It will also set out all the relevant information necessary for the tax authorities. Generally, the deed of gift indicates that the donor is the owner, makes the gift to the institution irrevocable, and identifies the work. The donee acknowledges receipt of the work, and acknowledges that it will be accessioned to the permanent collection by the institution. It will also note any restrictions regarding loans and deaccessioning, although restrictions of this type are best avoided wherever possible. Note in this regard that a gift "forever" may mean that the work cannot be deaccessioned. The deed should also indicate how the work is to be identified in the collection and the type of inscription to be used.

DEACCESSIONING

Selling or disposing of works of art has always been an area of conflict and concern, both to boards of directors and to the public generally. It is of special concern as well to donors and their family. Often, the donor's family will be angry or disappointed when, many years after the donation is made, the work is sold to finance the purchase of some other work which they inevitably believe to be inferior to the one originally donated.

This matter has to be looked at very carefully in light of the by-laws of the institution. If nothing is provided in the by-laws, a policy should be established by the institution to deal with deaccessioning rather than dealing with it on an ad hoc basis. The Canadian Art Museum Directors Organization recognizes that deaccessioning may be necessary at times, and therefore recommends written policy and procedures to cover this event. They recommend that the procedures for deaccessioning be initiated by the director of the gallery, with the knowledge and approval of the responsible curator, and receive the approval of the board. If a particular work is to be deaccessioned, it is recommended that the donor or the next of kin, if they can be found, be notified as a courtesy.

The museum must weigh carefully the interests of the public for which it holds the collection in trust. It must take into account all the surrounding facts regarding the original acquisition, such whether it was a donation or a purchase, whether the work is of importance to the scholastic and cultural community, or whether it is necessary for the institution's own financial well-being that the work be sold. The American Association of Museums believes that every institution should develop and make public a statement of its policy regarding the acquisition and disposal of objects. There has been a question raised by some writers as to whether a public institution has the right to deaccession anything once it has been accessioned and thus become part of the heritage of the public. It is suggested that the better view is that there is a discretion in the institution to dispose of those objects in the collection which in the reasonable opinion of the board are not, for any reason, required for the collection.

The museum, however, should be obliged to offer the work to the public for the best possible price. The museum should not allow its objects to be acquired privately by any museum employee, member of its governing board, or its representatives, unless this is done publicly and with complete disclosure. If it is decided that the work is to be sold to a particular collector, it is imperative that an independent valuation be obtained to show that the work is being sold at fair market value. The better approach is to sell the work at public auction and thus avoid any possibility of scandal.

NEW YORK DISCLOSURE OF MUSEUM TRANSACTIONS PROPOSAL

In New York State, a bill was recently passed by the Assembly (and is presently pending before the Senate) dealing with museum transactions. This Act would require public disclosure by museums of their records of acquisition and deaccession. This may, in fact, require the inclusion of price information as well. The only type of information specifically excluded from the proposed legislation is the identity of donors or vendors where anonymity is a condition of the donation or sale. The exact form and content of the disclosure would be determined by regulations drafted by the Attorney General after public hearings and consultation with a Commissioner of Education. The Committee on Art Law of the New York Bar Association has issued a statement opposing the proposed legislation. It supports the public disclosure aspect, but opposes certain specific provisions of the bill which might require museums to conduct a complete inventory of their collections. The association has objected to the fact that the only remedy mentioned for non-compliance is for the Attorney General to take action to remove any or all of the members of the board of trustees. The Committee has suggested that other remedies might be appropriate, such as fines, injunctions, etc.

There has been some question as well about possible legislation in Ontario, and in Canada generally, to deal with disclosure by public institutions and the right of access to information about the records of the institution by the public, or at least by the membership of the institution. Having regard to the public nature of most museums and art galleries, it would appear appropriate for information to be made available to the public if requested, as long as this does not violate any pre-existing conditions of gifts or accessions.

COPYRIGHT

Copyright has been dealt with in great detail in Chapter 1. Mention is made at this time only to note that institutions must consider copyright matters in their day to day dealings. It is not uncommon for institutions to forget that the ownership of the work of art by the institution may not have given the institution the right to reproduce it. Some institutions now pay an additional fee to the artist in order to acquire the copyright of the work at the time of purchase. The institution may also overlook the fact that permission to photograph a work on loan for an exhibition catalogue will often have to be obtained from the artist or his estate rather than the lender.

It is imperative that institutions respect copyright. They must be sure that they have the right to reproduce works for Christmas cards, posters, catalogues, and anything else commonly sold in their gift shops, and for any other commercial venture undertaken by the museum or gallery. This leads us to the question of art reproductions.

ART REPRODUCTION

More and more institutions are reproducing works of art from their collection in order to raise funds. Reproductions of works of art have now become a common form of "art." Recently, the series of reproductions from the Rockefeller collection has raised serious questions about the whole concept of reproducing works of art. Questions of copyright were not involved in those reproductions, since they were of works which either had been created many years before and thus had fallen into the "public domain," or on which the collector obtained the copyright. The question still arises of the ethics of such art reproduction, especially by public institutions. The Association of Art Museum Directors has now adopted a set of specific guidelines for the production and sale of reproductions by museums and art galleries, which have been approved by some Canadian gallery associations, including the Ontario Association of Art Galleries. The guidelines indicate that there is nothing wrong with offering reproductions to the public as an adjunct to the display of works of art. However, it would be wrong to offer the reproduction as a "surrogate" for the original work of art, and such confusion should be avoided. The Association indicated that it was deplorable, in its view, to tout the so called investment value of a reproduction, since the object offered for purchase is not the original, and the resale value of reproductions is very much in doubt. The association indicated that when advertising these reproductions in public media, the museum should not use language implying that there is any similarity in quality between the copy and the original, or which would lead the potential buyer to believe that, by purchasing the reproduction, he is in effect acquiring an original work.

To guard against the possibility that reproductions might eventually find their way into the art market as originals, they came out firmly against *exact* copies of the work. They suggested that the reproduction should differ from the original in material and/or size, and should be clearly marked on the object itself as a reproduction. They indicated that signatures, print edition numbers, and printer's symbols or titles should not appear in, or on, the reproduction if in the original they occur outside the actual border of the image. Similarly, signatures, edition numbers and/or foundry marks should not appear on sculptural reproductions.

CHAPTER 6 THE CULTURAL PROPERTY EXPORT AND IMPORT ACT

HISTORY

The Cultural Property Export and Import Act came into force in Canada on September 6, 1977. It was introduced as Bill C-33 on October 30, 1974 by the then Secretary of State, the Honourable Hugh Faulkner. The principles of the legislation were supported in the House of Commons by all the federal parties and received the support of all the provinces as well.

To date, more than 130 countries, in addition to Canada, have some kind of national heritage laws.

PURPOSES OF THE ACT

The Secretary of State indicated at the time of the second reading of the bill that the British Waverley Report on the arts and the French system of cultural control were used by his department as research materials and background to an examination of the Canadian experience and proposed legislation. He indicated that the following were the purposes of the Canadian Act:

1. to allow the state, in suitable cases, to retain the right to prevent the export of objects of high importance;
2. in every case in which export is prevented, to assure an offer to purchase at a fair price to the owner;
3. to strictly confine export control to limited categories of objects of high importance;
4. to have a time period during which the natural free flow of commerce in recently imported objects is allowed;
5. to have offers to purchase come from the marketplace rather than from government wherever possible; and
6. to establish a special fund which could be drawn upon to assist in financing the purchase of cultural property determined to be of national importance, for retention in appropriate institutions in the country.

The Secretary of State indicated that the British and French practice and principles that were utilized in preparing the Canadian Act, recognized the critical importance of enlisting the co-operation of collectors and the trade if the export system was to work effectively. In order to encourage the movement of national treasures into those institutions best able to preserve them, both countries offered tax incentives to encourage gifts and sales of national treasures to appropriate institutions.

THE CONTROL LIST

The Act establishes a "control list." This list contains seven classes of objects which are considered to be nationally important to Canada. In shortened form they are as follows;

Group I

Objects recovered from the soils or waters of Canada.

Group II

Objects of ethnographic art or ethnography. This group is important in a visual arts context because it covers "primitive art," that is, the art or artifacts of aboriginal persons, and therefore includes the art of the Innuit and other native peoples of Canada. The monetary minimum of such works must be a fair market value in Canada of more than $1,000.00. The Act also covers reworked or adapted items, used by an aboriginal person, having a fair market value in Canada of more than $3,000.00. As well, it covers items made, reworked, or adapted for use by, aboriginal persons in territory that is now the United States, Greenland or that part of the Soviet Union east of 135 degrees longitude, and which have a market value of more than $3,000.00.

Works by other aboriginal groups, such as those of Africa, Polynesia, and South and Central America, are also covered if they have been made, reworked, or adapted for use t aboriginal persons in those territories and have a fair market value in Canada of more than $5,000.00. Any works made, reworked, or adapted for use by any aboriginal persons other than those specifically mentioned in Group II, are covered if they have a fair market value in Canada of more than $8,000.00

Group III

Military objects.

Group IV

Objects of decorative art. This means art other than ethnographic art (covered by Group II) in which principles of design, ornamentation, enrichment, or decoration are applied to the production of functional and utilitarian objects such as pottery, glassware, earthenware, porcelain work, etc. To be included in the controlled group, these works must be more than 100 years old, made in Canada, and worth more than $500.00. This category also covers antique furniture, sculptured works in wood or precious metals, and other objects of decorative art, which have a fair market value in Canada of more than $2,000.00. The control list specifically defines a whole series of objects which are to be included in Group IV, and this list must be examined to determine whether a specific object is covered.

There is a second subclassification of decorative art, which covers work more than 50 years old, made in or out of Canada by a resident or former resident, and which has a value of more than $3,000.00.

There is a third subclassification dealing with decorative art made outside of Canada, but having in its history or origins a direct association with Canada. Such items must also be more than 50 years old and must have a value of more than $5,000.00 (except for Canadian coins, metals and medallions which must have a value of more than $3,000.00 to be controlled).

The fourth and final subclassification deals with decorative art made outside of Canada, having no direct Canadian association, and not made by residents or former residents. To be controlled, such items must have a fair market value of more than $8,000.00.

Group V

Objects of fine art. This category includes drawings, paintings, prints, and sculpture, and will be dealt with in detail below.

Group VI

Scientific or technological objects.

Group VII

Books, records, documents, photographic positives and negatives, and sound recordings. This group includes photographs and photographic art, cinematographic works, and motion pictures of all kinds.

The control list applies to photographs if they were made in Canada, or, were made outside of Canada by a person who at any time normally resided in Canada or were made outside of Canada but relate to the history or national life of Canada, and which have a fair market value of more than $500.00. The list also covers collections of photographs and film having a fair market value in Canada of more than $1,000.00.

Printed books of photographs, or sets of such books, are covered as well. A single book must be worth more than $2,000.00 and a collection of books of photographs must have a fair market value in Canada of more then $10,000.00.

Thus, although Group V deals specifically with fine art, not all works of fine art are included in that group. Innuit pieces would fall under Group II, photographs or moving pictures under Group VII, ceramic pieces under Group IV. It is important to determine in which group the particular work is included, since different tests must be applied in each category to determine whether it is necessary to make an application for an export permit.

Group V
Fine Art

This group contains three categories:
1. The following objects of fine art made in or out of Canada by a person who at anytime normally resided in the country:
    (a) a drawing or print that has a fair market value in Canada of more than $1,000.00; and
    (b) a painting or sculpture that has a fair market value in Canada of more than $3,000.00.

2. The following objects of fine art made *out* of the territory that is now Canada:
   (a) a drawing or print with a fair market value in Canada of more than $2,000.00; and
   (b) a painting or sculpture with a fair market value in Canada of more than $5,000.00. (Note the dollar differentiation between works which are made by a resident of Canada and a non-resident of Canada).

These "non-Canadian" objects which are now in Canada must not only have reached a particular dollar value, but they must have been either:
   (a) commissioned by a person who was anytime normally resident in the territory that is now Canada;
   (b) incorporate a Canadian theme or subject; or
   (c) be identified with a prominent person, institution or memorable event that relates to the art history, history, or national life of Canada.

3. The following objects of fine art other than the objects described in the second section above, made outside of Canada:
   (a) a drawing or print having a fair market value in Canada of more than $3,000.00; and
   (b) a painting or sculpture having a fair market value in Canada of more than $8,000.00.

This covers those non-Canadian objects that do not fit into the above section because they:
   1. were not commissioned by a person normally resident in the territory that is now Canada;
   2. do not incorporate a Canadian theme; or
   3. are not identified with a prominent person, institute, or memorable event, that relates to the art history, history, or national life of Canada.

What Works Need a Permit?

A permit is required for any object or work which fits one of the categories of the control list *unless* the object is less than fifty years old or its creator is still living.

HOW THE ACT OPERATES

Essentially, the system controls the export of cultural property. Therefore, the person who wishes to export an object which falls within those classes of objects covered by the control list *must apply* for an export permit. It will be up to the "exporter" to know what objects come under the control of the Act.

When cultural property is being exported, only a person ordinarily resident in Canada, or a corporation having its head office or establishment in Canada, may apply for the permit. However, a Canadian resident can apply as the exporter on behalf of a non-resident. The application is made to any one of the Canadian customs offices designated across Canada. Generally, the local customs office will have been designated and can provide the information required by the exporter.

It must be remembered, therefore, that the Act only applies if the owner of the work of art wishes to export it from Canada, and the work is "caught" by the control list. There is no interference with the collector who:

(a) wishes to export a work of art which is not on the control list, or which is exempt because it is less than 50 years old or because it was made by a living person;
(b) wishes to sell the work of art in Canada;
(c) wishes to donate it in Canada to a Canadian organization, institution, museum, etc.;
(d) wishes to gift it in Canada to a member of his family or otherwise deal with the work of art in this country, including making gifts by way of will. It would, however, affect a gift during the owner's lifetime or pursuant to a will, if made to a person, corporation, or institution resident outside of Canada.

Events if the Act Applies

Where the Canadian resident collector wishes to export a work of art, he must apply to a permit officer for an export permit. The form required to apply for an export permit is obtained from the local Canada customs office or the office of the Secretary of State.

After the form is filled in and submitted to the permit officer, he may determine that the work is not on the control list and a permit will issue immediately. The permit must also be granted *forthwith* if it is established that:

(a) the work was imported into Canada within the preceding thirty-five years and was not exported under a permit issued under the Act prior to that importation date;
(b) it was loaned to an institution or public authority in Canada by a non-resident; or
(c) it is to be removed from Canada for purposes prescribed by regulation for a period of time not exceeding such period as may be prescribed. For example, a work may be removed for display or exhibit outside the country, for restoration, or for display in a southern winter home, or on a signed undertaking not to sell it abroad.

The Permit Officer is Uncertain

If the permit officer does not know what to do, i.e., does not know whether to issue the permit, he will call a designated expert examiner (an appointed expert from a local museum or gallery). The expert examiner will determine whether the permit should be issued or not. He considers:

1. whether the cultural property is of outstanding significance under the Act because of:

(a) its close association with Canadian historical or national life,
(b) its aesthetic qualities, or
(c) its value in the study of arts or sciences; and
2. whether the object is of such a degree of national importance that its loss to Canada would significantly diminish the national heritage.

If the expert examiner determines that the object is not of outstanding significance or national importance, he advises the permit officer to issue the export permit *forthwith*. Where, however, the local examiner determines that the object has, in his opinion, outstanding significance, and meets the degree of national importance required, he advises the permit officer not to issue the permit. The permit officer then advises the applicant, listing the reasons why the work of art cannot be exported.

Appeal to the Review Board

The collector is therefore faced with a problem as to whether he should keep the object in Canada and not export it, or appeal the decision. If an appeal is taken it must be made to a review board within a thirty day period. This board is called the Canadian Cultural Property Export Review Board (the "Review Board"). The Review Board is composed of six to twelve members, appointed by the Secretary of State. The board members represent institutional interests as well as the interests of the trade, collectors, and the general public. The Review Board may use experts to give advice and make valuations, and can hold meetings whenever and wherever it considers it necessary in order to give effective and quick decisions. The Review Board has four months in which to render a decision. If a permit is refused, the board must then decide whether or not it is likely that an institution or public authority in Canada would be interested in purchasing the object. If this is unlikely, the permit will then be issued. If, however, this is likely, the board may establish a delay period of not less than two months and not more than six months (following the four months referred to above). The Review Board will then inform the Minister, and the Minister in turn will inform such institutions and public authorities in Canada as he deems necessary. Generally, he will inform those institutions which he is advised might be interested in the work. If no offer to purchase the work is obtained by the end of the delay period, a permit is issued.

OFFER AND POSSIBLE SALE

If an offer is made by an institution, and is acceptable to the collector, the transaction will be completed and payment made. In the event that the offer is not acceptable to the collector, the institution may request that the Review Board determine the amount of a fair cash offer. The board is authorized to do this. Once the Review Board has established what it feels is a fair market value it notifies the collector of this price. If he refuses a cash offer from an institution which is equal to that set by the Review Board, no export permit will be granted for two years. Thereafter, the collector may start the process over again (probably with little success).

Functions of the Review Board

One of the Review Board's functions, therefore, is to act as a court of appeal from the expert examiner, in order to determine whether he was correct as to the national importance of the work, and in refusing a permit. As well, the board will determine whether a Canadian institution may be interested in the work, and if so, institute a delay period. It also acts as a valuator to determine the fairness of any cash offer from an institution to a vendor. If the vendor does not wish to accept such an offer, he is still free to deal with the work in Canada by way of sale, gift or otherwise.

Another function of the Review Board is to certify cultural property for income tax purposes. Certification can apply to all cultural property in Canada which meets the criteria of being of outstanding significance and national importance, whether or not it would fall into one of the categories of the control list. The significance of obtaining certification is discussed below. Certification is valuable where the owner of a cultural property wishes to dispose of it by sale or gift to an interested institution or public authority which has been designated under the Act.

TAX BENEFITS OF THE ACT

Sale under the Act

The Act indicates that if the work of art is sold to a designated institution, the vendor will receive the proceeds of the sale *free of any tax on a capital gain.* (Because there is no taxable gain on works worth less than $1,000.00, this provision is relevant only to works worth more than $1,000.00). This means that if a certified work of art having an original value of $10,000 was later sold for $50,000 to such an institution, the $40,000 profit would come into the hands of the vendor tax free.

Gifts under the Act

If a person (including a corporation) wishes to donate a work of art to an institution, he may apply to the Review Board for a certificate for income tax purposes. Once the work is certified it enjoys the benefits of 100% deductibility (subject to certain limitations) under the Income Tax Act, and no deemed taxable gain accrues to the donor. Certification can be obtained presently only for gifts of property certified during the lifetime of the donor. At the time of writing, amendments were proposed which would give the tax benefits for bequests of property which are certified after death.

For a work of art to qualify for a certificate, it does not need to be on the control list or be over fifty years old or the work of a deceased artist. It must, however, be of outstanding significance to Canada and an object of such a degree of national importance that its loss to Canada would significantly diminish the national heritage. Works of art by both Canadian and non-Canadian living artists have been so certified. Individual works which might not by themselves be so certified may in fact be certified because they are part of a general collection of importance.

A late Borduas, early Riopelle, or early Jack Bush painting may not be affected by the provisions of the Act for export purposes, but could very well be certified under the Act for gift purposes.

General Tax Considerations

The tax considerations will be dealt with in more detail in Chapter 7, The Individual Collector: Taxation, Gifting, and Death. However, there are certain basic tax considerations which should be mentioned here. Under the Act, either the owner of a cultural property, or the institution which is its potential recipient, can apply to the Review Board for certification of the property. If the board determines that the property meets the criteria of national importance and outstanding significance, it will be certified. The board will then issue a Cultural Property Income Tax Certificate to the requesting party. However, the onus still remains with the donor or vendor to establish value for tax purposes under the Income Tax Act. The Cultural Property Export and Import Act does not change standard tax procedures. Proper valuations are extremely important. Valuations will be scrutinized carefully by the income tax authorities.

Professional Art Dealers Association Valuation Service

The Professional Art Dealers Association of Canada has established a service for evaluating works of art for tax purposes (as well as for insurance and other purposes). The Association generally requires photographs of the work and may also require it to be available for view by the valuators involved. A number of dealers are selected who are familiar with the type of work to be evaluated. Each sends the valuation to the chairman of the valuation committee. If there is more than a 10% or 15% differential, an investigation is held to determine why this has occurred. Once the matter is resolved, a certificate is issued under the letterhead of the Association. The fee charged is based on the value of the work or works.

Gifts of different types of interests in property can also be the subject of appraisal for income tax purposes. Reference is made to Chapter 7, The Individual Collector: Taxation, Gifting, and Death for a discussion of differing types of gifts.

Treatment of Art Collector, Dealer, and Artist

Though the Act applies to all art which meets the various tests in regard to export and import, regardless of who owns it, the tax benefits of sales or gifting under the Act are applicable only to donating art collectors. The benefit is not available on sales or donations by art dealers out of their inventory, nor sales or donations by artists of their own work. There would, however, appear to be nothing to prevent an artist or an art dealer from having a private art collection and utilizing the Act in regard to works of art gifted or sold from that collection, held separate and apart from business inventory.

Unless cultural property received by designated institutions or public authorities under the Act is kept by the institution for at least five years before it is disposed of or "deaccessioned," there is a 30% special tax payable by the institution on the fair market value of the work at the time of disposition.

CANADIAN HERITAGE PRESERVATION ENDOWMENT ACCOUNT

In order to assist in the purchase of these culturally significant works of art, a special account known as the Canadian Heritage Preservation Endowment Account has been established. Gifts to the fund from the private sector are tax deductible as gifts to Her Majesty. In addition, Parliament appropriates funds for the purposes of enabling institutions and public authorities to purchase works of art which have been determined to be of national importance, or in order to repatriate national treasures from abroad.

DESIGNATED PUBLIC INSTITUTIONS

Institutions and public authorities can be designated in a variety of ways to receive gifts pursuant to the Act. The Secretary of State may designate any institution or public authority indefinitely or for a limited period of time, and generally or for a specific purpose. The Secretary of State may also at any time revoke a designation. An institution or public authority designated indefinitely and for general purposes receives "category A" status. An institution or public authority designated indefinitely for the purpose of receiving a specific cultural property qualifying for certification which a person proposes to transfer to it, receives "category B" status.

"Institutions" are publicly owned, operated for the benefit of the public, and established for educational or cultural purposes. Institutions also conserve and exhibit objects or make them otherwise available to the public. For example, the National Gallery of Canada is such an institution, as is The Alberta-Glenbow Institute.

A "public authority" is Her Majesty in the right of Canada or a province, an agent of Her Majesty in either such right (consequently a provincial Heritage Foundation), a municipality, a regional municipality, a county, and some Crown corporations.

ADVANCE RULINGS

Neither an expert examiner nor the Review Board will give an advance ruling as to whether or not an export permit will be refused for a particular cultural property.

GENERAL PERMITS AND OPEN GENERAL PERMITS

General Permits

The Secretary of State with the concurrence of the Minister of Industry, Trade and Commerce, may issue a general permit to any resident of Canada who applies in writing and who demonstrates, on the basis of evidence gathered over a six month period immediately preceding the date of application, that a general permit is required to alleviate undue hardship, or interference in the conduct of normal business activities concerning cultural property which requires an export permit. Objects for which a general permit might be issued subject to ministerial terms and conditions are of a kind which, although included in the control list, would not meet the conditions of outstanding significance and national importance. If convinced of the need, and if satisfied that the person applying for the general permit will undertake to meet the terms and conditions he may establish, the Secretary of State may issue the permit.

Open General Permits

The open general permit may be granted by the Secretary of State, with the concurrence of the Minister of Industry, Trade and Commerce, to export objects within any class of objects included in the control list and specified in the permit, subject to such terms and conditions as the Secretary of State may require. Therefore, the Secretary of State, with the concurrence of the Minister of Industry, Trade and Commerce, may issue an open general permit where it is deemed advisable to exempt a particular type or class of object from control, even though it comes within the control list definitions (i.e., the Secretary of State can create exceptions to the control list in appropriate circumstances).

The Secretary of State has the discretion to amend, suspend, cancel, or reinstate any export permit other than one issued on the direction of the Review Board. As well, it is anticipated that the control list will be revised from time to time. Although the Governor in Council cannot set age and value limits below the minimum limits set out in the Act (the legislation would have to be amended), it is anticipated that the limits will be set higher as circumstances require.

UNESCO TREATY

The Act also deals with the importation into Canada of works of art which may contravene export legislation in another country. In order to implement this portion of the Act, Canada has ratified the 1970 UNESCO Convention on prohibiting and preventing the illicit importation, exportation, and transfer of ownership of cultural properties. This came into force in Canada on the 20th of June, 1978. On that date Canada became the 37th member state to accede to this Convention. The United States is not a member at the time of writing.

Illegal Imports into Canada

The Act sets out procedures which enable those foreign states who are signatories with Canada to bilateral or multilateral cultural property agreements to apply to the Secretary of State for the recovery and return of cultural property that has been illegally exported from that state to Canada. The Act also empowers our Attorney General to institute legal proceedings in Canadian courts to accomplish this end. The interest of bona fide Canadian purchasers is protected under the legislation, and the Canadian courts can decide what compensation, if any, is to be paid to the purchaser by the reciprocating state when an object is to be returned to that state.

Illegal Export of Canadian Heritage Objects

The control list defines cultural property that has been designated by Canada for the purposes of any cultural property agreements with foreign countries. This means that any of the objects included in the control list are illegal imports into countries with which Canada has a cultural agreement, as well as under the UNESCO Treaty, unless the work was exported from Canada with a proper Cultural Property Export Permit.

Penalties

The Act indicates that no person may export or attempt to export from Canada any object included in the control list except in accordance with a permit issued under the Act. It also indicates that it is an offence for a person applying for a permit under the Act to wilfully furnish any false and misleading information.

The Act makes it an offence to attempt to import foreign cultural property that has been illegally exported from a country that is a party to a cultural property agreement with Canada or a party to the UNESCO Convention. It is also an offence to export or attempt to export from Canada any work of art while it is under consideration by any of the persons or bodies designated under the Act.

Every person who contravenes the Act is guilty of an offence, and may be liable on summary conviction to a fine not exceeding $5,000, or to imprisonment for a term not exceeding twelve months, or both; or, if the Crown wishes to proceed upon indictment, to a fine not exceeding $25,000, or to imprisonment for a term not exceeding five years, or both. Where a corporation commits an offence under the Act, any officer, director, or agent of the corporation, who directed, authorized, assented to, acquiesced in or participated in the commission of the offence, is a party to and guilty of the offence and is subject to the penalties under the Act.

GENERAL BENEFITS OF THE ACT

1. In essence, the Act gives a "first right of refusal" to Canadian institutions to purchase works of art which are determined to be of national importance.
2. The Act establishes a fund to enable Canada to purchase important works of art for its institutions in order to make such works available to the viewing public. This may assist the smaller galleries even more than the larger ones, since smaller galleries have rarely had sufficient funds in the past to purchase works of major importance.
3. As already mentioned, the Act contains significant tax benefits to collectors who sell or donate works of art to approved institutions. Chapter 7, The Individual Collector: Taxation, Gifting, and death; and Chapter 8, The Corporate Collector: Taxation and Gifting, deal with the topic of gifting in more depth.
4. The tax benefits could enable dealers to improve and expand their sales. Collectors may purchase important works of art in Canada, with the hope that some day they can be sold or donated to institutions or public authorities while taking advantage of the provisions in the Act and the Income Tax Act. The tax benefits of the Act make it possible for a collector to donate a work of art to an approved institution and end up with almost the same benefits as he would obtain by a sale.

NEGATIVE ASPECTS OF THE ACT

1. By its very nature, the Act is an interference with private property rights. Collectors, by nature, and because of the operation of the marketplace, have generally kept information about their collections private. The Act allows the government to, in essence, enter the living-rooms of collectors and prevent them from dealing with their personal property in a normal, open, commercial manner. The Act could interfere with the opportunity for a collector to trade-in a particular work of art with dealers outside Canada. Since it is not uncommon for a collector to attempt to up-grade his collection, this legislation makes it more difficult to deal with this particular aspect of collecting. The Act could also interfere with the collector's need to make a quick out of the country private sale of all or a portion of his collection to raise ready cash, or his attempt to sell his work at auction in the international art market.
2. It is not impossible for the legislation to change and become more restrictive in the future. There is always the fear that

once the government has entered a particular area, the legislation will not remain static and will be subject to the whims of various governments coming into power. Tax benefits may be narrowed, control lists may be expanded, and greater interference with private property could occur.

3. There are no appeal procedures under the Act from the determination by the Review Board that the work of art is important to the nation. There is also no appeal in regard to decisions by the Governor in Council as to what works should be included in the control list.

CONCLUSION

After all is said and done, it must be recognized that the government has made a sincere attempt to increase the works of art available to Canadian institutions, for the benefit of the country as a whole. The legislation itself appears to be extremely sophisticated and in many ways sympathetic to both collectors and dealers. Since the enactment of the legislation, it would appear that a number of collectors who would not normally donate have made gifts of works of art to designated institutions. The Act would appear, therefore, to have had the desired effect of persuading collectors to make these works of art available to Canadian institutions. As well, the Canadian Cultural Property Export Review Board has been operating in an effective manner. The membership of the board has been extremely professional and sympathetic to the cultural community. It is hoped that the Act will continue to operate as successfully in the future as it is operating today.

CHAPTER 7 THE INDIVIDUAL COLLECTOR: TAXATION, GIFTING, AND DEATH

INTRODUCTION

The Income Tax Act of Canada was amended significantly effective January 1, 1972. One major reform was the introduction of a tax on the disposition or deemed disposition of capital property, including works of art. This tax is usually (somewhat inaccurately) referred to as the capital gains tax.

A taxpayer is obliged to include in his or her calculation of taxable income, an amount in respect of the increase in value of capital property disposed of in that year. Consequently, the amount of tax required to be paid varies with the taxpayer's marginal rate which, for individuals, can be as high as approximately 62%.

Art collectors are taxed under the provisions of that subdivision of the Income Tax Act which deals with capital gains and losses. Tax is usually exigible whenever art which has increased in value since acquisition is sold or gifted. Tax is also exigible when a collector dies or emigrates. This chapter will attempt to give an understanding of the various provisions of the Income Tax Act which serve to impose a "capital gains tax" on dispositions of works of art, and also those which allow tax deductions for gifts to public institutions. It is unfortunately impossible to give a comprehensive treatment of the capital gains area within the scope of this book, so only the provisions which are felt to be most commonly applicable or of interest to resident Canadian collectors of fine art and art related collectables are discussed in detail. There may be factors arising from other activities in the life of the collector which will influence his tax position, and the reader is advised to seek professional advice to determine whether the law as stated here is applicable in the collector's particular circumstances, and also whether the law is unchanged from the time of writing.

CALCULATION OF INCOME UNDER THE INCOME TAX ACT

The formula used to determine a taxpayer's income in the year for tax purposes (which is reflected in the tax forms themselves), is as follows:
(a) determine net business or employment income;
(b) determine the amount, if any, by which taxable capital gains and taxable net gains exceed allowable capital losses;
(c) add (a) plus (b) and subtract permitted deductions for moving

expenses, alimony, child care expenses, the purchase of income averaging annuity contracts (IAACs) etc.;

(d) if any income remains, subtract business, employment and allowable business investment losses;

(e) if anything still remains and the taxpayer is an individual (not a corporation), deduct the lesser of $2,000.00 and the amount, if any, by which allowable capital losses exceed taxable capital gains and taxable net gains.

Paragraphs (b) and also (e) require further examination in order to understand "capital gains tax" on individuals. What are "taxable capital gains," "taxable net gains," and "allowable capital losses"?

Taxable Capital Gains

The Income Tax Act of Canada defines the taxable capital gain of a taxpayer as being one half of his capital gain from the disposition of that property.

T.C.G. = $\frac{1}{2}$ C.G.

Accordingly, if a taxpayer has a $10,000 capital gain, he has a $5,000 taxable capital gain. The other $5,000 is a tax free capital gain.

But what is a capital gain? The Income Tax Act says it is the gain from the disposition of property, except certain properties and assets of importance in business, life insurance policies, and "an object that the Canadian Cultural Property Export Review Board has determined meets all criteria set out in paragraphs 23(3)(b) and (c) of the Cultural Property Export and Import Act and that has been disposed of to an institution or public authority in Canada that was at the time of the disposition, designated under subsection 26(2) of that Act either generally or for a purpose related to that object." This last exception for what we will term "certified cultural property" is of importance for donors of major works of art. Its effect is discussed in detail in the separate chapter on the Cultural Property Export and Import Act as well as below at page 138 under the heading *Disposition of Cultural Property*. In general, however, if a collector disposes of any property, whether by sale or gift, which is worth more than its value when it was acquired, he will have a taxable capital gain to include in his calculation of income.

The capital gains tax treatment of a collector should be contrasted with the tax treatment of an artist or a dealer dealing with the same property. The artist or dealer is taxed as having business income and must include the entire profit in calculating income, not just half of the capital gain.

Collectors should be aware of the problem that can arise if National Revenue authorities feel that a collector is really an art speculator or a private dealer who has inventory rather than a collection. This is a problem most frequently experienced by collectors who "turn over" their collections when their interests in art change. Some collectors will dispose of an entire collection in order to finance new acquisitions and obtain space in their homes for their new area of interest. This is true in particular of avant garde collectors who may wish to dispose of their collections at a favourable price once a style has become too popular and expensive for them to make further important acquisitions. Collectors should be prepared to offer a rational explanation for their changes in taste if questions arise, and should also be aware that a history of such dealings is not always a prerequisite to a finding adverse to the collector. The Revenue authorities may decide that the collector has engaged in "an adventure in the nature of trade," or has had one shot at acting like a dealer, and require tax to be paid on the entire profit from the sale.

Taxable Net Gains

The term "taxable net gains" is defined as one half of the net gain from dispositions of listed personal property.

T.N.G. = ½ N.G.

Listed personal property of a taxpayer means his personal-use property which is any:

1. print, etching, drawing, painting, sculpture, or other similar work of art;
2. jewellery;
3. rare folio, rare manuscript, or rare book;
4. stamp, or
5. coin.

Listed personal property also includes any interest to or right in any of the above.

Category 1 could include a serigraph or a limited edition fine art lithograph, but it is considerably more doubtful whether signed reproductions of paintings or sculpture are works of art, and consequently listed personal property. The definition of listed personal property includes another term — "personal-use property." Personal-use property is not defined outright, but is said in the Income Tax Act to include property owned by a taxpayer and used primarily for his personal use or enjoyment, or for the personal use of one or more individuals related to the taxpayer. Personal-use property, therefore, would include such things as furniture, antiques, and automobiles for personal use, as well as *listed* personal property such as art in the family home.

Allowable Capital Losses

A taxpayer's allowable capital loss for a taxation year is one half of his capital loss for the year from the disposition of the property.

A.C.L. = ½ C.L.

What is a capital loss? The Income Tax Act says it is the loss from the disposition of property except for certain properties and assets of importance in business and also life insurance policies.

(Note that these exceptions are identical to the parallel omissions in calculating a capital gain.) However, a person can have a capital loss if he disposes of "certified cultural property" where he cannot have a capital gain.

Summary of Inclusions in Calculating Income

In summary, when a collector disposes of *listed* personal-use property, he includes in income a taxable *net* gain equal to half of net gain. Capital properties which are not *listed*, but are personal-use property (such as butterfly collections and antiques), are subject on disposition to a calculation of taxable capital gain equal to half of capital gain. A loss on the disposition of personal-use property other than listed personal property is not recognized for tax purposes.

Inventory is not subject to capital gains tax treatment and is dealt with in Chapters 9 and 10. The disposition of depreciable property used in earning income is dealt with in Chapter 8, The Corporate Collector: Taxation and Gifting.

CALCULATION OF CAPITAL GAIN

The general rule for calculating a taxpayer's capital gain is to determine the amount, if any, by which the proceeds of disposition of capital property (other than property excepted from the calculation of capital gain such as certified cultural property), exceed the aggregate of the adjusted cost base of the property immediately before disposition and any outlays or expenses made or incurred by the taxpayer making the disposition.

Proceeds of Disposition

The proceeds of disposition is most commonly the sale price. If the property is gifted, the taxpayer is deemed to have received proceeds of disposition equal to the fair market value at the time of gifting. The fair market value is an expert's opinion of what the property would have been sold for by a willing vendor to a willing purchaser. If the taxpayer sells the property for less than fair market value to someone with whom he is not dealing at arm's length, he is nonetheless deemed to have received proceeds of disposition equal to fair market value. Related persons (you can be related to a corporation) are deemed not to deal with each other at arm's length. It is a question of fact whether persons who are not related to each other were at a particular time dealing with each other at arm's length.

Adjusted Cost Base

Adjusted cost base is the capital cost of the property to the taxpayer. There exist a set of rules, parallel to those which deem a taxpayer to dispose of property at fair market value, which deem a taxpayer to have acquired property at fair market value whenever there is a gift or acquisition from someone with whom he was not dealing at arm's length, so that the fair market value at the time of acquisition becomes the adjusted cost base.

V-Day Value

The topic of adjusted cost base requires consideration of "V-Day value." V-Day or Valuation Day value of most property is the value of that property on December 31, 1971, the day that the concept of capital gains was introduced into our tax system. Only capital gains which have accrued since January 1, 1972 are taxed.

Appraisers can theoretically determine V-Day value today from historical records if the object was acquired prior to December 31, 1971. There are special rules to ease taxation of persons who acquired property prior to December 31, 1971 at a price which was higher than the subsequent V-Day value. In the generally inflationary art market this is not the usual case, so we will assume that the adjusted cost base is the V-Day value, or the value at which the taxpayer acquired the property subsequent to December 31, 1971.

Expenses of Disposition

Outlays or expenses made or incurred in making the disposition could include dealer's commission, fees for professional advice in connection with the making of a gift, the cost of newspaper advertisements for private sale, etc.

Reserves

The Income Tax Act recognizes that when property is sold the entire proceeds of sale are not always realized immediately. For this reason provision is made for claiming a reserve. Suppose a collector has sold for $30,000 an antique toy-train set with an adjusted cost base of $18,000, and the collector has incurred no expenses in making the disposition. The terms of payment are $21,000 down and $4,500 for the next 2 years.

Obviously, the capital gain on the transaction as a whole is $12,000 ($30,000 − $18,000) and the taxable capital gain is half of that or $6,000.

The amount of the capital gain to be reported in year 1 is:

$$\frac{\text{proceeds in year } 1 \times \text{total capital gain}}{\text{total proceeds}}$$

$$= \frac{\$21,000 \times \$12,000}{\$30,000}$$

$$= \$8,400$$

The taxable capital gain to be included in income in year 1 is $4,200. The reserve carried forward into year 2 is $9,000 in respect of the two sums of $4,500 yet to be received.

The next year the taxable capital gain is:

$$\frac{1}{2} \left(\frac{\text{proceeds in year } 2 \times \text{total capital gain}}{\text{total proceeds}} \right)$$

$$= \frac{1}{2} \left(\$ \frac{4,500 \times \$12,000}{\$30,000} \right)$$

$$= \$900$$

The reserve carried forward into year 3 is $4,500, and the taxable capital gain in that year is again $900. The total taxable capital gain is $6,000 and the taxpayer has included the taxable capital gain in income proportionately as the funds have been received.

CALCULATION OF CAPITAL LOSS

The general rule for calculating capital loss is to determine the amount by which the aggregate of the adjusted cost base of the property immediately before the disposition and any outlays and expenses made or incurred by the taxpayer making the disposition, exceed the adjusted cost base of the property. There are no reserves for capital losses. The loss is taken for the year in which the disposition takes place.

A *capital* loss cannot be incurred on the disposition of any personal-use property whether it is the family car or listed personal property. A capital loss can be incurred for tax purposes on the disposition of things such as stocks, bonds, etc. As described below, losses on disposition of listed personal use property are deducted in calculating net gains.

CALCULATION OF NET GAIN

Net gains arise from the disposition of that type of personal-use property known as listed personal property. The kinds of property described as listed personal property — paintings, coins, stamps, rare books, etc., have an historical investment value, and perhaps for this reason have been singled out for special treatment. A deduction from the gains incurred on the disposition of listed personal property is allowed for losses suffered on the disposition of the listed personal property. This is why it is referred to as a "net" gain. The calculation requires a taxpayer to determine the amount by which the aggregate of his gains from the disposition of listed personal property (excluding cultural property) exceeds the aggregate of his losses from the disposition of listed personal property in that year. The taxpayer then applies against any excess, losses from the disposition of listed personal property incurred in the previous 5 years which have not been previously deducted from gains. The oldest losses, of course, are used first. If the taxpayer has a net gain in a year, and the next year has a loss from the disposition of listed personal property, he can refile the original tax return and deduct the loss from the net gain.

If a taxpayer has a listed personal property loss, and no listed personal property gains in either the preceding year or the next five years from which to subtract it, the tax advantages of the loss are lost.

Another difference in the tax treatment of listed personal property from that afforded to other capital property is that no reserves for amounts to be paid later in time are allowed in calculating the gain incurred for a particular taxation year.

SUMMARY OF GENERAL RULES

The formulas for taxable capital gain, allowable capital gain and taxable net gain are as follows:

1. $T.C.G. = \frac{1}{2}(P.D. - (A.C.B. + X.))$

   (Taxable capital gain (T.C.G.) is $\frac{1}{2}$ of the amount by which the proceeds of disposition (P.D.) exceed the aggregate of the adjusted cost base (A.C.B.) and any expenses or outlays made for the purposes of the disposition (X.).)

2. $A.C.L. = \frac{1}{2}((A.C.B. + X.) - P.D.)$

   (Allowable capital loss (A.C.L.) is $\frac{1}{2}$ of the amount by which the aggregate of the adjusted cost base (A.C.B.) and the expenses and outlays made for the purposes of the disposition (X.) exceed the proceeds of disposition (P.D.))

3. $T.N.G._{(L.P.P.)} = \frac{1}{2}(G_0 - L_0 - L_{-5} - L_{-4} - L_{-3} - L_{-2} - L_{-1} - L_{+1})$

   (Taxable net gain (T.N.G.) may only be incurred in respect of dispositions of listed personal property (L.P.P.) and is $\frac{1}{2}$ of the amount by which the gain G_0 for that year exceeds the losses for that year L_0 and the losses of the five preceding years L_{-5}, L_{-4}, L_{-3}, L_{-2}, L_{-1} and the forthcoming year L_{+1})

TAX USE OF ALLOWABLE CAPITAL LOSSES

It has been shown how losses incurred on dispositions of listed personal property can be utilized for tax purposes. Of what use are allowable capital losses?

Paragraph (b) of the general rules for determining income for tax purposes requires a determination of the amount, if any, by which the aggregate of the taxable capital gains and the taxable net gains exceeds the allowable capital losses for the year, or

$$T.C.G. + T.N.G. - A.C.L.$$

Note that this provision does not allow the use of allowable capital losses incurred in the five preceding and the immediately following year when calculating income. Paragraph (e) of the same general rules gives individuals (not corporations) a further tax break. If up to $2,000 of the allowable capital losses ($4,000 of capital losses) incurred that year still remains after being subtracted from taxable capital gains and taxable net gains, this amount can be subtracted from any other income.

Although a deduction of previous capital losses is not allowed in calculating income, a further deduction for net capital loss is permitted when calculating *taxable* income.

Net Capital Loss

Net capital loss in general means the excess of allowable capital losses over taxable capital gains and taxable net gains which were not deductible in calculating income for a taxation year or previous taxation years. An individual can, when calculating his taxable income, deduct net capital loss to the extent that his taxable capital gains and taxable net gains may exceed his allowable capital losses in that year. He can also deduct up to a further $2,000 of net capital loss against other (non-capital gains) income in calculating taxable income unless he has already applied $2,000 of allowable capital losses against other income in calculating income. However, the deduction of net capital loss must be taken before any personal deductions (donations to charities, medical expenses, etc.) may be made. This means that where the individual has net capital losses available, he must use them before applying his personal exemptions for the year; he may not preserve his net capital losses for future use by taking personal exemptions. Consequently, he loses the tax advantage of his personal exemptions.

Net capital losses can be carried back one year and forward indefinitely. They are not subject to the 5 year carry forward limitation applied to losses incurred on dispositions of listed personal property.

SPECIAL RULES

Some of the points to watch out for have already been mentioned.

1. Some works of art and other properties may be classified as cultural property pursuant to the provisions of the Cultural Property Export and Import Act, and be subject to different rules upon disposition. Please see *Dispositions of Cultural Property* at page 138.
2. A work of art has to be personal-use property before it can be classified as listed personal property.
3. There are no capital losses on personal-use property although there are on stocks and bonds etc.
4. "Deeming" provisions of the Income Tax Act take effect if the transaction is a gift or not at arm's length.
5. The provision for reserves facilitates the paying of tax and also allows some tax planning as to when it is best to incur a taxable capital gain. Reserves are not available for use in calculating allowable capital losses and taxable net gains.

There are a few other important rules.

The Personal-Use Property $1,000 Rule

One rule of great practical importance is the $1,000 deeming provision. This rule says that where a taxpayer disposes of personal-use property, including listed personal property, the adjusted cost base shall be deemed to be at least $1,000. If a collector buys an etching for his personal use and enjoyment for

130

$400 and sells it for $800 his gain for calculating taxable net gain is $0. He is deemed to have bought and sold it for $1,000. Likewise, if a sculpture is purchased for $900 and resold for $600 the loss for calculating loss for taxable net gain is $0. This rule frees the taxpayer from the necessity of keeping a myriad of records.

Part Dispositions

There is also a rule designed to prevent the taxpayer's delaying a realization of a capital gain by selling parts of the property. If a taxpayer sells part of a property, the adjusted cost base of that part of the property is deemed to be that portion of the adjusted cost base of the whole property that is reasonably attributable to that part.

The toy train buff who sells one of his four rooms of toy trains should be prepared to place on the portion sold an adjusted cost base of approximately 25% of the total adjusted cost base in calculating his taxable capital gain, or be prepared to explain why such should not be the case (best locomotives not sold, etc.)

There is a more specialized form of the rule which is a combination of the Personal-Use Property $1,000 Rule and the Part Disposition Rule. This says that if part of a personal-use property is disposed of, the adjusted cost base of that part is the greater of the adjusted cost base determined under the Part Disposition Rule and that proportion of $1,000 that the adjusted cost base of the part is of the adjusted cost base of the whole property.

Similarly, the proceeds of disposition are deemed to be the greater of the amount actually received (or the fair market value) and the proportion of $1,000 that the adjusted cost base of the part is of the adjusted cost base of the whole property.

E.g., suppose a stamp collector sells one quarter of his collection for $1,500. The adjusted cost base of the entire collection is $3,200. The adjusted cost base of the part of the collection being sold is the greater of $800 and $250.

The gain is $1,500 − $800 = $700 and if there are no losses in respect of listed personal property the taxable net gain is $350.

Properties Ordinarily Disposed of as a Set

An even more specialized form of the rule deals with property ordinarily disposed of as a set, e.g., matching chairs or the panels of a tryptych. This rule deems the set (not each component part of the set) to have an adjusted cost base of no less than $1,000 and the proceeds of the disposition in respect of the set to be not less than $1,000.

One problem that collectors face in dealing with sets is that the collector may actually have put the so-called set together from different sources at various points in time (e.g., limited edition serigraphs by the same artist all bearing the same number). Professional advice should be sought in cases where it is possible that a collection will be deemed a set.

The final reminder that you should not try to diddle the government is their attempt at a cure-all provision: "where the result of one or more sales, exchanges, declarations of trust, or other transactions of any kind whatsoever is that a taxpayer has disposed of property under circumstances such that he may reasonably be considered to have artificially or unduly
(a) reduced the amount of his gain from the disposition;
(b) created a loss from the disposition; or
(c) increased the amount of his loss from the disposition,
the taxpayer's gain or loss, as the case may be, from the disposition of the property shall be computed as if such reduction, creation or increase, as the casy may be, had not occurred."

GIFTING BY A COLLECTOR

This discussion of gifting by an individual collector resident in Canada will deal only with non-depreciable property, including personal-use property (and listed personal property). Depreciable capital property is dealt with in Chapter 8, The Corporate Collector: Taxation and Gifting. A gift requires a donor, a donee, and some property. The Income Tax Act provides that, except where a gift is made to a spouse, the donor is deemed to have received proceeds of disposition equal to fair market value for tax purposes. It is irrelevant who the donee is, if it is not your spouse; it could be a charity, the Queen, or your sister. It is also irrelevant what the gift of property is, unless it is "certified cultural property" in which case the calculation of taxable capital gains and taxable net gains excludes the deemed proceeds of disposition of certified cultural property to designated public institutions. This topic will be dealt with later at page138 under the heading *Dispositions of Cultural Property.*

Gifting of Different Property Interests

The common law, which is the basis for the non-criminal law of all the provinces except Quebec (which has based its civil law on the Napoleonic Code), has produced a rich variety of property interests. Consequently, in Canada we are beginning to see an increasing number of imaginative gifts of different interests in property, which are beneficial to both the donor and the recipient. Appraisers are able to put values on these different types of gifts. The most common is the outright gift of all interests, legal and possessory, in the property, but gifts can also be made of part interests of property measured in quantity or in time.

A person, for tax reasons, could gift a one-fifth interest in a major painting to a museum in each of five years until the museum owned all the painting. During the intervening years the person and the museum would have differing undivided interests which when totalled represent complete ownership of the whole painting. One disadvantage of this approach is that for a certain period of time ownership is divided between the donor and the museum, and this raises questions of responsibility and control. Another disadvantage is that the museum is not always assured of receiving the remainder of the gift.

Another approach would be to deliver the object and take back a number of promissory notes in payment, one of which would mature each year over a period of years. The donor then pledges to gift each note to the museum as it matures. In this fashion, the museum buys the art with the donor's gifts of money and the donor makes a charitable donation each year for the value of the promissory note.

One area of gifting for tax deductions that has not been explored sufficiently is the loan of works of art. This is a limited gift of property: it is the gift of possession for a period of time, but the donor still owns the object. Galleries that wish to assemble touring exhibitions would have a tangible benefit to offer collectors who may be reluctant to have their art absent from their collections and subject to the rigors of public exhibition. The value of the gift, it is suggested, would be the rental cost of the same work.

A gift could be made of a right-of-way across real estate to give the public more convenient access to an historical home. An easement over the historical facade of a building has been given. A gift has also been made of the use of some land, for the relocation of an historical home, to which the owner has retained legal title.

A person could also give title to an historical home to a Heritage Foundation, subject to a life interest for the donor so that he could continue to enjoy the possession of his home during his lifetime. The person could deal with the house as he wished during his life as long as it was not exposed unduly to damage, but upon his death all rights in the home would belong to the Heritage Foundation. The advantage of this type of gift is that it gives an immediate tax deduction without loss of possession of the property.

When dealing with these unusual types of gifts it is important to have proper documentation so all parties know what interests have been gifted. In some cases income tax rulings might be obtained from the Minister of National Revenue as to the tax effect of the gift.

Gifts to Spouses   If non-depreciable capital property was transferred after 1971 to a spouse (not including a common-law spouse), or to an inter vivos (between living persons) spousal trust, as opposed to a testamentary trust (which is made in a will), the taxpayer is deemed to have disposed of the property and the spouse is deemed to have acquired it at the adjusted cost base to the taxpayer. Therefore, no immediate tax effects arise on a transfer between a husband and wife whether or not it involves a gift.

133

Then, when the recipient spouse disposes of the property, any taxable capital gain, allowable capital loss, or gain or loss from the disposition of listed personal property, is deemed to be that of the spouse who was the original owner, if he is resident in Canada and the person disposing of the property is still his spouse. This latter qualification to the general attribution rule prevents divorced spouses from having unexpected tax problems, but still may leave some separated spouses with headaches. Remedial legislation has been proposed at the time of writing to assist separated spouses in certain circumstances.

This provision dealing with dispositions to a spouse is part of an attempt by Revenue Canada to prevent income splitting between spouses which is designed to take advantage of one spouse's lower marginal rates. However, this provision applies even to those cases where one spouse purchases in arm's length fashion from the other.

Tax-planning in this area to decide which spouse will buy particular capital assets requires very long range vision as to the state of the art market, the state of the income of each spouse, and the state of the marriage.

Gifts to Minors

If property is transferred to any person under the age of 18 (whether related or not) either directly, indirectly, or by means of an irrevocable trust, the transferor is deemed to have received proceeds of disposition equal to the fair market value, and the minor is deemed to have acquired the property at fair market value. The transferor is obliged to report, for the year of transfer, any taxable capital gain or taxable net gain.

When the minor, even if he is a child of the transferor, disposes of the property, whether before or after he attains the age of 18 years, the capital gains or losses realized on the property transferred are those of the minor in most cases, not of the transferor. In no case is there attribution of gains or losses from dispositions of listed personal property to the transferor. This differs substantially from the treatment provided for transfers to a spouse.

It should be pointed out, however, that any income earned on a transferred asset while it is the property of the minor and before the minor reaches the age of 18 years is deemed to be that of the transferor even if the parties are not related.

By virtue of a special provision of the Income Tax Act, the minor who has received the property is jointly and severally liable with the transferor to pay any tax exigible in respect of the transfer and any other income taxes owing by the transferor not exceeding the value of the transferred property. This stops people transferring assets to their children and depriving Revenue authorities of their tax. The same rule applies to the transfers to spouses.

Gift Taxes

A word should be said about gift taxes. Prior to the inauguration of the capital gains tax, the federal government had levied a gift tax since 1935. This tax was repealed effective January 1, 1972. The provinces had shared in the revenue from the federal gift tax and so, when the federal government repealed it, all of the provinces except Alberta introduced a gift tax effective January 1, 1972. As more tax began to be collected on deemed capital gains arising on gifts, the provinces (who assess their tax on generally the same taxable income base as the federal government) either discontinued or reduced their gift taxes. By January 1, 1980, only Quebec still had a gift tax.

TAX DEDUCTIBLE DONATIONS

The advantages of gifting works of art to various institutions are widely touted. The intangible advantages are personal to the donor. The tax advantages are substantial but varied. The tax advantages depend on the characterization of the recipient for tax purposes, and also on the type and value of the property being donated.

The character of the donee becomes important when determining the limit to the size of the deduction from income that can be made in calculating taxable income.

Tax deductible gifts can be made to

1. charities
2. Her Majesty, and
3. designated public institutions pursuant to the Cultural Property Export and Import Act.

Charitable Donations

Gifts to registered charities (this includes charitable organizations, public foundations, and private foundations), registered Canadian amateur athletic associations, Canadian municipalities, the United Nations and its agencies, certain universities outside Canada at which Canadians are ordinarily students, and charitable organizations outside Canada which the federal government has donated to in the recent past, etc., are generally referred to as charitable donations.

Donors of art objects should be aware that their charity of choice may also be a "designated public institution" or may be able to obtain that status for the purposes of their gift, pursuant to the provisions of the Cultural Property Export and Import Act (CPEIA). Since there are greater tax benefits arising from the disposition of cultural property so certified under that Act, other than listed personal property whose adjusted cost base and fair market value are less than $1,000, reference should also be made to *Dispositions of Cultural Property* at page 138.

Receipts issued by the charity must be filed with the tax return showing the amount or value of the donation when claiming a deduction.

135

Revenue Canada will, as a matter of practice, allow either spouse to claim charitable expenses regardless of whose name is on the receipt. If those donations exceed $100 the spouse with the higher taxable income, and hence the higher marginal tax rate, should claim all the donations as a deduction. The spouse with the lower income and marginal tax rate is still able to claim the standard charitable/medical deduction of $100.

The one problem that can arise with charitable donations is that they may not be fully utilized for tax purposes because the total deduction for all gifts to charities in one year is limited to 20% of income (it used to be 10%). Some flexibility is allowed, in that any excess donations may be carried forward for use in the next year.

E.g., suppose a collector donates a painting worth $20,000 to a gallery. His income including the deemed taxable net gain is $45,000. In the year of giving, a deduction can only be made for $9,000 instead of the entire $20,000. If his income remains constant for the next year, $2,000 of potentially deductible donation has been lost.

Suppose that the same collector has instead an income of $80,000. The collector is not free to use $10,000 of the deduction this year and save $10,000 for use next year in order to more fully exploit the deduction in conjunction with the increasing marginal rates. The collector is obliged to use $16,000 the first year and $4,000 the second.

The one great advantage to a collector in donating to a local gallery or museum is that he may be able to have special conditions attached to his gift. He may wish to have some personal recognition for the gift, such as identification on labels when the cultural property is exhibited or reproduced in publications. Donors should be aware, however, that galleries and museums much prefer to accept gifts with no strings attached, as this reduces their need to keep records and perform otherwise unnecessary tasks, the costs of which must be met from their operating budgets.

Gifts to Her Majesty

Gifts to Her Majesty in the right of Canada or in right of the provinces are limited to 100% of income remaining after deductions have been made for charitable donations. Any amount that cannot be used in the year of giving can be carried forward for use in the next year. Again, the taxpayer cannot choose how much of the deduction he wishes to carry forward. The effective use of personal deductions in the year of giving may be lost if the gift is of such a size that the personal deductions may not be used.

Gifts to Her Majesty are becoming more common. Gifts are being made to provincial heritage foundations who are agents of Her Majesty in right of their respective provinces. Property acquired by Foundation is the property of Her Majesty in right of the

136

province. (Heritage Canada is a registered charity which, by agreement with the Crown, can hold property in trust for the Crown in order that donors to Heritage Canada may receive the same treatment as donors to the Crown.)

Prior to the general tax reform that culminated in the introduction of the present Income Tax Act effective in 1972, gifts to Her Majesty were limited to Her Majesty in the right of Canada and the only donations of art eligible for the 100% deduction from income were those made to the National Gallery of Canada in Ottawa.

A word of caution is in order. The taxpayer should always check that the intended recipient is indeed considered in law to be an agent of Her Majesty. Appearances can be deceiving. A fund established by Her Majesty may not be Her legal agent.

Heritage foundations are aware of the limitations of donations to charities and for this reason will frequently entertain requests to receive the gift but make it available by deposit, or on loan, to the local municipality or gallery where in the opinion of the donor the work really belongs. However, there is no guarantee that the Crown authorities will abide by such a request, and there cannot be a guarantee of any personal recognition for the donor.

Heritage foundations which are agencies of Her Majesty may also apply for designated public institution status pursuant to the provisions of the Cultural Property Export and Import Act. A prospective donor to a heritage foundation is well advised (for tax reasons) to determine whether the foundation has, or is prepared to seek, designation for purposes of receiving a gift of property capable of being certified as cultural property under the Act. A discussion of the tax advantages appears under *Disposition of Cultural Property* at page 138.

Election on Gifts of Tangible Capital Property

The federal government realized that although there was flexibility in gifting to either a charity or Her Majesty, a taxpayer could sometimes still be penalized if a gift of very valuable capital property was made by a taxpayer whose income was not very great. The penalty would arise because tax would be paid as if the proceeds of disposition were equal to the fair market value, but the full value of the deduction (the fair market value of the gift) would not be available for deduction. Consequently, the Act was amended to provide that where a taxpayer made a gift to either a charity or Her Majesty of tangible capital property that could, at that time, reasonably be regarded as suitable for use by the donee directly in the course of carrying on its charitable public service or other similar activities, he could elect any amount to be the proceeds of disposition, which was between the fair market value and the adjusted cost base of the property (assuming the fair market value was greater than the adjusted cost base). This elected amount would be deemed to be the taxpayer's proceeds of disposition and the value of the gift.

E.g., suppose an individual who otherwise would have a taxable income of $25,000 donates a painting, whose fair market value is $35,000 and whose adjusted cost base is $5,000, to a charity. Without the election, in the year of donation the taxpayer's income prior to the deduction for his charitable donations is

$$\$25,000 + \frac{1}{2}(\$35,000 - \$5,000) = \$40,000.$$

The maximum charitable donation is $8,000, so the taxpayer pays tax on $32,000 in the year of donation, and tax the next year on $20,000 ($25,000 less $5,000 from the $27,000 charitable deductible carry forward). The taxpayer has paid higher taxes than he would have, because of the tax on the deemed capital gain, and $22,000 of charitable deduction has not been used in calculating taxable income.

But suppose instead the taxpayer elects that the proceeds of disposition and the amount of the gift be $10,000. The taxpayer's taxable income prior to the deduction for his charitable donation is

$$\$25,000 + \frac{1}{2}(\$10,000 - \$5,000) = \$27,500.$$

The taxable income after the charitable donation has been deducted is

$$\$27,500 - \$5,500 = \$22,000$$

in the year of donation, and the next year the taxable income is

$$\$25,000 - (\$10,000 - \$5,500) = \$20,500.$$

Approximately $4,000 in tax is saved through use of the election.

However, restrictions on the use of this election should be noted. The gift must be suitable for use by the donee in carrying out its activities. The gift of an abstract sculpture to grace the environs of a welfare organization would probably not be regarded as suitable for use by the donee in carrying out its program of poverty assistance. In contrast, the gift of a sculpture to an art gallery would be useful to a gallery. Note also that the gift must be of capital property; it cannot be inventory.

Dispositions of Cultural Property

Gifts of Certified Cultural Property

It has already been seen that a collector taxpayer does not include in his calculation of capital gain, or gain on the disposition of listed personal property, his deemed proceeds of disposition from the disposition of "an object that the Canadian Cultural Property Export Review Board has determined meets all criteria set out in paragraphs 23(3)(b) and (c) of the Cultural Property Export and Import Act and that has been disposed of to an institution or public authority in Canada that was at the time of the disposition, designated under subsection 26(2) of that Act either generally or for a purpose related to that object." This has been the law since September 5, 1977. This tax advantage does not accrue to dealers or artists unless the work comes from their private collections. Taxpayers in Quebec will also not receive the benefit of this omission from income for purposes of calculating provincial tax until their taxation acts have been amended. The tax advantages of this non-inclusion are tremendous. For example, suppose a wealthy collector, whose taxable income after charitable gifts and gifts to Her Majesty have been deducted is $150,000 a year, decides to donate a painting worth $250,000, which he acquired for $50,000 on January 2, 1972, to a Heritage Foundation. His taxable income in the year of donation is nil

$$[\$150,000 + 1/2 (\$250,000 - \$50,000) - \$250,000]$$

and the next year his taxable income returns to $150,000.

But suppose he donates the painting to a designated institution after having it certified as cultural property. In this case, his taxable income in the year of donation is still nil

$$(\$150,000 - \$250,000)$$

but he has a $100,000 donation to use the next year to reduce his taxable income to $50,000.

One important feature of the deductibility of donations of certified cultural property to designated institutions (as well as charitable donations and gifts to Her Majesty), is that the deduction must be made from income before personal deductions and deductions for supporting dependents can be made. The benefits for deductions available in respect of such things as medical expenses, education allowances, interest and dividend income, and pension income may be lost. The taxpayer is not allowed to arbitrarily spread his deductions over the permitted 2 years to take maximum advantage of the deductions by obtaining the lowest possible marginal tax rates for both of the years.

As mentioned previously at page 132, there are different property interests which can be gifted, and it is not necessary to gift all rights in an object in one year. Donations of part interests could be made over a number of years, of a monetary size which allows full use of all deductions and prevents losing the advantage of those initial portions of taxable income on which no tax is payable in any case. Notice that it is also possible to have the donation spread over more than 2 years in this fashion.

Certified Cultural Property

The criteria necessary for an object to be certified as cultural property are set out in paragraphs 23(3)(b) and (c) of the Cultural Property Export and Import Act. First, the object must be of outstanding significance for one or more of the following reasons:

1. its close association with Canadian history or national life,
2. its aesthetic qualities, or
3. its value in the study of the arts or sciences.

Secondly, the object must be "of such a degree of national

importance that its loss to Canada would significantly diminish the national heritage." It is irrelevant whether or not the object is less than 50 years old, or was made by a living person, or has a value less than the minimum prescribed on the control list which affects exports of art. (The significance of this age and these values will become apparent on reading Chapter 6, which is devoted entirely to the Cultural Property Export and Import Act.)

In order to have the work certified as cultural property for donation purposes, and to have a value placed on the donation, an application for certification of cultural property for income tax purposes is completed and forwarded to the appropriate authorities in Ottawa. An example of the application is attached as Appendix A to this chapter. The application may be submitted by either the prospective recipient or by the donor collector.

When the property has been certified, the donor receives a Cultural Property Income Tax Certificate signed by an officer of the Canadian Cultural Property Export Review Board. An example is attached as Appendix B to this chapter. The donor does not receive a receipt for tax purposes from the institution or public authority which has received the gift.

A donor who wishes to give an important article to a local museum or gallery, but is reluctant to do so because of the 20% limitation on deductions, and who is also unwilling to lose local recognition by making a gift to a heritage foundation, may be able to make a gift to a local public institution after exploring the possibility of using the opportunities available through the Cultural Property Export and Import Act.

A further advantage of gifting pursuant to the provisions of the CPEIA is that the donor can be assured that the work will not be sold by the recipient institution or public authority for at least five years. This is because the federal government imposes on the institution or public authority a tax of 30% of the fair market value of the object at the time of disposition if it is disposed of within five years, unless it is given to another designated institution.

Sales of Cultural Property

The other tax effect of the introduction of the Cultural Property Export and Import Act comes into play when a collector has sold (not gifted) an object to a designated institution after he has unsuccessfully sought an export permit for that object under the CPEIA. Reference is made to export under CPEIA in Chapter 6.

The scenario would be approximately as follows. The collector applies for an export permit pursuant to the CPEIA. The permit officer refers the application to an expert examiner, who decides that the object is on the control list and meets the criteria of outstanding significance and national importance, and an export permit is denied. Following the expert examiner's ruling, the collector appeals the decision (within 30 days of the date of the notice of refusal given by the permit officer) to the Canadian Cultural Property Export Review Board. The board, in the 4 months following, affirms that the object is on the control list and is of outstanding significance and national importance. The board believes that a fair cash offer to purchase the object will be made by a Canadian institution or public authority and establishes a 1 to 6 month delay period. During the delay period, the collector and prospective purchasers negotiate the purchase price. An institution then makes an offer which is refused by the collector, and more than 30 days before the end of the delay period the institution requests the review board to determine the amount of a fair cash offer. The board seeks the advice of expert evaluators and determines a fair cash offer. The institution offers the collector this amount and the offer is accepted.

The capital gain realized is not included in the calculation of income. The collector, of course, does not receive a receipt to be used as a deduction when calculating taxable income.

In the hypothetical example of the wealthy collector, this would mean that if he was paid $250,000 he would have a tax free gain of

$$\$250,000 - \$50,000 = \$200,000.$$

As his marginal tax bracket is approximately 60% the tax saving is

$$60\% \times \frac{1}{2} (\$200,000) = \$60,000.$$

However, in negotiating a price, it is expected that the collector and the institution will take into account any tax relief for which the collector may qualify, in order to reduce the price to be paid by the purchasing institution or public authority. Consequently, the collector would realistically only be offered $190,000 for his object. His tax free capital gain is then

$$\$190,000 - \$50,000 = \$140,000,$$

which is the same amount he would have had in hand if he had sold the painting outside the country for $250,000 and paid tax.

$$[\$250,000 - 60\% \times \frac{1}{2} (\$250,000 - \$50,000) = \$190,000].$$

It should be remembered that a certified cultural property object will not be purchased by an institution or public authority unless an export permit is refused. The object not only has to be of outstanding significance and national importance, but also has to appear on the control list. Reference is again made to Chapter 6.

DEATH OF A COLLECTOR AND TAXES

When an individual dies, he is deemed to have disposed of all of his capital property, including his art, immediately before his death.

The rules for collectors are as follows:

1. the taxpayer is deemed to have received proceeds of disposition equal to fair market value for each property that was a capital property (other than depreciable property);
2. the heir or legatee is deemed to have received the property at an adjusted cost base to him equal to the value at which the collector is deemed to have disposed of the property.

The one outstanding exception to this rule is that capital property which is bequeathed to a spouse who is resident in Canada, or a trust set up in the will for the sole benefit of the spouse, is deemed to have been disposed of by the taxpayer and acquired by the spouse or trust, at the taxpayer's tax cost. This means that no taxable capital gain, or allowable capital loss, or taxable net gain occurs on the deemed disposition of capital property to a spouse. However, when the property passes to persons other than the spouse, the rules governing deemed dispositions take effect.

Some of the provisions can cause difficulty. The wording used in the Income Tax Act says that the taxpayer is deemed to have disposed, immediately before his death, of *each* capital property (other than depreciable property) and to have received proceeds of disposition equal to the fair market value of the property at that time. The Act does not say that the taxpayer is deemed to have disposed of *all* capital property (other than depreciable property) and to have received proceeds of disposition equal to the fair market value of *all* the property at that time. The estate of a collector with a large collection of one artist's work, which places this collection on the market, may not be able to realize as great a value from the entire collection as may someone who can gradually release the works of art for sale over a period of time. Recognition of the effect of the laws of supply and demand on the price which could be obtained in the market when a large number of works are available, could be given by a so-called blockage discount. The wording of the Income Tax Act, however, appears to preclude calculation of a blockage discount when determining fair market value. Please refer to page 171 for a more thorough discussion of what is meant by a blockage discount.

The Income Tax Act also does not allow for any reasonable hypothetical expenses and outlays in the making of the disposition. This could cause serious problems where a dealer or auction house which actually sells the work for the estate, demands a commission or a discount in the case of outright purchase, of 10% - 60% depending on the work. If, in that case, the Department of National Revenue fails to exercise its discretion and insists that fair market value means the retail price which would be paid for the object by a willing retail purchaser, instead of the price that would be received by a willing vendor who uses the services of a dealer (or who sells to a dealer, or who acts as his own dealer and incurs expenses), serious capital losses will be incurred by the estate of a deceased collector. It should be noted that all capital losses are deductible in the terminal year.

A taxpayer can also give a bequest of works of art to a charitable organization or to Her Majesty. A gift made in a will to a gallery, museum, heritage foundation, etc., is deemed to have been made by the taxpayer in the year in which he died. Such a gift, of course, reduces the amount of tax payable by the estate on the terminal return of the taxpayer, since while only half the deemed gain is taxable, the entire value of the gift is deductible in calculating taxable income on the terminal return. However, the 20% limitation on gifts to charities is in effect, and there is no carry forward of excess charitable contributions for use by anyone beyond the terminal return.

Gifts to Her Majesty are similarly restricted to the 100% deduction on the terminal return in the year of death with no carry-forward of excess donations. The Income Tax Act again provides relief by allowing an election on the gift of tangible capital property as to the deemed proceeds of disposition and value of the gift.

It is clear that it may be to the benefit of an estate to argue that in the case of a donation of a work of art, the fair market value is the price which would be paid by the institution to purchase from a dealer; whereas if the estate is selling, it would argue for a value which took into account dealer's commissions, blockage discounts, etc. It is easy to see the difficulty that faces the authorities at Revenue Canada also.

Bequests of Cultural Property

If a taxpayer wills cultural property, which could be subsequently certified, to a designated public institution, it would be logical to think that his estate could take advantage of the exception for certified cultural property in calculating both capital gains and gains from dispositions of listed personal property for the taxpayer's terminal return. However, at the time of writing, such is not the case. The relief can apply only in the unusual case where the property has been certified before the taxpayer's death. This is clearly an oversight, and a resolution to amend the legislation retroactive to September 5, 1977 has been proposed. It is expected that the legislation implementing the resolution will provide that the bequest will be exempt from taxes applicable to capital property if it is certified by the Review Board, and disposed of to a designated institution or public authority, within a reasonable period of time after the death of the testator.

The Income Tax Act has already had one retroactive amendment providing that the deduction may be allowed against income and deemed income in the year of death.

The anticipated amendment is expected to encourage bequests of cultural property to Canadian institutions. The British law in this area of cultural property is even more generous. There, an heir to an object which forms part of the national heritage is not subject to estate duties as long as the object is not sold. In addition, since 1972, gifts to public collections of important works of art may be accepted in lieu of payment of taxes. The French government has adopted similar provisions.

Estate Taxes and Succession Duties

A discussion of death taxes reminds many people of the old estate taxes and succession duties. Prior to April 1, 1947, every province and territory, as well as the federal government, levied and collected succession duties. In 1958, the federal government replaced the Dominion Succession Duty Act with the Estate Tax Act. All of the provinces eventually shared to some extent in the revenue collected by the federal government, although Ontario and Quebec still had their own Succession Duty Acts.

As with gift tax, up on the introduction of the capital gains concept, the federal government vacated the inheritance and death tax field effective January 1, 1972. All of the provinces which were not already in the succession duty field, except Alberta, moved in to fill the vacuum by re-introducing succession duties. At the time of writing, however, only Quebec was still levying such a tax. The other provinces presumably felt that their share of the revenue collected by virtue of the inclusion of capital gains and gains on listed personal property in income, no longer justified the continuation of a provincial tax.

Some tax observers in Canada feel that Canadians are going to see the re-introduction of some form of wealth tax, either provincially or federally, in the not so distant future, possibly levied once again at the time of death.

DEPARTURE FROM CANADA

If a taxpayer ceases to be a resident in Canada, he is deemed to have disposed of all his property (with some exceptions) at its fair market value. This includes all his capital property – his personal-use property and listed personal property. His taxable capital gains (not including taxable net gain) for these purposes are the amount, if any, by which the taxable capital gains from the deemed disposition exceed $2,500.

The net gain on the deemed disposition of listed personal property for these purposes is the net gain otherwise determined less the amount, if any, by which $5,000 exceeds the capital gains. Half of the net gain is his taxable net gain. Basically, the government lets a person have a tax-free $5,000 gain on capital property when leaving the country, if the property has not actually been disposed of.

A taxpayer may elect to pay the tax exigible in up to six annual instalments, provided that appropriate security is given to the Minister of National Revenue.

A taxpayer may also elect, provided acceptable security is given, to pay no departure tax in respect of some or all of his capital property which has not been disposed of. If the property is subsequently disposed of while the taxpayer is non-resident, he becomes liable for the tax. This election cannot be made in such a way as to effectively realize capital losses and defer capital gains, although it can be used in this fashion with respect to losses and gains on dispositions of listed personal property.

Appendix A

Secretary of State
Secrétariat d'État

APPLICATION FOR CERTIFICATION OF CULTURAL PROPERTY FOR INCOME TAX PURPOSES / **DEMANDE D'ATTESTATION RELATIVE À UN BIEN CULTUREL AUX FINS DE L'IMPÔT**

(Please see notes and instructions on reverse before completing)
(Consulter les remarques et instructions au verso, avant de remplir la présente formule)

Return completed Application to: Movable Cultural Property   Biens culturels mobiliers
A retourner à l'adresse suivante: Ottawa, Canada K1A 0M5   Ottawa Canada K1A 0M5

Date

1. Owner – Propriétaire
   Name – Nom _____

   _____
   Address – Adresse   Tel. – Tél.

   Applicant (if other than owner or recipient institution or public authority)   Requérant (si ce n'est ni le propriétaire, ni l'établissement ou l'administration bénéficiaire)

   Name – Nom _____

   _____
   Address – Adresse   Tel. – Tél.

2. Recipient institution or public authority – Établissement ou administration bénéficiaire

   Name – Nom _____

   _____
   Address – Adresse   Tel. – Tél.

   _____
   Person in Charge – Responsable   Title – Titre

   Institution or public authority is – L'établissement ou l'administration
   ☐ designated under Category A – est désigné dans la catégorie A
   ☐ seeking specific designation under Category B for the / demande à être désigné dans la catégorie B pour le bien
      cultural property described herein.   culturel décrit ci-après.

3. Cultural Property will be disposed of by – Le bien culturel sera aliéné par
   ☐ sale – vente   or – ou   ☐ donation – donation

4.   **DESCRIPTION OF CULTURAL PROPERTY – DESCRIPTION DU BIEN CULTUREL**

   Photograph or copy is attached – Photographie ou reproduction ci-jointe ☐

   (if above space is insufficient, continue on a separate sheet) – (Au besoin, annexer une feuille)

5. State briefly why cultural property described above is of outstanding significance and of national importance   Indiquer brièvement pourquoi le bien culturel décrit ci-dessus présente un intérêt exceptionnel et revêt une importance nationale:

6. Declaration of authenticity for cultural property is attached – La déclaration d'authenticité du bien culturel se trouve ci-jointe ☐
   Authenticated by – Elle est authentifiée par   Name – Nom _____
   Qualifications – Titres et qualités

7. Estimated Fair Market Value of cultural property – Juste valeur marchande du bien culturel estimée à _____

   We the undersigned hereby certify that the information given in this application and any accompanying documentation is true and correct.   Nous soussignés certifions que les renseignements ci-dessus et les documents ci-joints sont véridiques et exacts.

   _____   _____
   Owner – Propriétaire   For Recipient Institution / Pour l'établissement ou
                                                        or Public Authority   l'administration bénéficiaire

   FOR INTERNAL USE ONLY – RÉSERVÉ À L'ADMINISTRATION

   _____   _____
   Date received – Date de réception   Reference No. – Numéro de référence

   SEC4-12 (1/77)

146

Appendix B

Revenue Canada
Taxation

Revenu Canada
Impôt

1 FOR APPLICANT FOR ATTACHMENT TO OWNER S INCOME TAX RETURN
POUR LE REQUERANT, À ANNEXER À LA DÉCLARATION D IMPOT
SUR LE REVENU DU PROPRIÉTAIRE

CULTURAL PROPERTY INCOME TAX CERTIFICATE

- For use by an authorized officer of the Canadian Cultural Property Export Review Board to certify that a particular cultural object(s) meets specified criteria namely:

    (A) that it is of outstanding significance for one or more of the reasons set out in paragraph 8(3)(a) of the Cultural Property Export and Import Act, and

    (B) that it meets the degree of national importance referred to in paragraph 8(3)(b) of the Cultural Property Export and Import Act.

- This Certificate when signed by an authorized officer is evidence that the property herein described is such that its disposal to an institution designated by the Secretary of State of Canada, will qualify for the following treatment under the Income Tax Act:

    (A) where the property is donated, the donor may deduct an amount up to the value of the donation in computing taxable income if the claim is supported by a receipt (paragraph 110(1)(b.1) of the Income Tax Act);

    (B) a gain, which would otherwise be a capital gain, arising from the disposition of the property is not subject to tax (subparagraph 39(1)(a)(i.1) of the Income Tax Act).

- The Certificate is valid for income tax purposes only in circumstances where:

    (A) disposition is of the object as herein described,

    (B) the condition, composition, texture, etc. of the object(s) has not been altered since an application for certification was sent to the Review Board, except any measures for repair and/or conservation authorized by the Review Board,

    (C) disposition is made to the designated institution indicated below, and

    (D) ownership rests in the designated institution and possession of the object by the institution is obtained by the last day of the calendar year following that in which this Certificate is issued.

- Further particulars may be obtained from your District Taxation Office.

CERTIFICAT FISCAL VISANT DES BIENS CULTURELS

- À l'usage d'un agent autorisé de la Commission canadienne d'examen des exportations de biens culturels pour certifier qu'un ou plusieurs objets culturels particuliers sont conformes aux critères établis, à savoir:

    (A) qu'ils présentent un intérêt exceptionnel pour l'une ou plusieurs des raisons énoncées à l'alinéa 8(3)a) de la Loi sur l'exportation et l'importation de biens culturels, et

    (B) qu'ils revêtent l'importance nationale dont fait mention l'alinéa 8(3)b) de la Loi sur l'exportation et l'importation de biens culturels.

- Le présent certificat une fois signé par un agent autorisé, établit que les biens décrits ici répondent aux conditions requises, de sorte que leur disposition au profit d'un établissement désigné par le Secrétaire d'État du Canada ouvre droit au traitement suivant en vertu de la Loi de l'impôt sur le revenu:

    (A) si les biens sont donnés, le donateur peut déduire dans le calcul de son revenu imposable un montant n'excédant pas la valeur du don, pourvu qu'il présente un reçu à l'appui (alinéa 110(1)b 1) de la Loi de l'impôt sur le revenu);

    (B) un gain, qui serait par ailleurs un gain en capital, résultant de la disposition des biens n'est pas assujetti à l'impôt (sous-alinéa 39(1)a) (i.1) de la Loi de l'impôt sur le revenu).

- Ce certificat est valable aux fins de l'impôt sur le revenu dans les seuls cas où:

    (A) il y a disposition de tout objet décrit dans le présent certificat;

    (B) il n'y a eu aucune modification de l'état, de la composition, de la texture, etc. desdits objets depuis qu'une demande d'attestation a été envoyée à la Commission d'examen, à l'exception de toutes mesures autorisées par la Commission d'examen en vue de la réparation et (ou) de l'entretien desdits objets;

    (C) la disposition est faite au profit de l'établissement désigné dont il est fait mention ci-après; et

    (D) le droit de propriété est dévolu à l'établissement désigné et celui-c devient le propriétaire desdits objets au plus tard le dernier jour de l'année civile suivant celle où le présent certificat est délivré.

- Pour obtenir plus de détails, veuillez consulter votre bureau de district d'impôt.

NAME OF DESIGNATED INSTITUTION (to which disposal of the property has been or will be made)
NOM DE L'ÉTABLISSEMENT DÉSIGNÉ (au profit duquel la disposition des biens a été ou sera faite)

ADDRESS — ADRESSE

Pursuant to section 26 of the Cultural Property Export and Import Act a determination has been made by the Canadian Cultural Property Export Review Board with respect to the object(s) described as follows: (If space below is insufficient, attach a statement.)

Conformément à l'article 26 de la Loi sur l'exportation et l'importation de biens culturels, la Commission canadienne d'examen des exportations de biens culturels a rendu une décision concernant l'objet ou les objets décrits ci-après: (Si l'espace ci-dessous est insuffisant, annexer une feuille.)

Estimated Fair Market Value
Estimation de la juste valeur marchande ▶ $_____

NOTE: The description of object(s) should commence with some general terms followed by such specific terms as dimensions, colour, date and any other particular marks such as creator's signature, hallmarks, serial numbers, etc.

NOTE: Il faut d'abord donner une description générale de l'objet ou des objets, puis des précisions comme les dimensions, la couleur, la date et autres caractéristiques comme la signature de l'auteur, le cachet de contrôle, les numéros de série, etc.

---CERTIFICATION---

IT IS HEREBY CERTIFIED that the above-described object(s) meets the criteria provided in paragraphs 23(3)(b) and (c) of the Cultural Property Export and Import Act.

---ATTESTATION---

IL EST CERTIFIÉ PAR LES PRÉSENTES QUE l'objet ou les objets décrits ci-dessus sont conformes aux critères énoncés aux alinéas 23(3)b) et c) de la Loi sur l'exportation et l'importation de biens culturels.

Signature of Authorized Officer — Signature de l'agent autorisé

Date

Form prescribed by the Minister of National Revenue — Formule prescrite par le ministère du Revenu national

CHAPTER 8 THE CORPORATE COLLECTOR: TAXATION AND GIFTING

OWNERSHIP OF ART BY A CORPORATION

A corporation can own fine art and other collectables in the same way as an individual. The number of ways in which the art can be classified for taxation purposes, however, is likely to be greater for the corporation.

Depreciable Property

Many corporations are conscious of the importance of having attractive offices. Well executed design and layout contributes to the office landscape. Good original art also adds greatly to the quality of the environment, and can be an excellent long-term investment as well. Ordinary furniture bought for an office may become dated and obsolete, but fine art is timeless.

Both office furniture and fixtures, including fine art in many cases, can be depreciated for tax purposes. Presently, a capital cost allowance of 20% a year is allowed on the class of property which includes office furniture and fixtures.

The Income Tax Act provides that " ... in computing a taxpayer's income in a taxation year from a business ..., there may be deducted ... the following amounts as are wholly applicable to that source or may be reasonably regarded as applicable thereto: ... such part of the capital cost to the taxpayer of property ... as is allowed by regulation ...."

The Regulations provide that "there is ... allowed to a taxpayer in computing his income from a business ... deductions for each taxation year equal to such amounts as he may claim in respect of property of each of the following classes in Schedule B not exceeding in respect of property ... of Class 8, 20% ... of the undepreciated capital cost to him as at the end of the taxation year ... of property of the class."

Class 8 of Schedule B is a catch-all, defined by exception to include tangible assets not specifically included in another class, and which also excepts certain specific items. The assets commonly thought of as being included in this class are machinery, equipment, and office furniture. Present practice is to also include fine art and reproductions in this class.

This ability to claim a capital cost allowance considerably reduces the amount of money actually put at risk in buying fine art for its investment possibilities.

The concept of using classes of assets has important tax ramifications. The cost of all assets acquired in a year of a particular class, is added to the undepreciated capital cost of the assets of the same class acquired in previous years. The proceeds of disposition (not exceeding the original cost of the asset sold) of each asset in the class which is disposed of during the year are deducted from the balance of the undepreciated capital cost of the class of assets, and capital cost allowance is then claimed on the undepreciated capital cost of the class. This means that, while the corporate collector is increasing the size and value of the art collection by disposing of some works and acquiring others, there may be no recapture of capital cost allowance to be included in income. The balance of the undepreciated capital cost for the class will vary, of course, with acquisitions and dispositions of art work and other class 8 assets such as furniture, and thus the capital cost allowance capable of being claimed will also vary from year to year.

For example, suppose the Class 8 assets of a small corporation had an undepreciated capital cost (U.C.C.) of $50,000. Last year, capital cost allowance (C.C.A.) of $10,000, (20% x $50,000), was claimed, leaving for this year a base for calculating capital cost allowance of $40,000. The corporate collector buys office furniture for $8,000 and two works on paper for $1,000 each, and sells a small canvas for $6,000. Its capital gain on disposition of the canvas was $3,000. Determining the capital cost allowance to be claimed this year involves this calculation:

U.C.C. of Class 8 assets at beginning of year	$ 40,000
Add - cost of furniture	8,000
- cost of works on paper	2,000
	50,000
Subtract - proceeds of disposition equal to original cost of canvas	3,000
U.C.C. on which to claim C.C.A. this year	$ 47,000
C.C.A. to be claimed this year	9,400
U.C.C. of Class 8 assets at beginning of next year	$ 37,600

The corporation would also include a taxable capital gain of $1,500 in income. The painting was depreciable property. It could not be listed personal property because it was not personal-use property.

One result of this type of calculation is that if art is bought and sold later at a loss, the loss may be realized as an expense against income. If, on the other hand, the value of the art which is bought holds steady or increases, the corporation obtains a valuable deduction in present dollars and may only have to bring that sum back into income at a future time. Since this time can be almost indefinitely postponed, by then the value of the dollar will, if present trends continue, have shrunk considerably.

There is one caveat to be observed in the area of corporate art collecting and claiming capital cost allowance. The art being purchased and included as Class 8 assets should be reasonable in the circumstances. It may not be reasonable for a corner grocery store to claim capital cost allowance on a painting by Ken Danby. Relevant circumstances would include the nature of the business, the amount of art purchased, and the location of the art. The Internal Revenue Service in the United States is concerned about the tax savings being recognized by some corporations who are buying fine art. Noises are being made about amending the rules to prevent depreciation being claimed on art which may increase in value. Echoes of these rumblings have been heard in Canada, too.

Personal-Use Property and Listed Personal Property

Art is obviously capital property and can be a corporation's depreciable property. Art owned by an individual, in contrast, is usually classified as personal-use property, that is, property owned by a taxpayer that is used primarily for his personal use or enjoyment, or the enjoyment of individuals who are related to the taxpayer. Personal-use property is termed listed personal property if it is a print, etching, drawing, painting, sculpture or similar work of art, jewellery, a rare folio, rare manuscript, or a rare book, stamp, or coin.

The advantage of classifying property which is appreciating in value as personal-use property, is that its adjusted cost base is deemed to be no less than $1,000 for the purposes of calculating any gain on disposition. This can provide small tax shelters.

Can a corporation have personal-use property? The answer would appear to be affirmative in certain limited circumstances.

It should be possible to argue successfully that a corporation has personal use of a work of art, in that it is used to embellish its offices and add to its prestige. An even stronger argument can be made in the case where the art is used for the personal enjoyment of an individual who controls, or is a member of a group which controls, a corporation.

If, however, it is decided that art is personal-use property, in order to take advantage of the personal-use property $1,000 rule (discussed briefly at page 153 in this chapter and more extensively at page 130 in Chapter 7, The Individual Collector: Taxation, Gifting, and Death), it may be difficult to claim capital cost allowance on the same art. This position requires the taxpayer to argue simultaneously that the art is for personal use or enjoyment and that it is also required for the purposes of earning income. If this is done, the rules dealing with dual usage of property should be consulted.

As a matter of policy, it would be prudent to decide whether art owned by the corporation is to be personal-use property of the corporation and consequently listed personal property in the majority of cases, or whether it is to be depreciable property. It may be possible that a corporation has both types of art if it has a prestigious corporate collection which is distinct from the art which adorns the offices of employees.

TAXATION OF DISPOSITIONS OF CAPITAL PROPERTY

It is important to remember that many provinces have their own tax laws for corporations and that while they closely follow the federal Income Tax Act in many particulars, there can be important differences.

The following are some salient points in considering the federal taxation of dispositions of corporate owned art:

1. The taxation of the proceeds of disposition of depreciable property differs from the tax treatment given on dispositions of personal-use property and from that given on dispositions of listed personal property. (A more complete discussion of some aspects of the taxation of capital property is given in Chapter 7, The Individual Collector: Taxation, Gifting, and Death, commencing at page 123.)

2. The disposition of depreciable property involves a possible adjustment to business income and a possible taxable capital gain, as has been shown above. If the last depreciable property of a class is disposed of for less than the undepreciated capital cost of the class of assets, the taxpayer may deduct the difference from his business income as a terminal loss. For example, suppose a desk is the last remaining class 8 asset in a business. The undepreciated capital cost of the class 8 assets is $500 and the desk is sold for $300. In this case the terminal loss of $200 is deducted from business income, but note that there are no other class 8 assets. If there had been other assets in that class, their undepreciated capital cost would have become $200 and no deduction of terminal loss from income would have been allowed.

3. If depreciable property is disposed of for an amount equal to or greater than its original capital cost, only an amount equal to the original capital cost is deducted from the undepreciated capital cost of the class of assets. This was demonstrated in the example on page 150.

Taxable Capital Gains

The capital gain is the amount by which the proceeds of disposition exceed the cost base of the property and any outlays made or expenses incurred for the purpose of making the disposition.

Tax is payable only on the taxable capital gain, which is one half of the capital gain. The other half of the capital gain is tax free. It is the taxable capital gain which is included in the income on which the corporation pays tax. In Ontario, the combined federal and provincial corporate tax rate is approximately 49%. Actual rates of tax paid by corporations can vary because of the availability of the small business deduction, the manufacturing and processing profits deduction, and other adjustments in the Income Tax Act. However, the effective rate of 24.5% tax on capital gains can only be bettered by the approximate rate of 20% paid on manufacturing and processing income by a Canadian controlled private corporation which is eligible for the small business deduction. Another advantage of realizing a capital gain is that Canadian controlled private corporations which buy art and subsequently realize a capital gain may give the tax free half of the gain as a tax free capital dividend to their shareholders. Also, this capital dividend does not reduce the adjusted cost base of the shareholder's investment.

Capital Losses

A capital loss for tax purposes cannot be incurred on the disposition of depreciable property, and a loss for tax purposes cannot be incurred on the disposition of personal-use property that is not listed personal property. Capital losses can be incurred on the disposition of income producing assets such as stocks, bonds, etc.

Taxable Net Gains

Both gains and losses on the dispositions of listed personal property may be recognized for tax purposes. Losses incurred in the year of disposition, as well as those incurred in the five previous years and the succeeding year, are deductible from gains in order to arrive at the net gains from dispositions of listed personal property. Half of this net gain is taxable and is included in income as a taxable net gain.

The personal-use property $1,000 rule applies to dispositions of listed personal property and states that "where a taxpayer has disposed of any personal-use property (which includes listed personal property such as art) the adjusted cost base ... shall be deemed to be the greater of $1,000 and the amount otherwise determined to be its adjusted cost base ... ; and his proceeds of disposition ... shall be deemed to be the greater of $1,000 and his proceeds of disposition otherwise determined." This is why no tax is payable if transactions involve art worth less than $1,000. Gains or losses will be taken into account for tax purposes only if either the proceeds of disposition or the adjusted cost base exceed $1,000.

ART RENTAL

Corporations are considering the benefits of renting art for a number of reasons: an introduction to art, particularly contemporary art, may be thought necessary for the staff; shareholders may not be convinced of the investment value of art; and rented art can improve the aesthetics of the work environment while staff and shareholders reconsider their prejudices. Corporations may also rent if they do not wish to make a major cash outlay, but still want to have significant works by important artists to enhance their offices. The rental paid is deductible from income in the year of outlay as a business expense.

Original Canadian art can be rented from many public galleries. The profits from the rental shop, which is usually staffed by knowledgeable volunteers, goes to the local gallery. If the works for rent have come from the consignment inventories of commercial galleries, the artist may also receive a portion of the rental fee.

There are also professional art consultants who may enter into lease arrangements with interested corporations for works from their own stock.

In many cases the lease agreements contain an option to buy.

Hire-Purchase or Lease-Option Arrangements

Some corporations enter into lease arrangements with fairly definite prospects of purchase. If the option to purchase is exercised, some credit is usually given toward the purchase price for the rental paid. The rent paid before the option is exercised is deducted as an expense of business. In a properly structured arrangement there will be no recapture into income, for tax purposes, of the rental fees. The adjusted cost base of the work of art is the price paid to exercise the option. No part of the rent is included in the adjusted cost base. Consequently, a taxable gain will be realized if the art is sold in excess of the option price.

The benefits of a hire-purchase arrangement are obvious. A prospective purchaser has an extended period of time after seeing the work in place to decide whether or not to acquire it permanently. The lessor takes the short-term risk of whether or not the work will appreciate in the art marketplace, and may also provide ancillary services such as insurance coverage and responsibility for repair. The tax advantages of the 100% write-off for rental, and the benefits of the low rate of tax on capital gains realized, are also very inviting.

Because of the obvious tax advantages of hire-purchase arrangements, abuses have occurred. Corporations considering entering into such arrangements involving significant amounts of money, should have the agreement scrutinized by a knowledgeable lawyer or accountant. Some agreements are considered shams by the Revenue Canada authorities and the promised tax benefits do not accrue to the purchaser. Revenue Canada has issued a policy statement, called an Information Bulletin, expressing their views of the lease-option agreements. The Department of National Revenue may ignore the wording of the agreement and determine for its own purposes whether payments are, in substance, toward rent or toward the purchase price of the art. They will do this in the light of the factual circumstances surrounding the entering into and the performance of the agreement. If a corporation disagrees with Revenue Canada it may find itself disputing the matter in court.

One key question asked is whether it is the object of the

transaction, from its inception, to eventually sell the art to the lessee. The answer, in the tax authorities' view, is "yes" in those cases where one or more of the following occur:

(a) the lessee automatically acquires title to the art after payment of a specified amount in the form of rentals;

(b) the lessee is *required* to buy the art from the lessor during or at the termination of the lease, or is required to guarantee that the lessor will receive the full option price from the lessee or a third party (except where such guarantee is given only in respect of damage inflicted by the lessee);

(c) the lessee has the right, during or at the expiration of the lease, to acquire the art at a price which, at the inception of the lease, is substantially less than the probable fair market value of the art at the time or times of permitted acquisition by the lessee; or

(d) the lessee has the right during or at the expiration of the lease to acquire the art at a price, or under terms or conditions, which at the inception of the lease are such that no reasonable person would fail to exercise the option.

The information bulletin goes on to state:

Where an agreement is a lease, the annual payments are made as rentals, and for income tax purposes a subsequent exercise of the option to purchase does not change their character to that of payments on account of the sale price of the property, even if the agreement provides that some part of them will be so applied should the option be exercised. Where a part of the rentals are to be so applied, for the purpose of determining whether a specified option price approximates fair market value at the time the option can be exercised, the option price is reduced by the amount of the rentals that would be applied....

....

The Bulletin also states the following:

... The option to purchase may be part of or separate from the lease agreement itself or may be a verbal agreement or undertaking. Where, although not specified in the agreement, it becomes apparent, for example, as a result of previous similar transactions undertaken by the parties involved, that it is the intention that the lessee be allowed to acquire the property at the termination of the lease for an amount that is less than its probable fair market value, the transaction is considered to be a sale.

The Department is aware that many lease contracts are in the nature of "financial leases" in which the lessor is providing a financial service only. As a result certain costs or obligations that are usually considered incidental... become the responsibility of the lessee. In the Department's view the assumption of these obligations by the lessee or any other conditions of the lease that may be indicative of a sale, are not, in and by themselves, conclusive in determining whether the transaction is in substance a sale. Such conditions only add corroborative support....

One private art gallery attempted to lease works using the standard form of a leasing company, whose services were also used at a fee. This program ran into difficulties because Revenue Canada questioned what sum could be properly deducted as an expense by the lessee, i.e., what part was rental and what part was on account of purchase price.

The one aspect of art lease-option which distinguishes it from lease-options for typewriters, cars, etc., is that art can appreciate in value while the other products generally do not. Consequently, the Department's concern is that significant sums paid for the purchase of property will be charged against income as rent. The lessee who exercises his option can subsequently sell the art for a price which reimburses him for all or part of the "rent" but avoids recapture of capital cost allowance.

CORPORATE GIFTING

Gifts can be made by corporations to other corporations, to individuals, and to public institutions. Different types of gifts can be made and reference is made to Chapter 7, The Individual Collector: Taxation, Gifting, and Death at page 132 for a discussion of this topic.

There are a number of tax provisions of which a corporation should be aware before gifts are made. Firstly, whenever a gift is made, the donor is deemed to have received proceeds of disposition equal to the fair market value of the gift. Secondly, situations can arise in which the donor is deemed to have received proceeds of disposition equal to fair market value whether or not the donor actually has received this value. These situations involve non-arm's length transactions, or transactions with related persons who are deemed not to deal at arm's length.

Gifting to a Related Person

The Income Tax Act provides that corporations can have "relatives." Individuals can be related, of course, by blood relationship, marriage, or adoption. A person (whether an individual, a trust, or another corporation) who controls a corporation is related to that corporation. A person who does not control a corporation, but is a member of a related group that does control the corporation, is also related to that corporation. Further, a person who is related to another, who is related to a corporation, is also related to the corporation. For example, the granddaughter of a man who owns a small number of shares in a corporation, the majority of the shares of which are held by his brothers, is related to that corporation.

Corporations can be related to each other if control is held by the same person or by persons who are related to each other. Generally, if a control relationship (which may in some cases be very tenuous) can be traced through a corporate family tree then the corporations are related.

A husband who wishes to benefit his wife by having his corporation sell a work in its collection to her at a bargain price, will cause his corporation to be deemed to have received proceeds of disposition equal to the fair market value of the work. However, the attribution of income and capital gains from gifts to spouses, discussed in Chapter 7, The Individual Collector: Taxation, Gifting, and Death at page 133, are avoided.

Gifts to Minors

As is the case with an individual, if a corporation transfers property to a minor or a trust for a minor, any income produced by the property while the minor is still less than 18 years of age is deemed to be that of the corporation, but any capital gain will be that of the minor.

A kindly grandfather, who has his corporation give a sculpture from its collection to his grandchild, may cause his corporation to have a deemed taxable capital gain. Any subsequent accretion in value upon disposition by the grandchild, however, will be without tax effect to the corporation. Reference is made to Chapter 7, The Individual Collector: Taxation, Gifting, and Death for a more complete discussion of this matter.

Gifting to Charity

Corporations who donate to charities are subject to the same rules as are applicable to individual donors. (Reference should be made to the discussion commencing at page 135 concerning gifting by individual collectors.) These rules may be summarized as follows:

1. The donor will be issued a charitable donation receipt showing the fair market value of the gift. This amount can be deducted from income in calculating taxable income.
2. The donor must include the fair market value of the gift in its tax calculations unless it has elected a lower value to be the deemed proceeds of disposition and amount of the gift.
3. Deductions for donations to charities are limited to 20% of income but any excess in a year may be carried forward for use in the forthcoming year.

    Generous corporate donors should be aware of precedent in which a business was giving donations in excess of the limit then allowed for charitable gifting, and that business was able to deduct the excess as a business expense.
4. No deemed gain or loss from the disposition of personal-use property by the corporate collector will accrue for tax purposes unless that property has a fair market value or an adjusted cost base of in excess of $1,000.

    An example of the tax advantages of donating a work of art

is as follows:

Suppose a corporation bought a painting for $3,000 in 1973 and donated it in 1979 to a public gallery. A tax deductible donation receipt is issued for $10,000, based on a Professional Art Dealers Association of Canada appraisal.

Proceeds of disposition from painting	$ 10,000
Original cost of painting	3,000
Capital gain	$ 7,000
Taxable Capital gain	$ 3,500
Approximate amount of capital cost allowance claimed in 6 years added to income on which recapture could occur, in the unlikely event that there were no other Class 8 assets	2,215
Net inclusion in taxable income assuming recapture	$ 5,715
Less charitable donation assuming there is other income	– 10,000
Amount of taxable income saved	$ 4,285
Tax saving 49% x $4,285 =	$ 2,100

If it is assumed that there would be no recapture of capital cost allowance because there are other Class 8 assets, the calculation of tax saving would be as follows:

Net inclusion in taxable income assuming no recapture	$ 3,500
Less charitable donation	–10,000
Amount of taxable income saved	$ 6,500
Tax saving 49% x $6,500 =	$ 3,185

As well, the tax free portion of the capital gain ($3,500) is added to the notional capital dividend account for tax free distribution to shareholders of a Canadian controlled private corporation.

Consequently, if a good purchase is made as theorized here, a corporation enjoys a work of art for six years, begins to take 20% depreciation immediately upon purchase, enhances its reputation in the community at the time of giving, and ends by enjoying a tax saving in excess of the purchase price.

Gifting to Her Majesty

Gifts to Her Majesty in right of Canada and the provinces are subject to the same rules as those applicable to individuals, and reference should be made to page 136 for a more complete discussion. The great difference between a gift to a charity and one to Her Majesty is that the deduction for the latter is not limited to 20% of the donor's income, but extends to 100% of his income.

**Gifts
of Certified
Cultural Property**

Charities, Her Majesty, and other public bodies, can be designated public institutions and authorities for the purpose of receiving certified cultural property. When capital property has received the designation of being certified cultural property, no portion of capital gain, or gain on the disposition of listed personal property has to be included in income. Again, reference is made to Chapter 7, The Individual Collector: Taxation, Gifting, and Death, particularly to the section commencing at page 138, and to Chapter 6, The Cultural Property Export and Import Act.

Deductions for donations of certified cultural property to designated institutions are limited to 100% of income as are those to Her Majesty.

In the previous example, if the work was donated in accordance with the CPEIA provisions, the tax saving would be as follows:

Net inclusion in taxable income assuming recapture	$ 2,215
Less CPEIA donation	−10,000
Amount of taxable income saved	$ 7,785
Tax saving 49% x $7,785 =	$ 3,815
Tax saving if no recapture occurs because assets remain in Class 8 49% x $10,000 =	$ 4,900

No amount would be added to the notional capital dividend account for tax-free distribution to the shareholders of a Canadian controlled private corporation as there has been no capital gain.

CHAPTER 9   THE ARTIST: BUSINESS ARRANGEMENTS AND TAXATION

INTRODUCTION

The artist is not singled out for special treatment by federal or provincial taxing authorities. The particular effect on artists of rules of general application is not considered when laws are made. This chapter considers various taxes and their effect on the artist. As well, the chapter discusses some of the different forms in which an artist can carry on business and how this choice can affect taxation.

TAXES

Federal Sales Tax

Federal sales tax, which in 1980 was 9% (reduced from a previous 12%), is a hidden or indirect tax. It is not added at the cash register when goods are bought, but is incorporated into the price of retail goods. Producers or manufacturers, importers, and wholesalers must include this tax (imposed only once) in the price of finished goods and remit the tax to Revenue Canada, Customs and Excise. This tax is imposed under Part V of the Excise Tax Act, but should be distinguished from excise tax, which is a special additional tax imposed on specific goods such as wine, tobacco, jewellery, watches, etc. Goldsmiths and other jewellery craftsmen should be aware of these provisions of the Excise Tax Act, not discussed here, which are of particular application to them. These taxes must also be distinguished from duties collected under the Customs Tariff on certain goods imported into Canada.

A producer or manufacturer, for the purposes of Part V of the Excise Tax Act, includes commercial artists, lithographers, and engravers, but no specific mention is made of other fine arts artists. If it is assumed that a fine arts artist is a producer or manufacturer, what are the rules which apply to the artist?

All producers or manufacturers are required to apply for a federal sales tax licence unless they produce less than $50,000.00 worth of taxable goods per year. A licenced producer or manufacturer is obliged to collect the federal sales tax on all taxable products sold, but has the privilege of buying materials free of that tax. Artists, of course, want to purchase their materials free of federal sales tax. Revenue Canada, however, is reluctant to licence any person unless he manufactures taxable goods worth at least $50,000.00 a year. Moreover, no licence whatsoever will be granted if no taxable goods are made. Consequently, fine art artists will usually not qualify for a licence because they do not produce goods which are taxable under Part

V of the Excise Tax Act. The following art works are federal sales tax exempt (the wording used here is that of the federal government):

69505-1 Paintings, drawings and pastels by artists, all of the foregoing when valued at not less than twenty dollars each; paintings and sculptures by artists domiciled in Canada but residing temporarily abroad for purposes of study, under regulations by the Minister.

69510-1 Hand-made drawings, sketches or designs, but not including patterns, *viz.*: – drawings, sketches or designs of wearing apparel, including boots and shoes, wall or floor coverings and textile fabrics, when imported in single copies of each such drawing, sketch or design for use in the manufacture of wearing apparel, boots or shoes, textile fabrics, wall or floor coverings or of patterns.

69515-1 Original sculptures and statuary, including the first twelve replicas made from an original work or model; assemblages: the professional production of artists only and valued at not less than seventy-five dollars each.

69520-1 Engravings, etchings, lithographs, woodcuts, maps and charts, printed prior to 1st January 1900; original engravings, etchings, lithographs, woodcuts, unbound, printed by hand from plates or blocks wholly executed by hand, and signed by the artist.

69525-1 Hand-woven tapestries, suitable only for use as wall hangings, valued at not less than twenty dollars per square foot.

(The reference numbers appearing above are used in the Excise Tax Act Schedule and are a cross reference to the Customs Tariff.)

In connection with tariff item 69520-1 it should be noted that all engravings, etchings, lithographs, and woodcuts must be printed by hand, not by machine, and the plates or blocks used have to be wholly executed by hand in order to be exempt from federal sales tax. Expressly excluded are serigraphs, photographic representations, and photomechanical representations whether or not these are signed and numbered. Where an artist engages a printer to produce images from an original, for purposes of resale, it is the printer and not the artist who is considered the manufacturer or producer.

In conclusion, if a fine art artist is not a producer or manufacturer under the Excise Tax Act, he cannot apply for a licence and obtain the tax exemption or purchase privileges available to licenced manufacturers. As a matter of administrative policy, even if the artist is a small producer or manufacturer, he cannot usually obtain a licence. Small manufacturers of taxable goods who do not have federal sales tax licences may obtain refunds for federal sales tax paid for materials incorporated into their taxable items. However, production of the tax exempt art items enumerated in the Tariff does not entitle the artist to obtain a refund of the tax paid on the materials incorporated into that art work.

Ceramists, potters, and other artisans who produce over $50,000.00 of taxable goods, must obtain a licence and levy and collect tax on all goods sold, not just the amount exceeding $50,000.00.

Sculptors – Exemption Certificate

It has been recognized, however, that hardship may be suffered by some artists, particularly sculptors, whose materials have a proportionately high cost to the price of the finished product. Consequently, as a matter of administrative practice, an exemption certificate has been developed for sculptors only. Procedures to obtain this exemption certificate vary across the country among the different district taxation offices. Basically, the sculptor is required to satisfy the Regional Chief of Compliance, Excise Division, that the finished work would fall into the classification 69515-1 set out above. Usually the sculptor must provide a detailed description (in writing) of the work, and sometimes drawings or even a maquette, to obtain a favourable ruling. A new ruling has to be obtained for each sculpture for either an exemption from, or refund of, federal sales tax. The Sales Tax Branch of the District Office then allows a form of exemption certificate rather than a licence. This form authorizes the purchase of basic materials without the payment of the federal sales tax. Despite this policy, kinetic sculptors sometimes still have to pay the sales tax on the purchase of completely manufactured components such as motors and hydraulic systems, but can obtain a refund of tax after these parts have been incorporated into the sculpture. The same procedure can sometimes be used to import materials for a sculpture free of customs duty.

Artists should be aware that federal sales tax on some items is reduced from 9%. For instance, federal sales tax on building supplies in 1980 was only 5% whether or not they were used for that purpose. The 5% tax also applies to aluminum paint, artists' paints, cement paint and plastic cement paint, ceramic colours (powdered or liquid), cleaning compounds, cold water paint, colours in oil, dry colours, dyes, enamels, gold or aluminum or silver leaf, liquid colours, paint oils and water colours, and vitreous glazing enamels – powdered or liquid.

In summary, federal sales tax is not a major issue to most artists, as they are not obliged to include the tax in the sale price of works they produce. It was of greater importance to artists involved in crafts when the exemption from having to obtain a licence and collect tax was only available where the artist produced less than $3,000.00 in taxable goods a year rather than the 1980 cut off level of $50,000.00. Producers of serigraphs and similar works of art, however, are still affected by the tax.

Customs Duties   A general discussion of customs duties as they affect a work of art is dealt with in Chapter 10, The Commercial Art Dealer: Business and Taxation at page 183.

Provincial Sales Tax   A tax which concerns many more Canadian artists is provincial sales tax. Only residents of Alberta escape this consumption tax, variously known as a retail sales tax, a social services tax, etc. In all provinces exemptions from this tax are available. In Ontario, an artist can obtain goods exempt from retail sales tax if the goods are to be processed, fabricated into, attached to or incorporated into other tangible personal property (i.e., included in a work of art), and if the artist provides the vendor with the appropriate purchase exemption certificate bearing the number of the artist's vendor's permit. With this privilege of buying goods free of Ontario provincial sales tax, comes the responsibility of filing retail sales tax returns and collecting tax where necessary. Some artists who are not required to collect retail sales tax (because their dealer does so), feel the additional time and effort to file returns required to obtain exemption is not worth the tax saved.

An artist who sells to the retail market is required to have a vendor's permit and remit tax to the province. An artist who sells to the retail market without a vendor's permit should still remit the tax payable to the government. Artists should be aware that in Ontario, the Ministry of Revenue is conducting investigations into retail sales of art. One method by which they are obtaining information involves securing lists of participating artists at art fairs and shows.

Artists should be aware that buying materials outside a province may not relieve them of the liability to pay tax. Also, sales to persons resident outside the province from which the artist is selling may not be tax exempt. The artist should check with the local tax office to determine whether a particular out-of-province sale will be tax exempt.

Municipal Taxes   Other taxes which affect artists are realty taxes on their premises (these may be included in rent) and business taxes. Both of these taxes are levied at the municipal level. Canadian Artists' Representation has had some success in persuading some city taxing authorities that an artist's studio is not a commercial use and subject to business tax, even if the occasional sale takes place through the studio.

INCOME TAX

The other important tax of concern to individual artists is, of course, income tax. Income tax is levied at both federal and provincial levels. All the provinces, except Quebec, have the federal government collect their taxes on individuals for them, and levy their income tax as a percentage of the federal tax.

A sad fact of life for artists in Canada is that many are not concerned with the amount of tax they are required to pay, but rather with the fact that their art earnings alone are not great enough to require them to pay any income tax at all. Only one in five artists earned $5,000 or more from the sale of their own works in 1978.

Unemployment Insurance and Canada (Quebec) Pension Plan

Artists may or may not be self-employed. Artists who are employees have the benefit of coverage by their employers under both the Unemployment Insurance Act and the Canada Pension Plan (in Quebec, the Quebec Pension Plan). If an artist is an employee, his expense deductions for tax purposes are limited to the lesser of 3% of gross income or $500.00.

Artists who are self-employed cannot be covered under the Unemployment Insurance Act, and must pay their own contributions to the Canada Pension Plan (or the Quebec Pension Plan). These contributions are based on their net self-employed earnings. Self-employed artists, however, can deduct all expenses which are related to earning their income.

Almost three-quarters of the artists in Canada do not fall clearly into either category but are both employed and self-employed. Part of their income may be earned as ordinary employees, perhaps working in art related fields, because their art sales cannot yet be relied on to support them. Their employers make contributions on their behalf, as required by law, under the Unemployment Insurance Act, and also contribute to the Canada Pension Plan/ or Quebec Pension Plan. These artists may then make further contributions to the Canada Pension Plan and or the Quebec Pension Plan, if the maximum required contribution has not been made based on their employment earnings and they have net self-employed earnings.

Deduction of Art-related Expenses from Other Income

An interesting question has arisen regarding the extent to which many art related expenses may be deducted from art income and then from other income. Can these expenses be deducted only against self-employed art earnings or can they also be deducted from employment income as well?

A recent case heard by the Tax Appeal Board (the first level of appeal when a taxpayer disagrees with the revenue authorities) allowed an unsuccessful painter to deduct her expenses (which were several thousands of dollars more than her self-employed income) from her non-art employment and other income. The test applied was that of "a reasonable expectation of profit." This artist was in her 30's, and had obtained a B.A. and an M.A. in English, and also had received a Canada Council grant. She had sold some poetry and paintings. The chairman of the Tax Appeal Board refused to say that at this early stage in her career she did not have "a reasonable expectation of profit."

165

Revenue Canada did not appeal this case to the Federal Court of Canada, and so some precedent exists for the deduction, from employment or other income, of art related expenses which are incurred in attempting to produce self employment income. This does not mean that Revenue Canada will not challenge another artist in the future.

Record Keeping

Because a business person keeps records, an artist can assist his cause and demonstrate business intent by keeping records. The Income Tax Act also requires that they be kept, and Revenue Canada will disallow expenses that cannot be proved. Consequently, receipts should be kept for all payments for art supplies, paper, typewriter ribbons, stamps, other office supplies, professional fees, and other disbursements. Records must be kept for at least five years and written permission obtained from the local office of Revenue Canada to destroy older records.

Calculation of Art Income

Accrual Method of Accounting

Self-employed artists are required to calculate their income for tax purposes on the accrual basis, as are all other types of business except farming, which uses the cash basis of accounting. Under the accrual method, all materials, work in progress, and unfinished inventory must be valued at the lower of its cost and its fair market value in order to calculate income. The theory of the accrual method of accounting is that the income has been made available to the taxpayer artist. The reasoning is that the artist could have sold the completed inventory, partially completed inventory, or material inventory anytime he liked. This obviously ignores the realities of the situation. However, it appears that Revenue Canada is willing to ameliorate the situation by accepting, as a matter of administrative policy, that no value whatsoever will be ascribed to the work in progress and finished inventory of an artist. Consequently, work in progress and finished inventory is valued at nil.

However, there has been no change of official policy concerning the inclusion of the value of materials inventory in the calculation of income. This may be of significance to some sculptors and other visual artists whose works embody a high proportion of costly materials in relation to the final price. One argument advanced for also valuing materials inventory at nil is that its value when used may become lower, or even disappear, upon incorporation into the finished work, and that this should be taken into account when calculating the value of such inventory in determining the income of artists. If this argument were accepted, artists, like farmers, would be taxed on a strictly cash basis, where transactions are taken into account only when cash is exchanged. Some artists may feel that there is a philosophical justification for taxing artists and farmers in the same fashion.

At the present time, an artist should calculate the present value of his inventory of material at the beginning of the year, add the purchase price of material bought during the year, and subtract from this total the value of the material on hand at year end. This calculation yields the cost of producing the works that were created during the year.

What is more commonly done by artists, though it is technically incorrect, is to deduct as an expense the material bought during the year against sales made and to disregard any inventories of material in stock. This shortcut is not recommended.

Expenses and Depreciation

If an artist has bought tools in a year, their purchase price can be deducted as an expense, provided that none costs more than $200.00. Equipment which costs over $200.00, such as kilns or printing presses, must be treated as capital items and capital cost allowance (depreciation) for tax purposes claimed at the prescribed rates using the declining balance method.

Inclusions in Income

When calculating income an artist must include:
1. all income from sales or rentals,
2. honoraria and expenses for jury work for the Art Bank, Canada Council, etc.,
3. the amount by which all grants, scholarships, prizes, etc. exceed $500.00,
4. rental income for renting part of a studio or residence to others,
5. interest and dividend income,
6. employment income,
7. unemployment insurance benefits, and
8. fees for commissions whether or not completed. The artist will be entitled to claim a reserve (i.e., a deduction) if the commission is not completed.

Deductions

Deductions from income which an artist can claim in calculating taxable income include:
1. administrative costs – stationery, typing costs, etc.,
2. rental of a studio, and
3. expenses of using part of the home as a studio.

Doing work at home does not automatically entitle the artist to a deduction. It is necessary for a part of the home to be set aside and used solely as a studio. A percentage, based on the ratio of floor areas, or other appropriate measure of the rental or the cost of running the home, can be deducted as an expense from income. Costs such as heat, electrical costs, water rates, taxes, mortgage interest, insurance, repairs and maintenance are deductible. If capital cost allowance is claimed on part of the home, the status of the home as a principal residence, which is otherwise entirely free from capital gains, will be affected. If the house is sold at a profit, recapture of the capital cost allowance will occur and capital gains tax will be payable on that portion of the house for which capital cost allowance was claimed. In most cases, therefore, it is not advisable to claim capital cost allowance on that portion of the family home in which the artist works.

It is interesting to contrast the present state of Canadian tax law with that in the United States. A commercially unsuccessful Canadian artist can presently deduct the costs attributable to the studio portion of his residence from his art business income, and if this produces a loss, deduct the loss from other income. In the United States, the artist can only deduct costs attributable to the business portion of a residence from his gross income from the art business, after first subtracting his non-business deductions (personal deductions available without regard to art business income).

Other deductions from income include:
4. child care expenses (an expense which can usually only be claimed by the mother),
5. tuition fees to designated institutions, and student expenses,
6. RHOSP contributions (Registered Home Ownership Savings Plans),
7. RRSP contributions (Registered Retirement Savings Plans),
8. investment income from Canadian sources (chiefly interest from arm's length transactions and dividends) up to $1,000.00, and
9. an amount used to purchase an IAAC (Income Averaging Annuity Contract). This is of great assistance when an artist has an unusually high income in a year and wishes to receive and pay tax on the amount over a number of years.

Instalments

Self-employed artists are required to pay their taxes in quarterly instalments due on March 31, June 30, September 30, and December 31 in each year unless:
1. tax is deducted at the source from at least 75% of income,
2. federal income tax does not exceed $400.00, or
3. the chief source of income is farming or fishing.

Instalments can be based on the amount of tax the artist expects to pay for the year or the amount he paid the previous year. Interest must be paid on any deficiency of tax owed if an underestimate is made.

Finally, the importance of keeping accurate and full records cannot be over emphasized. The agony and expense of suffering and defending a prosecution launched by Revenue Canada, when there are inadequate records, should not be risked. The fact that a prosecution is not successful, as in the case of noted Vancouver artist Jack Shadbolt, does not repay or reimburse the taxpayer in any way. Revenue Canada goes by the exact wording of the law, not its spirit, and the law is enforced by people who generally have little affinity for art or knowledge of artists' problems. Consequently, an artist should keep good records, and if at all possible obtain the services of a good accountant to assist in compiling records and filing tax returns.

Taxing in Other Jurisdictions

The Canadian and American tax situations for artists might be contrasted with those in Mexico and Ireland. In Mexico, artists may pay their taxes by donating works of art at fair market value to government sponsored institutions and museums. Ireland has abolished income tax on earnings from works of cultural merit — books, plays, painting, sculpture and music. The aim is twofold — to create a tax incentive for local artists, and to attract other artists to come and live in Ireland.

Partnership

While most artists practice their profession alone it is also possible to have an art career in partnership with other artists. One example of artists working in partnership is *General Idea* of Toronto, a trio of internationally renowned performance and video artists. A partnership calculates its profit (or loss) at the partnership level, and then divides the profit (or loss) among its partners for inclusion in personal income. There are a number of special tax rules for partnerships and an accountant's help is advisable when filing tax returns.

A partnership can be a most fulfilling and rewarding method of carrying on a business of art, but it does present certain drawbacks on its dissolution. Dissolution can be voluntary (by agreement) or involuntary (as in the case of the death of one of the partners or unilateral action by one of the partners). In all cases, individual interests in property including copyright have to be dealt with, and taxes paid.

A good partnership agreement, drafted with professional assistance, can anticipate many of the problems which arise during the term of a partnership or on its dissolution, and can provide a philosophy for dealing with unexpected events.

Incorporation

Self-employed artists and partnerships can also carry on business through a corporation. A corporation offers a variety of advantages to artists who wish to enjoy some of the benefits available to other businessmen. A corporation has certain tax benefits, and can also offer a useful vehicle to a commercially successful artist during his lifetime, and for his estate after his death. There are, however, also disadvantages to the corporate mode of carrying on business. Some of the advantages and disadvantages of having a corporation are discussed following the analysis of the tax consequences of an artist's death.

Some tax provisions may have a very harsh effect on an artist's estate, and therefore on his family, and may also frustrate attempts to enhance or at least maintain the artist's reputation after death. What follows is a brief examination of the taxing statutes that affect an artist's estate, together with a brief comparison with the situation in the United States and other jurisdictions.

Succession Duties

By 1980, succession duties had been abolished in all provinces except Quebec. Consequently, nine provinces no longer levy a wealth tax on the passing of property from one generation to another, or to a person outside the family. The provinces now share in the revenue collected under the federal Income Tax Act on deemed dispositions of all property owned by the artist taxpayer. For long range planning, the artist should be aware that a number of commentators feel that some form of provincial wealth tax will be reintroduced in the future.

Estate Taxes

Federal estate taxes, which also used to be levied in connection with the death of an individual, were abolished in Canada in 1972 with the introduction of a tax on capital gains from deemed dispositions at death under the Income Tax Act.

Deemed Disposition on Death

The Income Tax Act of Canada has a general rule that a taxpayer is deemed to have disposed of all of his property immediately before his death. All capital property, such as a house, household furnishings, shares, bonds, or a personal art collection (not the artist's inventory) is deemed to be disposed of for fair market value. All depreciable properties (property on which capital cost allowance is claimed) such as a car used for business, a kiln, etc., are deemed to have been disposed of for a value midway between their undepreciated capital cost and their fair market value. No allowance is made for the actual cost of disposing of these assets.

RIGHTS OR THINGS AND THE VALUE THEREOF

Another category of property is called "rights or things." All rights or things, (a term which appears to include an artist's inventory) may be deemed to have been disposed of for "the value thereof." There has been very little written on what constitutes "rights and things." Revenue Canada has said that the inventory of a taxpayer who is taxed on a cash basis is included in rights or things. From the discussion above, on taxation of living artists, it has been seen that artists usually report their income in such a way as to effectively have themselves taxed on a cash basis. The Income Tax Act also says that land included in the inventory of a business is not included in rights or things. This statement would indicate that works of art forming the inventory of an artist's business are rights or things. Consequently, on the death of an artist, all his inventory may be deemed to have been disposed of for "the value thereof" as at the date of death.

Is copyright also a "right or thing"?

The other question that arises is what is meant by the phrase "the value thereof." Does it mean the retail fair market value? Under some of the old Succession Duty Acts, inventory was valued at fair market value, and in the United States inventory is valued at fair market value on death. Does the "value thereof" mean retail fair market value less the dealer's commission, i.e., the wholesale fair market value? Does it mean the wholesale fair market value less a discount for "blockage"?

BLOCKAGE DISCOUNT

Blockage is a term which refers to a discount allowed when pricing a large number of similar assets. One painting by an artist might be saleable on the date of death for $20,000. The blockage principle postulates that 100 paintings of a similar size and quality could not be sold for $2,000,000 on the same day, since the demand would not exist to support such a price. The blockage principle argues that the market value of the 100 paintings on a given day should be the price which would be paid for the entire lot of 100 by an interested dealer or specialized collector, which would presumably be at a discount from the aggregate of the unit prices. The blockage theory would claim a fair market value for the lot of paintings considerably below $2,000,000.

This problem of blockage discount has been litigated in the American courts. In the David Smith estate which held over 425 sculptures, the executors argued for a sizable discount on account of blockage, and for deduction of a hypothetical commission to reflect the usual commission payable. The Internal Revenue Service ignored the blockage discount and refused to allow any deduction for the dealer's commission. Although the court, after a lengthy hearing, decided on a value which happened to be approximately midway between that submitted by each side, it is noteworthy that in its reasons for judgment the court did not allow any deduction for gallery commission and specifically rejected the contention that a sale in bulk would necessarily result in lower prices.

The estate of Mark Rothko battled privately with the IRS in the United States to arrive at a valuation for the hundreds of paintings left in his estate, but it is not known whether a blockage discount was allowed.

One American artist had his own solution to the problem. He destroyed large numbers of his works to avoid burdening his heirs with large tax bills. This kind of do-it-yourself tax planning does not always recommend itself.

Another argument for a discount from the fair market value is the weakness of the assumption that all pieces in the estates are equally saleable.

VALUATION

A factor which has to be considered, is that the value of works of art often changes shortly after death, when a determination of the value of the works of art as at the date of death has to be made. When an artist's works were selling consistently and at steadily increasing prices, the remaining works frequently soar in value following the artist's death when collectors and museums realize that there will be no more work created by this artist. Revenue authorities, in common with the rest of the world, have excellent hindsight, and what happens in the period following the artist's death can often affect the value, as at the date of death, placed on works in an artist's inventory. For this reason, current price lists used by a successful artist can be very important to ensure that art is not valued at too high a price using hindsight.

A good argument can be made that the "value thereof" is not equal to the fair market value of an artist's inventory, but it certainly is not clear what "the value thereof" is. This question could be expensive and time consuming to discuss with Revenue Canada or to argue before a judge, and to date, no significant case has arisen in Canada. This may be because any significant inventories held in estates have been disposed of in such a way as to avoid the problem, or because little or no valuable inventory has been held directly by an estate. It is common to use a corporate structure where there are significant art holdings, to avoid the problem by ensuring that the inventory is not held directly by an individual.

DISTRIBUTION TO A BENEFICIARY

Problems of valuation on death can be avoided if the art inventory is transferred or distributed to a beneficiary within approximately one year of death, and the prescribed election is made. If a beneficiary receives the inventory and makes the election, the Income Tax Act states that the amount realized on disposition of the inventory shall be included in the beneficiary's income for the year of disposition. This means that a bequest of inventory which becomes part of a beneficiary's private art collection does not change its nature in the hands of the beneficiary and become listed personal property, but maintains its character as inventory for tax purposes. As a matter of interest, this is now also the law in the United States.

In Canada, if the property is not transferred to a beneficiary, and the election is not made, the value of the inventory is included in the taxpayer's income for the terminal year. The estate can lower the taxes otherwise payable by electing to file a separate tax return in respect of the rights and things. All of the artist's personal deductions can be taken on the "rights and things" return as well as on the regular return. Tax savings will result both from the benefit of obtaining these deductions twice, and from the fact that lower marginal rates will apply than if the value of the inventory was included in a single return with other income.

Once taxes are paid by the estate, the property can pass to the heirs and beneficiaries and will be treated as capital property in their hands.

Avoiding the problems of tax litigation by outright bequest is not always in the best interest of an artist and his reputation, however. A beneficiary may choose to sell no works at all, in which case the artist's name may pass from the public eye, or he may wish to obtain cash, in which case the market could be flooded and the reputation of the artist adversely affected.

WILLS AND ESTATE PLANNING

The artist will avoid some of the more onerous tax ramifications of death through a well-drafted will, but the tax problems that face an artist's estate are only one reason why an artist should give serious consideration to having his own will rather than allowing his estate to be dealt with under the statutory will provided by the provinces under Devolution of Estate Acts or similar legislation.

A will ensures that the artist will have the executor or executors of his choice, and it will not be necessary for these executors to buy and post a bond. A will also allows the testator freedom to divide his estate as he, not the government, sees fit. Proper clauses inserted into a will obviate the necessity for court applications and notices to Official Guardians before property can be disposed of or money used. Where there are infant children, the Official Guardian could well require that the entire inventory be sold and the funds be invested in "blue chip" approved securities.

Executors

A will is, of course, useful for anyone, but it has particular advantages for an artist. An artist can assist the promotion of his reputation after death by choosing knowledgeable and interested executors to administer the art assets. It is possible to name executors to deal with personal assets, and nominate separate executors to deal with the art and to dispose of it advantageously. While it may be natural for an artist to want to appoint the dealer who has assisted in promoting his reputation, this presents a severe conflict of interest problem for the dealer and is not recommended to the artist. How can a dealer be, or even appear to be, uninfluenced by his personal interest in collecting a commission on the sale of works while making decisions affecting the artist's estate? The legal situation can be intolerable for the dealer. Fellow artists may also be poor choices as executors, particularly if they are likely to show at the gallery which represents the artist. If this is the case, the artist-executor may be under some pressure to act in a manner which is advantageous to the dealer, in order to improve his own relations with that dealer.

The successful lawsuit brought by the heirs of the estate of Mark Rothko against the executors, one of whom was an officer of the Marlborough gallery (which was Rothko's dealer), and another of whom was an artist who showed with Marlborough, should be sufficient to warn artist testators of potential conflict of interest problems. A judge awarded the heirs damages of $9,250,000, against those executors who were found to have not acted in the best interests of the estate. Anyone who is named an executor is always free to refuse the position and should do so if a continuing conflict of interest will arise.

Holograph wills (wills written by hand and generally not witnessed) are legal in some jurisdictions in Canada. Although a professionally drawn will may appear expensive, it is a good investment which can save taxes. Professional drafting can also ensure that the document will not be litigated in the courts because of uncertainty about what the testator meant, or what he wanted to happen in unforseen circumstances.

GIFTS MADE BY ARTISTS

A gift by an artist of one of his own works of art is not governed by the same rules as apply to gifts made by collectors. Some important tax concessions available to collectors are of no assistance to the artist. For the purposes of the discussion that follows, it will be assumed that the artist is gifting his own work from his inventory unless otherwise specified.

General Rule

When an artist makes a gift, he is deemed to have received proceeds of disposition equal to the fair market value of the inventory. No allowance is made for the hypothetical dealer's commission, and the artist is required to include the entire notional profit in calculating income. This is to be contrasted with the capital gains tax treatment applicable to a collector, whether individual or corporate, who only includes half of the gain in income.

This is not to say that it is impossible for an artist to be a collector, but he must be prepared to demonstrate clearly that his personal collection is not for sale in the way that inventory is. This is most easily done by conducting all business through a corporate vehicle which owns all the inventory. The principal of the corporation may then hold his own personal collection and have capital gains treatment on it so long as he does not engage in dealing, or adventures in the nature of a trade, with the works in the art collection. In an analogous case, Revenue Canada authorities recognized that a house builder who builds a home to live in can treat the disposition of that house as a capital rather than a business transaction.

Gifts to a Spouse

In Chapter 7, The Individual Collector: Taxation, Gifting, and Death, at page 133, the rules regarding the transfer of *capital* property to a spouse are discussed. There is another tax rule which deals with the transfer of non-capital property to a spouse. This rule deems that any income or loss from the property remains the income of the transferor while he is resident in Canada. Revenue Canada has stated that there is no attribution of business income or losses to the transferor, and has drawn a distinction between income from property and income from business.

Unlike an apartment building, or a piece of farmland, a work of art is not usually property which produces income. Royalties received for permission to copy a work of art is income from the copyright and not income from the work itself. An artist's income is not from the work of art itself, but from the business of disposing of the work of art. For this reason, it might be argued that since the spouse making the transfer was in the business of selling works of art, there should be no attribution of income.

Suppose, for example, the artist's spouse was given the work of art for his art collection. National Revenue has recognized that it is possible to have a permanent change in the nature of the use of the property by virtue of a transfer, but has not issued any opinions (to the date of writing) on the tax consequences of a spousal transfer where inventory becomes personal-use property and listed personal property. Nor has Revenue said whether the change in the nature of the property takes place in the hands of the transferor or the spouse transferee. In conclusion, a generalization concerning the tax effects of an artist's gifting works to the legal spouse is not possible. The particular aspects of each situation must be carefully considered before a conclusion can be reached.

The preferred course of conduct is to have the work held by a corporation which sells or gifts inventory to the artists' spouse. The corporation would be deemed to have received proceeds of disposition equal to the fair market value of the work, and the spouse would receive the inventory as personal-use property with an adjusted cost base also equal to fair market value. Further, when the spouse disposes of the property, he could do so without any question of attribution of the gain to the corporation.

Gifts to Minors

The general rules dealing with gifts to minors may be summarized as follows:
1. there is no attribution of gains or losses on dispositions of listed personal property; and
2. attribution of taxable capital gains and allowable capital losses occurs only in a few cases.

However, a problem may arise when there is a change in the nature of use of the property from inventory to personal-use property or listed personal property. Again, no policy statement has been issued by the Department of National Revenue to the time of writing, and the law will depend on all the circumstances of the case.

Gifts to Charities, Her Majesty and Gifts of Certified Cultural Property to Designated Public Institutions

There is no tax relief for artists making gifts of inventory to a public institution or authority similar to that which allows collectors to obtain deductions from income. This is so in spite of the fact that the works may be comparable in value to the institution or authority.

When a gift is made to a charity, Her Majesty, or a designated public institution under the provisions of The Cultural Property Export and Import Act, the artist must include his deemed profit on the disposition as income. In accordance with the general rule, the artist is deemed to have received proceeds equal to the fair market value of the art with no deduction or allowance being made for the dealer's commission. The artist is then allowed a deduction from income equal to the work's fair market value. This means that the gift is the same as if the artist had given the organization cash amounting to the cost of the materials incorporated in the work.

It is, of course, open to an artist to make a donation from his own private collection and be treated as a collector.

The gifting situation in the U.S. has been approximately the same as that in Canada since the introduction of their Federal Tax Reform Act in 1969. For federal tax purposes, an American artist may only deduct from income the cost of the materials utilized to create the work. Lobbies for amendments to the Act are achieving some success in the United States. Opposition to amendments is based on the argument that artists are providing services (e.g., putting paint to paper) which for other groups in similar circumstances would generally be non-deductible, and why, therefore, should the successful artist be able to paint one or two tax deductions for himself every year?

Artists have been successful, however, in obtaining amendments to some state laws. California now allows artists to deduct from taxable income the fair market value of art work donated for charitable use, provided that at least one fifth of the artist's income is derived from the sale of art. Similar provisions have been adopted in Oregon and Kansas.

INCORPORATION

Disadvantages

As has been seen, there are a number of advantages to incorporation for an artist to consider. Disadvantages also exist, which must be overcome before an artist goes to the expense and bother of creating a separate legal entity, and consequently becoming responsible for its well-being. Some of the disadvantages are:

1. It is not inexpensive to incorporate. There are fees to be paid to the government, costs of acquiring forms and record books for the requisite registers and records, and fees to be paid to professional advisers to assist both in determining the best structure for the artist's particular needs and desires and in drafting the necessary documentation and ancillary contracts.
2. It requires money to keep the corporation working well and performing its proper functions. Financial statements must be prepared each year from separate books of account kept for the corporation, and separate tax returns must be filed. The people involved in the corporation must also pass certain resolutions and perform certain annual administrative tasks which are prescribed by law.
3. In addition, because a corporation is otherwise invisible, steps must be taken to bring the corporation to the attention of the world. A corporation should have its own phone listing and its own letterhead. It needs its own bank account and record books. A corporation should enter into written employment contracts with its employees – particularly those who do not deal at arm's length with it. It, not the artist, should contract with suppliers, dealers, and purchasers, and also lease premises. These and other details all require time and some money.
4. Another disadvantage is that the artist must be prepared to deal, and have his suppliers and market also deal, with this abstract legal being. While the corporate structure offers a variety of ways to reduce taxes, these alternatives may be available only at the price of giving up a certain amount of absolute control. Some artists do not have the temperament to work within the structure prescribed by law.

If the artist ignores the legal being because of its administrative disadvantages and complications, he cannot complain if the world denies him the advantages that a corporation offers.

The disadvantages can be summarized as money, time, and possible lack of flexibility and control.

Advantages

The advantages of incorporation are many. Some of them are as follows:

1. A corporation is an ideal vehicle to reduce taxation on death. The artist is deemed to dispose of the shares of the corporation, which has as its chief asset inventory which is valued at less than fair market value. The disposition of the shares in the corporation is treated as a capital disposition as contrasted with the deemed disposition at fair market value of inventory by an unincorporated artist, which is an income transaction.
2. As demonstrated above, the tax ramifications of gifting can be ameliorated.

177

3. If the artist is earning more than he requires to live on, a corporation can be used to save tax dollars. The income earned by some Canadian artists' corporations is taxed at approximately 25%, and some other artists' corporations have paid tax at the rate of 20%, based on the argument that they are engaged in manufacturing and processing activities. These rates are considerably lower than the marginal rates of over 60% paid by some successful artists.

Up to $750,000 of profit can be retained by the corporation at these low tax costs and used by the corporation to earn more income.

4. A corporation also offers a method of income averaging for the artist whose income changes significantly from year to year.

5. Amendments to the Income Tax Act had been proposed at the time of writing which would make it possible, in some instances, for an artist to employ his spouse. Without these amendments, however, a spouse must be paid by a corporation in order to achieve an income split between the spouses, and to avoid the attribution of income rules.

6. There are a number of other tax saving devices available to corporations which vary according to particular circumstances.

7. Limited contractual and tortious liability is an advantage often touted for corporations. This means that only the corporation is liable for debts incurred in the art business, etc., and that assets which do not belong to the corporation cannot be affected. This advantage can be largely illusory however, because lenders such as banks will require personal guarantees before they will deal with the corporation, which means that the artist will again be personally responsible.

8. A corporation provides a good commercial vehicle which enables the artist's executors to control the promotion of the reputation of the artist and provide dividends to the heirs. This can produce a considerable tax saving because of the favourable tax treatment given to dividends.

Incorporation should be seriously considered by any artist living comfortably (perhaps with an income over $25,000) and earning his income from his art. Artists earning less than this amount may also have valid reasons for incorporating. Again, the artist is urged to obtain professional advice to determine the structures best suited to his needs and desires.

CHAPTER 10   THE COMMERCIAL ART DEALER: BUSINESS AND TAXATION

DEALER BUSINESS

There are many different types and forms of business or service which can be grouped together under the heading "art dealer." This chapter will consider some of these different activities, and problems that can arise operating an art selling business.

The words "art dealer" usually connote the commercial art gallery which displays works of art for sale to the public. There are many dealers, however, who operate privately, without the benefit of a public showroom. Some of these dealers operate from an office, with or without facilities for storing art works; some operate from their homes, which may have been modified to allow some display of works in that setting; some have neither offices nor physical possession of any works of art but, rather, visit prospective purchasers and show photographs of works which are available for purchase.

Dealers may also engage in a wide variety of subsidiary businesses such as appraisal, art rental, restoration, and framing. Others act as advisers to collectors and represent both artists and their estates or specialize in a particular style or period of art.

In short, art dealers are engaged in a wide variety of businesses and services. This chapter makes no attempt to analyze all of the details and problems of dealing in art, but rather focuses on some elements of taxation which are common to everyone in the trade, and discusses some functions, such as valuation, which are not dealt with in detail elsewhere in this book.

Dealing with Artists

Owners and managers of commercial art galleries, as well as other dealers, should consult Chapter 2, The Artist, The Dealer, and The Patron, which discusses such matters as consignment contracts and other forms of contract between the dealer and the artist. The checklists of matters to be dealt with in such contracts are directed to both the artist and the dealer.

Purchases by Dealers

There is an important difference which must be kept in mind by the dealer when reading the material on purchases by collectors: the dealer is an expert and the law recognizes this fact in dealing with cases where a dealer has made a bad purchase. The collector who purchases a forgery, a painting which is wrongly attributed, or an oriental vase credited to the wrong dynasty, may have recourse against the seller for any false representations made at the time of purchase. The dealer, however, will rarely, if

179

ever, be in a position to show that he relied on information given by the vendor. As an expert he is assumed to be in as good a position as the seller to evaluate the nature of the works he is purchasing. Any guarantees of authenticity, etc., would have to be carefully detailed in writing before they were effective to allow the purchasing dealer any remedy against the seller.

Selling to Collectors

Chapter 3, The Collector: Purchase of Works of Art, contains information about such things as contracts of sale, warranties of authenticity, etc. The dealer should be aware of the growing number of consumer protection laws being enacted in various jurisdictions to govern contracts of sale. It is not unlikely that specific legislation dealing with the sale of art works will be enacted in some Canadian jurisdictions. Such legislation was enacted in New York in 1978 as section 219(c) of that state's general business law, and provides that when an art dealer gives a written *description* of the authorship of an art object to a buyer who is not a dealer, that description shall create an express warranty of the authenticity of such authorship.

Appraisals

Dealers are often approached in the normal course of business by collectors who want appraisals of works of art. Most commonly, these appraisals are for insurance purposes. It is usual for a private collector to have a home owner or "floater" type of policy, and unless a work is specifically scheduled or "listed," only a small amount (often a maximum of $500.00) can be collected on the loss or damage of a work of art. If the work is worth more than this amount, insurance companies insist that it be added specifically to the policy and that an additional premium be paid. For this reason, collectors require each work to be appraised by someone having knowledge of its value. The appraisal is then filed with the insurance company, and the work specifically added to the policy as a "scheduled item" for its fair market value or replacement cost value, which is payable separately from the non-scheduled items of the policy.

Collectors also require valuations for income tax purposes. The valuation can be an attempt to establish a value for a work of art as of V-Day (December 31, 1971). For tax purposes, the V-Day value usually becomes the "adjusted cost base" to the collector of a work bought prior to V-Day. Alternatively, the valuation may be required to establish the value of a work being gifted to an institution so that the capital gain and the value of the deduction from income may be calculated. As well, a valuation may be required after the death of a collector to establish the fair market value of the work at the time of death, in order to calculate the capital gain arising from the deemed disposition of the work.

Dealers will often provide clients with insurance valuations for a nominal sum or no charge at all. This is generally considered to be an ancillary service provided by the dealer and one of "good will."

For tax purposes, a collector should obtain at least two independent valuations. The collector should also pay a fee for these valuations so that he may properly rely upon the service provided by the dealer and be able to hold the dealer responsible for the opinion.

Recently, a prosecution was conducted in the province of Saskatchewan for tax fraud involving inflated valuations for works of art donated to a public institution. The tax authorities disputed the values submitted to establish the allowable deductions for the donations. The government authorities brought independent appraisers from the United States to testify as to the inflated value of the appraisals. A number of donors, and the selling dealer (who also happened to be the appraiser supplying the valuations used), were found guilty and sentenced to jail terms.

Because of the responsibility involved, many dealers are reluctant to place themselves and their reputations in jeopardy, and refuse to give valuations other than for insurance purposes. A dealer who gives an appraisal for income tax purposes may be questioned by the income tax authorities as to the value and how it was determined, and may later be required to testify in court. In order to fill this void in the industry, and to provide a service to the art collecting community, the Professional Art Dealers Association of Canada provides income tax valuations for a fee. The large auction houses also provide this service for a fee. The difference between the two services is that the opinion received from the Professional Art Dealers Association is a "multiple opinion" which has been received from at least two members of the Association and is issued under the certificate of the Association.

Warranties of Authenticity

Does appraising the value of a work inherently include a warranty by the appraiser that the work so appraised is genuine? If the appraisal shows a market value in the same range as for authentic works by the artist to whom the work is attributed, then the argument is that this reflects the appraiser's opinion that the work is authentic. A recent incident involved a valuation, for a substantial sum, of a painting purported to be by one of the Group of Seven. The donor filed his income tax return showing a deduction for a donation to an institution, based on the valuation. In a subsequent investigation, the Revenue authorities determined from museum specialists that the work was a forgery and disallowed the deduction. Does the donor, who at all times believed the work to be an original, have a cause of action against the appraiser for negligence? The donor relied upon the skill and professional competence of the appraiser. The appraiser was obviously wrong in his valuation, and the donor was caused damage by the improper appraisal. It would appear that this might give rise to liability on the part of the appraiser for the damage incurred by the collector.

Importing

Another activity in which dealers are frequently engaged is that of importing art into the country. This activity requires some knowledge of both the Excise Tax Act, as it affects federal sales tax, and the Customs Tariff (which is the act under which customs duty is levied).

Federal Sales Tax

Fortunately for dealers and collectors, most works of art produced in Canada are not subject to federal sales tax, and most works of art which are imported are also free of this tax. The following works of art, whether Canadian made or imported, were, in 1980, free of federal sales tax levied under the Excise Tax Act:

69505-1 Paintings, drawings and pastels by artists, all of the foregoing when valued at not less than twenty dollars each; paintings and sculptures by artists domiciled in Canada but residing temporarily abroad for purposes of study, under regulations by the Minister.

69510-1 Hand-made drawings, sketches or designs, but not including patterns, *viz.*: – drawings, sketches or designs of wearing apparel, including boots and shoes, wall or floor coverings and textile fabrics, when imported in single copies of each such drawing, sketch or design for use in the manufacture of wearing apparel, boots or shoes, textile fabrics, wall or floor coverings or of patterns.

69515-1 Original sculptures and statuary, including the first twelve replicas made from an original work or model; assemblages: the professional production of artists only and valued at not less than seventy-five dollars each.

69520-1 Engravings, etchings, lithographs, woodcuts, maps and charts, printed prior to 1st January 1900; original engravings, etchings, lithographs, woodcuts, unbound, printed by hand from plates or blocks wholly executed by hand, and signed by the artist.

69525-1 Hand-woven tapestries, suitable only for use as wall hangings, valued at not less than twenty dollars per square foot.

(These numbers used in the Excise Tax Act Schedule are a cross reference to the Customs Tariff as it existed immediately prior to June 19, 1971.)

Canadian producers of works of art which are not included in the above list are obliged to include the federal sales tax in the price of the goods. This poses no problem for the dealer selling these works, however, for he has no obligation to collect and remit this tax. Dealers who are involved in the framing business should be aware that they may be obliged to charge and remit federal sales tax from this part of the business. If a dealer imports works of art which do not appear on the above list, he will be obliged to remit federal sales tax to the federal government. This most frequently arises when a dealer is importing serigraphs, or photographic and photomechanical representations, whether or not these are signed and numbered, as these items are not covered by tariff item 69520-1. Note that the items from the Customs Tariff which are incorporated by reference into the provisions concerned with federal sales tax are *not* the provisions that govern whether or not customs duty must be paid.

CUSTOMS DUTIES

In 1980, the Customs Tariff exempted from customs duty the following items:

69510-1 Hand-made drawings, sketches or designs, but not including patterns, *viz.*: − drawings, sketches or designs of wearing apparel, including boots and shoes, wall or floor coverings and textile fabrics, when imported in single copies of each such drawing, sketch or design for use in the manufacture of wearing apparel, boots or shoes, textile fabrics, wall or floor coverings or of patterns.

69515-1 Original sculptures and statuary, including the first twelve replicas made from an original work or model; assemblages:

The professional production of artists only and valued at not less than seventy-five dollars each.

69516-1 The production of artists domiciled in Canada but residing temporarily abroad, under regulations by the Minister.

69520-1 Original paintings, drawings, collages and pastels by artists;

Engravings, etchings, lithographs, woodcuts, maps and charts, printed prior to 1st January 1900;

Original engravings, etchings, lithographs, woodcuts, unbound, printed from plates or blocks wholly executed by hand and signed by the artist or, under regulations by the Minister, authenticated by or on behalf of the artist;

Serigraphs and photographic or photomechanical representations, numbered and signed by the artist or, under regulations by the Minister, authenticated by or on behalf of the artist;

Any combination of the foregoing media, numbered and signed by the artist, or under regulations by the Minister, authenticated by or on behalf of the artist, and

69525-1 Hand-woven tapestries, or hand-made appliques, suitable only for use as wall hangings, valued at not less than twenty dollars per square foot.

A comparison of the lists itemizing which items are federal

sales tax free and those which can enter the country customs duty free shows that they are not identical. Tariff item 69505-1 has been deleted and Tariff item 69520-1 is expanded considerably to cover in part those items previously covered in tariff item 69505-1.

Because of the differences in the two lists, it may be necessary to make payments under either the Excise Tax Act or the Customs Tariff or pursuant to both acts. One of the contentious areas has been the payment of levies on signed and numbered serigraphs entering Canada. Customs duties do not have to be paid because the serigraphs are included in Tariff item 69520-1. However, federal sales tax must be paid on these serigraphs under the wording of Tariff item 69520-1 applicable to the Excise Tax Act. Federal sales tax is also payable on signed and numbered serigraphs produced in Canada.

The meeting of bureaucracy and modern art, particularly in the customs duties area, has produced some amusing incidents. One such incident was the attempted levying of customs duty on an Anthony Caro sculpture on the basis that it was a farm implement. Another customs officer tried to levy customs duty on unframed lithographs by Jules Olitski on the basis that the dealer was importing wallcovering which was subject to the wallpaper tariff.

The problem, of course, lies in the lack of knowledge by the public as to the scope of what constitutes art today. In 1928, a modern sculpture by Brancusi called *Bird in Flight* was imported into the United States. The customs officials indicated that in their view it was not a work of art. It was created of bronze and therefore should be charged a 40% tariff because it was a "thing" manufactured of metal and should be included in their paragraph dealing with articles or wares manufactured in various metals, including bronze. The case was taken to the courts and the plaintiff introduced expert evidence from various curators and directors of museums drawn from across the United States indicating that in fact the "thing" was a work of art. The judge came to the conclusion that the definition of a work of art must be expanded to include "non-objective" objects as well as those items which were generally conceived by the public at that time to be art and the work was allowed to enter the United States tariff free.

About fifteen years ago, in the United States, another leading art import case arose. It dealt with original glass works of art which had been created by a European glass blower. These, too, met with objections from customs officials who said that they were not works of art. It was argued by customs that since most of the items were decanters, vases, bowls, ashtrays, etc., and had utilitarian uses, they should not be exempt as objects of fine art. The judge in this case was also of the view that these were, in fact, works of art, and should be allowed into the country under the art tariff rather than as goods or wares.

We, in Canada, as illustrated above, still encounter these same kinds of problems. In order to have works of art passed under the appropriate tariff it is necessary both to have Canada Customs agree that the work is an original work of art and also to have them decide that the original work of art should be designated as an object covered by an appropriate tariff item.

A problem that may be encountered from time to time involves the levying of duty on a frame surrounding a painting that is itself duty free. Persuasion is the best remedy in this case. Future difficulties can be anticipated involving works that have been fabricated in factories outside of Canada and then shipped into this country. The solution may again lie in convincing the customs officials that this is a work of art rather than a manufactured object. Other problems could arise in regard to "found objects" which form the basis of art and art works made of unusual materials. Glass blowing and ceramics have again become important areas of the art world, and dealers acting as importers could run into difficulties because of the utilitarian nature of the work.

However, the picture is not bleak. Customs officials in Ottawa have been most helpful in discussions with dealers, and Revenue authorities are concerned about avoiding unnecessary conflict with dealers and artists regarding the importation into Canada or export from this country of original works of art. So-called "modern" art is no longer treated as the stepchild of the art world. Real problems may occur, however, in dealing with conceptual art, organic art, and minimal art.

PROVINCIAL SALES TAX

Only some dealers are concerned with federal sales tax and customs duties. Many more are concerned with provincial sales tax, because art dealers in all provinces, except Alberta, must collect retail sales tax on most of their sales. There are some exemptions available of which the dealer should be aware in order to save his client this tax. Do public institutions and authorities in his province have to pay the tax on purchases of art? Does a person who is not resident in the province have to pay the tax? Does it make a difference if the art is delivered to a client's out-of-province residence rather than if the client takes the art with him?

How often does the dealer have to remit the tax to the government? If a work of art is sold and arrangements made for instalment payments, when does the government receive its tax? What sorts of records have to be kept?

These are a few of the questions to which a dealer must have the answers.

BUSINESS AND REALTY TAXES

Business and realty taxes are both levied by municipal governments. Realty taxes relate to the value of the real estate occupied by the gallery. Business tax is the tax paid for the privilege of carrying on business in the municipality, and is related to the type of premises occupied — warehouse, retail, office accommodation — as well as the type of business carried on. Neither of these taxes depend on the value of sales made.

INCOME TAX

The tax that does vary with the success of the gallery is income tax. This tax is levied at both the federal and provincial levels. The provinces in large part either adopt, or repeat almost exactly, the provisions of the federal Income Tax Act for taxing both individuals and corporations. Some of the particular provisions that are of interest to dealers will be examined below.

Calculation of Income

The Income Tax Act states that subject to any express provision to the contrary, a taxpayer's income for a taxation year from a business or property is his profit therefrom for the year. (The chief provision to the contrary, is that "income from a property" does not include any capital gain from the disposition of that property.) The art owned by a dealer is inventory, not capital property, from which he earns a profit.

Inventory

The Income Tax Act requires the dealer, in calculating his profit, to take an annual inventory which reveals the quantities and nature of the art in sufficient detail to ascertain its value for calculating the dealer's income.

The dealer adds to the value of the inventory he had at the commencement of the year the cost of all the inventory he purchased during the year, and then deducts the value of the inventory at the year-end pursuant to the accrual method of calculating income. The difference yields the cost of the sales that he made during the year. A dealer may not use the cash basis of calculating income and thereby postpone the payment of tax by building valuable inventories.

The entire inventory is valued at the lower of its cost to the dealer or its fair market value. The dealer cannot value some inventory at fair market value and other inventory at cost. A small tax break was introduced in 1977 which permits the dealer, in common with other businessmen holding inventory, to deduct 3% of the cost of his opening inventory in each year when calculating income. Inventory, for tax purposes, does not include works on consignment because the dealer has not purchased such works and does not have legal title to them. Any costs incurred in connection with shipping, crating, etc., of the consigned works are an expense to be deducted from gross income in calculating profit.

Sales and Trades

Inventory includes works traded in as partial payment on other art. Suppose a dealer sells a work on consignment from an artist for $2,400, to be paid by $1,900 cash plus an allowance for $500 on a work traded in. This work is not resold by year end. The dealer commission is 50% so that after paying the artist the dealer retains $1,200; $700 cash and a work traded in whose cost to him is $500. The dealer includes $1,200 in his gross income when calculating profit.

While for tax purposes the dealer has realized the full profit of $1,200 on the sale, and has realized the full expenses of making the sale, he only has received $700 cash. He must sell the work that was traded in to realize the remainder of the cash; and must receive an amount in excess of $500 sufficient to cover his costs of holding inventory and making a second sale, to place him in the same position as if he had sold the first work for $2,400. This is why many dealers are reluctant to accept trades on the purchase of works or do not usually allow credit for the full retail value of the traded work.

Another fact of life for a dealer, is that he has to pay tax on all amounts receivable notwithstanding the fact that he may not be paid until the subsequent year. No reserve, such as that allowed to a taxpayer in respect of a capital gain, is allowed for monies not yet due unless the terms of payment are for a period in excess of two years. A dealer may, however, claim a reserve for doubtful debts; these are amounts that a dealer has reason to believe will not be paid. Because of the requirement that tax must be paid notwithstanding the fact that money has not been received, dealers prefer not to give terms for payment extended beyond their tax year-end.

TAX PLANNING

Need for Tax Planning

Everyone who is successful in business will pay some income tax. However, the amount of income tax paid can usually be lessened through tax planning. Taxes arising from an operating business may be reduced. Taxes arising on death and on the making of gifts may also be reduced through proper tax planning.

Unincorporated dealers, or dealers in personal partnerships, should be aware that they share many problems in common with artists, and reference is made to Chapter 9, The Artist: Business and Taxation at page 170, dealing with the tax treatment of inventory on the death of the owner and the tax problems of making gifts of inventory, discussed at page 174.

The aim of tax planning is to give taxpayers more disposable income to enjoy. But if the structures adopted in the plan interfere with the enjoyment of life, compromises have to be found. There is no one approach which offers solutions for everyone's concerns. Many persons obtain benefits from incorporating their businesses and this is one approach that an unincorporated dealer should always investigate.

Incorporation

Everyone's personal objectives are different. One person might wish to have a partnership arrangement, another a limited partnership arrangement. A dealer might wish to ensure that the profits of the business provide for his children's education. Another dealer might wish to open a series of galleries. A spouse might wish to be involved only on a limited basis. A dealer could be concerned with the possible tax consequences to his estate because he owns inventory. A dealer might wish to clearly separate his private collection from his inventory and make gifts from his private collection with the maximum tax saving. He may wish to provide for the continuance of his business on his death. All of these problems will give rise to different solutions which have to be tailored to the individual concerned.

Incorporation does not merely involve setting up a corporation. Many questions have to be asked in order to have the proper structure. Some items a professional adviser would endeavour to have answered are itemized below.

1. How many corporations should there be? Should the real estate be held in a separate company? Should each partner have his own corporation? Should different business aspects of the gallery be owned by separate corporations?
2. What should the share capitalization be? Who will control the gallery? How will it be financed? Is the spouse going to have an interest in the gallery? What happens if the marriage dissolves? Are children going to have an interest in the gallery? Who should be receiving dividend income?
3. Who will the directors and officers of the corporation be? Who will have the power to contract on behalf of the gallery?
4. How broad or narrow should the objects of the corporation be? What name would the owners of the corporation prefer? Can it be used without problems?
5. How much flexibility can be worked into the structure of the corporation for unforseen changes and is this desirable? Does the corporation not wish to file reports with the relevant securities commissions?
6. Is there an unincorporated business that is going to be transferred into the corporation?

Unfortunately, no generalizations can be made about the structure most suitable for a gallery. That is a matter to be discussed by the dealer with his legal and financial advisers. A corporation is a flexible vehicle and can accommodate a number of varying needs and directions, including tax benefits where applicable.

CHAPTER 11   OBSCENITY AND ART

INTRODUCTION

While the main focus of this chapter will be on obscenity provisions in the Criminal Code, it should be noted that censorship is exercised in this country in a variety of ways and by a number of different authorities. For example, the Postmaster General and the Customs and Excise Department, have the power to restrict the movement and availability of certain material, and censorship also occurs through the Broadcast Act, various municipal by-laws, and provincial film censorship boards.

In regard to the visual arts and their exhibition in public, from time to time the morality squad of a particular police force may find it appropriate to visit a particular art exhibition. The visit is usually initiated by a call from one or more members of the public, who may or may not have seen the particular works of art in issue. At other times the morality squad may be motivated by itself to investigate a particular exhibition.

TYPES OF OFFENCES

Disgusting Objects

In the past, using the City of Toronto as an example, the police have basically shown interest in two types of exhibitions. The first is the kind of exhibition which has appeared from time to time at the Isaacs Gallery and primarily involved the work of the sculptor, Mark Prent. The Isaacs Gallery has twice been charged with showing "disgusting objects," a somewhat medieval offence still contained within the Criminal Code of Canada, i.e., "everyone commits an offence who knowingly, without lawful justification or excuse... publicly exhibits a disgusting object or an indecent show...." These exhibitions have consisted of various tableaux or scenes with lifelike figures or objects created primarily from fibre glass based material. Such scenes have consisted of, for instance, various parts of the human body hanging from hooks inside a large meat freezer. The viewers are invited to look into the cold storage vault and see the hanging meat. Another scene is of an outdoor washroom. The door has a half moon carved into it and the viewer can look in and see a paraplegic on the toilet. Another work invites the viewer to walk up some steps and peer into an operating theatre where an abortion is being performed on a figure which is half woman and half pig. Another tableau invites the viewer to pull the handle on an electrical switch and electrocute a figure which has been manacled into an electric chair. These, and other scenes like them, have caught the attention of the police. The charges laid against the Isaacs Gallery have never been successfully prosecuted, once being dismissed on a technicality, and once being dismissed at the preliminary hearing without ever reaching a trial on the merits. One show was taken to York University where it was exhibited in the visual arts department without interference by the authorities, and works by the artist of a similar nature have been exhibited in the most reputable public museums in Europe and pieces have been purchased for major public and private collections.

Sexual Obscenity

The second kind of work which occasions visits by the police are works which might be considered sexually permissive. The police may request that various works be removed from public view. If the gallery owner complies with this request the matter is usually dropped. It is when the gallery owner refuses to comply with the request that the problem truly begins. This was the situation when the police charged Dorothy Cameron of the Cameron Gallery in Toronto with obscenity on the 21st of May, 1965. Before dealing with that case in detail, we should look at the origin of obscenity, its history, and the definitions which have been applied in determining it.

Obscene and Blasphemous Libels

Since literature has always been the prime target of censorship, it is not surprising that the earliest recorded obscenity case involved the publication of *Venus in the Cloister or The Nun in her Smock* which gave rise to "Curl's case" in 1727. The court held that its obligation to protect the King's peace extended beyond offences involving physical force. Thus, the common law offence of "obscene libel" was created. In this regard it is interesting to note that an action was brought recently in Quebec by a group of private individuals against a play (performed on stage and later published) entitled *Les Fées Ont Soif.* The plaintiffs alleged that the play "libelled the Virgin Mary." The case, however, was dismissed, as it was held that the plaintiffs had no standing to bring the action. As well, the Canadian Criminal Code still contains an offence known as "blasphemous libel," which had been virtually ignored for fifty years until charges were laid in 1979 (in northern Ontario) against Monty Python's movie *Life of Brian.*

JUDICIAL TESTS

The Hicklin Case

To return, however, to an examination of the history of obscenity laws, the offence of obscene libel seems to have been rarely applied, at least in the context of erotic literature and art, until the Victorian age. The Victorian period gave rise to the first book-burning legislation in the common law world, the British *Obscene Publications Act* of 1856. Shortly thereafter, the famous case of *R. v. Hicklin* was heard and gave rise to the following test of obscenity which has been with us almost ever since:

> The test of obscenity is this, whether the tendency of the matter charged as obscene is to deprave and to corrupt those whose minds are open to such immoral influences and into whose hands a publication of this sort may fall.

The first Canadian legislation dealing with obscenity was enacted in 1892 as a section of the Criminal Code. The statute did not define obscenity and the matter was therefore left to the courts to determine. They used the *Hicklin* test referred to above. Obviously, the test requires a judicial appraisal of what constitutes depravity and corruption, as well as conjecture as to who might come in contact with the work and what their sexual and moral susceptibilities are likely to be. Artistic merit seems to be irrelevant.

Few cases appear to have been heard between the time of the adoption of a statutory prohibition in 1892 and the middle of this century. It may be speculated that either little material was available which could be thought obscene, or that the public was not particularly offended or concerned by "obscene" works.

In the 1940's, the *Hicklin* test began to be interpreted somewhat less harshly, particularly in the Province of Quebec. For example, the case of *Conway* v. *The King* held that a woman's breasts could be revealed during a theatrical performance if this was necessary for artistic effect. Less lenient courts had previously even held that material which described lewd performances on the stage was obscene although it was published in order to call attention to the fact that such performances ought to be suppressed.

In 1951, the court hearing the case of *Regina* v. *Stroll,* held that a window display showing ties draped over female silhouettes in a manner which revealed breasts was not obscene. The judge in the case stated that "the law is made to protect the modesty of normal persons, not to bridle the imagination of the hot blooded, vicious or overly-scruplous." He went on to say that if the display was suggestive, "then it would be necessary to put brassieres on cows and diapers on dogs."

The 1950's and early 1960's saw a tremendous increase in the production of "girlie" magazines and various sexually oriented books. This literature is of particular interest to the study of obscenity and the visual arts because it usually was the cover "art" which was found most objectionable. Objections arose because one often was forced to see the covers, whether or not one was interested in the contents. It is to be noted that the covers were almost invariably more sexually explicit than the writing or photographs within. Sometimes prosecution was, and is, regarded as a positive factor. Nothing seems to incite more interest than a book that has been banned, a show that has been closed, or a magazine under attack for being obscene. In fact, some U.S.

publishers would have a publication banned in one state in order to generate sales in another. "Banned in Boston" could then be emblazoned on the cover.

The New Test

In 1959, Bill C-58 was introduced by the Justice Minister to amend the Criminal Code as it related to obscenity. That Bill provided a new definition aimed at the commercial "pulp" magazines and was stated to be "capable of application with speed and certainty, by providing a series of simple objective tests...." It was intended to operate in addition to the Hicklin test. This purportedly objective test reads:

> Any publication a dominate characteristic of which is the undue exploitation of sex, or of sex and any one or more of the following subjects, namely, crime, horror, cruelty and violence, shall be deemed obscene.

This definition remains today in the Criminal Code of Canada.

Confusion of Tests

Parliament recognized that interpretation of the terms "dominant" and "undue" involves an element of subjectivity, but stated that "the word undue is one with which the courts are familiar as meaning generally something going beyond what men of good will and common sense would normally tolerate." Unfortunately, the courts did not seem able to read the intentions of parliament into the legislation itself. A few cases decided immediately after the amendments were passed did examine the legislative debates and attempt to apply the guidelines proposed at that time. In later cases, however, the new definition was not confined to the kind of writing that would be objectionable to "men of good will and common sense." No works which would have been found obscene under the *Hicklin* test escaped under the new definition.

Confusion then reigned as to which was the proper test to be used, the old *Hicklin* test, or the new test in the Criminal Code. Cases went every which way, some holding that the new test was meant to supersede the *Hicklin* test, others indicating that the *Hicklin* test could be relied upon as well. The old *Hicklin* test was used in a case in Nova Scotia in 1960. There, a father had taken photographs of his nude son, for artistic purposes. The father was found guilty of obscenity, despite the fact that it was conceded by the Crown that the photographs were not intended for publication.

The question of the coexistence of the two tests arose again in the prosecution of Lady Chatterley's Lover (*R. v. Brodie*). At trial, in spite of the evidence of noted authors Hugh MacLennan, Morley Callaghan, and others, that the novel was a serious work of fiction which was no more sexually frank than other serious literature of the time, and despite the production of no expert testimony by the prosecution, the trial judge held that the book was obscene. On appeal, the court ruled that some of the earlier cases were wrong in not recognizing that the definition in the Criminal Code was now exhaustive. The Court of Appeal felt that this new test in the Criminal Code was an objective test which precluded expert literary opinion, since literary merit was irrelevant in interpreting the various elements required to prove the offence.

In 1962, the Supreme Court of Canada overruled this decision by a bare majority of five to four. As to whether the *Hicklin* test continued to exist, however, there was no consensus. Since the Crown had conceded that the Criminal Code provisions provided the exclusive test of obscenity, two judges found it unnecessary to decide the question and another simply ignored it. Of the five judges in the majority, three stated that the Hicklin test had been superseded and that the jurisprudence concerning it was therefore irrelevant, one felt that the two tests continued to co-exist, and one that it was unnecessary to decide the question. For the minority, one stated that the Code provisions were now exclusive, another that the two tests co-existed, a third that the question was unnecessary to decide, and the fourth made no reference to the question at all.

A majority of the court did hold, however, that *expert evidence* was admissible. They stressed that the work had to be examined as a whole in order to determine the "dominant characteristics" of the work, and in this context the purpose of the author was relevant in order to show what the author was doing, or trying to do, and whether his purpose was serious or one of "base exploitation." Evidence regarding the purpose and artistic merit of the work was also useful in helping the judge decide whether offending passages constituted an undue exploitation of sex when measured against the "internal necessities of the work."

It is unclear, however, against which of three tests put forward in court "undueness" is to be measured. The tests were, the "internal necessities of the book," the "usages of contemporary novelists and writers," and the "standards of the community." The most important aspect of the majority decision is its approval of the last of these tests (which originated in Australia). Approval was given to a lower court decision of that country which stated that "there does exist in any community at all times — however the standard may vary from time to time — a general instinctive sense of what is decent and what is indecent, of what is clean and what is dirty. . . ." The application of this test, it was felt, would be useful in avoiding the application of the judge or jury's personal opinions about a work. No final resolution of what test or tests should be applied was made, however, since the majority stated that they did not find that the novel offended under any test.

Another 1962 decision by the Supreme Court of Canada, dealing with two magazines, *Dude* and *Escapade,* also adopted the community standards approach. Once again, the viability of the *Hicklin* test was not resolved. Of interest is the Court's adoption of the trial judge's tolerant attitude toward artistic expression:

... in cases close to the border line, tolerance is to be preferred to proscription. To strike a publication which is not clearly obscene may have repercussions beyond what is immediately visible.... Suppression may tend to inhibit those creative impulses and endeavours which ought to be encouraged in a free society.

In 1965, the Ontario Court of Appeal adopted the community standards test in reversing a lower court finding that *Fanny Hill* was obscene.

THE CAMERON CASE

This was the state of the law in Canada when, in 1966, the Ontario Court of Appeal considered what is perhaps the most famous case in the visual arts, *R. v. Cameron.* Dorothy Cameron, the owner and operator of a commercial art gallery in Toronto, was charged with seven counts of exposing obscene pictures to public view, each count referring to a different picture. The seven offending works were included in an exhibition entitled *Eros 65* displaying some sixty drawings representing the work of 22 artists. Two signs were displayed in conjunction with the exhibition, one giving the title of the exhibition, and the other reading "adults only." Five of the works giving rise to charges were black and white drawings by Robert Markle, the other two were a chalk drawing by Lawrence Chaplin and one in red pencil by Fred Ross. The Markle drawings all portrayed nude female figures, three of them apparently showing lesbian acts and another a single nude female in what the court called "an attitude of sexual invitation." The Chaplin piece showed "a male nude figure and a female nude figure with the female figure grasping the nude male's genitalia with her right hand." The Ross work displayed "a female and a male in the nude in a position or in the act of sexual intercourse."

After the first visit by the Toronto morality squad to the gallery, Dorothy Cameron agreed to remove one of the Markle drawings from the exhibition and not display it again without notifying the police. Sometime later, her lawyer informed the police that Miss Cameron felt strongly about the picture and that she felt that the gallery had no alternative but to show it again. This resulted in another visit by the morality squad, this time with a search warrant, and all seven works were seized.

The evidence showed that the artists whose drawings were at issue were all professional craftsmen well known in the art field, and the art gallery one of the best in Ontario, if not in Canada. At trial, five expert witnesses testified for the defence. According to the court, "these witnesses were experts in the field of art; some were teachers of art with or without actual experience as artists; some were connected with well-known art galleries; one was described as an art critic." Each of the experts testified as to the artistic merit of the drawings. The Crown called no expert witnesses at all; their case consisted entirely of the police testimony relating to the seizure of the drawings, together with a description of the drawings and the drawings themselves. Nevertheless, the magistrate convicted Miss Cameron on all seven counts.

The appeal was unsuccessful. Four judges of the five judge court upheld the trial decision, and found that for the purposes of the charges in question the exclusive definition of obscenity was to be found in the Criminal Code, although they noted that the question was still an open one for the Supreme Court of Canada. They held that the magistrate was correct in holding that each of the pictures showed an excessive emphasis on sexual themes for a base purpose, having regard to both the internal necessities of each drawing and to community standards. The majority also held that the manner and circumstances of exposure are relevant only in establishing that the work was exposed to "public view," and the exposure here was held to have been a general invitation to the public to view and purchase the works. The court also made it clear that artistic merit was only relevant in determining obscenity or assessing the purpose of the artist in doubtful cases, or as the court expressed it, where the work falls into some "grey area of doubt." Art and obscenity are seen as being able to co-exist in a given work. The community standards to be applied are those of Canada as a whole, in contemporary times. They are not the standards of those "who have an intense interest in art" but rather represent the "middle path" of interest and tolerance in the community. The court felt that there was ample evidence before the magistrate, by inference or otherwise, including the drawings themselves, to conclude that the works were obscene. As well, the defence of "public good" resulting from the benefit to students of art or the public generally of seeing works of artistic merit which displayed the human form, was rejected. The court held that this end could be achieved without "the exposure of these obscene drawings."

The majority of the judges also indicated that the offence of exposing obscene pictures to public view "knowingly and without lawful justification or excuse" does not mean that the accused must possess the legal knowledge of whether or not the pictures were obscene; it is sufficient that the accused knew the subject matter and caused the pictures to be publicly exhibited. Since the Crown's onus of proving that the exposure was done without lawful justification or excuse requires proof of a negative, little proof will often suffice and such proof may be drawn by inference from other proven facts. Moreover, the conduct of the accused may afford that proof. The majority of the judges went on to indicate that the Crown had discharged the onus of showing the absence of lawful justification or excuse, beyond a reasonable doubt, where the accused, who was an educated person and well represented by a lawyer, brought nothing forward during interviews with police raising any pretense of lawful justification or excuse, failed to advance any such excuse even in argument, and failed to testify at her trial.

Dissent   On the other hand, Mr. Justice Laskin (now the Chief Justice of the Supreme Court of Canada) registered the sole dissent. He felt that the following propositions could be distilled from previous cases:

1. Determination of whether exploitation of sex is a dominant characteristic of the challenged work, be it a book or a drawing or something else, involves consideration of the work as a whole and the purpose of the author or artist.
2. Evidence of the author or artist or of others qualified to express an opinion is admissible on the question of purpose.
3. Consideration of the work as a whole, in the case of a painting or drawing, means that the composition, the method and manner of execution of the work, and the treatment in terms of materials and their expression on the board, canvas, or paper, cannot be disassociated from the theme or themes, and it is the overall result or effect that must be appraised.
4. Exploitation of sex as a dominant characteristic does not offend the law unless the exploitation is "undue," a term which reaches for an objective standard based on an average of contemporary Canadian attitudes and the quality of the work in question.
5. Expert evidence is admissible on the issue of "undueness" but it must be weighed by the court even when it is all one way and stands uncontradicted.

Mr. Justice Laskin also clearly felt that the evidence of experts was necessary in order to prevent the judge from relying merely on his personal opinion based on his own inexpert appraisal of the work. He also stated that "if the artistic purpose of the author emerges as a dominant characteristic... it will be a rare instance indeed in which that dominance can be said to be so suppressed by a sexual theme as to make the exploitation of sex a dominant characteristic which is undue."

In regard to the onus on the Crown of proving the exposing of the works to the public "knowingly," and "without lawful justification or excuse," Mr. Justice Laskin felt that the Crown had failed to discharge its onus of proving the absence of lawful justification or excuse by the accused beyond a reasonable doubt. He felt that the failure of Crown counsel to address this issue, though invited by the magistrate to do so, as well as the fact that the magistrate himself ignored the question completely in his reasons for judgment, were additional reasons why the case should be dismissed against Miss Cameron.

Since the case was not appealed further, the decision of the Court of Appeal stands as a precedent for any future prosecutions.

PRESENT OBSCENITY LAW IN CANADA

The Statutory Law

The present Criminal Code provisions dealing with obscenity are grouped under "Offences Tending to Corrupt Morals." The relevant sections of the Criminal Code are as follows:

Section 159(1) Every one commits an offence who

(a) makes, prints, publishes, distributes, circulates, or has in his possession for the purpose of publication, distribution or circulation any obscene written matter, picture, model, phonograph record or other thing whatsoever, or

(b) makes, prints, publishes, distributes, sells or has in his possession for the purpose of publication, distribution or circulation, a crime comic.

Section 159(2) Every one commits an offence who knowingly, without lawful justification or excuse,

(a) sells, exposes to public view or has in his possession for such a purpose any obscene written matter, picture, model, phonograph record or other thing whatsoever,

(b) publicly exhibits a disgusting object or an indecent show,

(c) offers to sell, advertises, publishes an advertisement of, or has for sale or disposal any means, instructions, medicine, drug or article intended or represented as a method of causing abortion or miscarriage, or

(d) advertises or publishes an advertisement of any means, instructions, medicine, drug or article intended or represented as a method for restoring sexual virility or curing venereal diseases or diseases of the generative organs.

Section 159(3) No person shall be convicted of an offence under this section if he establishes that the public good was served by the acts that are alleged to constitute the offence and that the acts alleged did not extend beyond what served the public good.

Section 159(4) For the purposes of this section it is a question of law whether an act served the public good and whether there is evidence that the act alleged went beyond what served the public good, but it is a question of fact whether the acts did or did not extend beyond what served the public good.

Section 159(5) For the purposes of this section the motives of an accused are irrelevant.

Section 159(6) Where an accused is charged with an offence under subsection (1) the fact that the accused was ignorant of the nature or presence of the matter, picture, model, phonograph record, crime comic or other thing by means of or in relation to which the offence was committed is not a defence to the charge.

Section 159(7) In this section "crime comic" means a magazine, periodical or book that exclusively or substantially comprises matter depicting pictorially

(a) the commission of crimes, real or fictitious, or

(b) events connected with the commission of crimes, real or fictitious, whether occurring before or after the commission of the crime.

Section 159(8) For the purpose of this Act, any publication a dominant characteristic of which is the undue exploitation of sex, or of sex and any one or more of the following subjects, namely, crime, horror, cruelty and violence, shall be deemed to be obscene.

It is this last section, of course, which has led to so much confusion, and so many conflicting judgments and unresolved questions. Firstly, the question of whether the Criminal Code contains the sole definition of obscenity remains in doubt. Although recent cases have leaned toward an affirmative answer to this question, the presence of the word "deemed" in this section argues against its being an exclusive definition. As generally used in the law, and certainly as used in the Criminal Code, the word "deemed" implies the existence of another definition. For example, if a person injures another in the course of a robbery, and the victim later dies, the crime committed is "deemed" to be murder but this, of course, is by no means the sole definition of murder.

Many authors over the years, however, have speculated that the question of whether the test of obscenity is an objective one, or a subjective one, or both, is really irrelevant. Legal writers sometimes fear that cases are really won or lost depending upon whether a particular judge personally regards a work as obscene. The court in the Cameron case stated more than once that "the drawings themselves remain the most eloquent and the best evidence upon the subject [of obscenity]. This sounds suspiciously like the American judge who said of pornography simply that "I know it when I see it."

Acceptability and Tolerability

Following the Cameron case two lines of authority have developed concerning the present definition of obscenity. One line of authority indicates that only material which is "acceptable" to the average member of the community should be available to anyone. This standard appears to have been approved in the Cameron case. The second line of authority establishes a "tolerability" test, which involves a determination of what the community would tolerate having available. This standard was applied, for example, in cases involving the publication of the book *Show Me* and the stage performance of *An Evening with Futz*. Where tolerance is the test, evidence regarding the manner and circumstances of exposure is highly relevant. Thus, in the *Show Me* case, the price, packaging, and manner of distribution were introduced into evidence and the court accepted that these would exclude the book from indiscriminate exposure. Since children would only have access to the book through the agency of their parents, the court held that the community would *tolerate* selected use by parents, the issue being whether "a general average of community thinking and belief would entail no objection to the book being seen and read by those members of the community who wished to do so."

Several Ontario cases decided after the Cameron case used the "acceptability" standard. Now, however, it appears that the Ontario Court of Appeal, in a recent decision involving Sudbury News Services Limited, has adopted the "tolerability" standard. Nevertheless, the Supreme Court of Canada has yet to examine this question and at the moment the standard used could well differ from province to province.

The Community

Later cases have also established that the "community" that must be looked at is a cross-section of the entire Canadian community, both rural and urban. It is not a local community, and most emphatically not the artistic community or university community. Nevertheless, the question still arises of whether a judge or jury in a rural area would reach the same decision as one sitting in a highly urbanized city. In a very recent case involving Penthouse magazine, the Ontario Court of Appeal used the "tolerability" standard. They also held that it was possible to bring expert evidence regarding standards from other parts of the country, such as by testifying about observations of performances or exhibitions elsewhere. However, they held that opinion evidence relating only to general standards of tolerance of the contemporary Canadian community is not useful. It is therefore, they stated, the judge and the judge alone who in the final analysis must determine the prevailing standards of tolerance.

CENSORSHIP

A recent Supreme Court of Canada case has decided that there was no constitutional barrier to provincial censorship boards. A variety of other cases have determined that approval by a censorship board, or by the Customs and Excise Department for importation purposes, will *not* prevent a prosecution and conviction under the obscenity provisions of the Criminal Code. Thus, a work could enter the country, be approved by a provincial censorship board, and yet, following a complaint by a member of the public, charges could be laid (and, in fact, successfully prosecuted) under the obscenity provisions of the Criminal Code.

SUMMARY

From the foregoing, it can be seen that obscenity legislation raises a number of questions and creates a variety of problems in the visual arts and elsewhere. Every time a work of art which has sexual overtones is shown by a public or commercial gallery there is a risk that the morality squad of the local police will intervene, either on their own initiative or following a complaint by a member of the general public.

It also becomes apparent that since obscenity is not as easily defined as theft, for instance, or arson, whether an action is brought at all, or brought successfully, will depend upon discretionary actions by a number of individuals.

It may depend, for example, on whether a member of the public, or an individual police officer, is offended by a work. Even if someone is offended, no further action will be taken unless a complaint is made or an officer decides to lay charges. Once a charge has in fact been laid, there is still a discretion on the part of the Crown Attorney's office as to whether or not to proceed to trial, and where a trial in fact takes place, there is, as we have seen, a great deal of judicial discretion involved in determining whether or not a work is obscene. Expert evidence may or may not be admissible in assisting the court to make this determination, and the weight accorded to such evidence may well differ from one court to another. Even the questions which are reputed to be objective in nature may be difficult to answer. What, for example, is a Canadian standard of morality?

ALTERNATIVE APPROACHES

Should obscenity, which seems to be primarily a matter of religion and morality, even be in the Criminal Code? What alternatives are available to deal with sex and violence in the arts? In some of the Scandinavian countries, the view has been expressed that a differentiation should be made between "voluntary" and "involuntary" exposure to pornography. This is taken to mean that a person should be free to attend a store which sells pornography, or a pornographic film, or a nightclub act, if he so desires. "Involuntary" exposure to pornography, however, would be prevented, so that such works would not be thrust upon the unsuspecting, and particularly not upon children. Control would be exercised over displays in store windows, or posters displayed in public, and performances or films would be accompanied by some form of warning or rating system to alert those who might be offended. This is not, of course, the law of Canada, and is unlikely to be in the near future. The issue of obscenity is an emotional one which leads, therefore, to emotional arguments from both sides. An example of the vehement arguments against obscenity is the statement made in the Canadian Senate by a former Attorney General of Ontario, during debates on the amendments to the Criminal Code in 1959:

> Obscenity does not develop only carnal passions; it also develops other pleasures such as sloth, because the sensual person is generally lazy and vicious, and as he has to do something to live, he tries to steal so as to work as little as possible, and once he has stolen he may not stop at killing.

The U.S. Position on Obscenity

In the United States, pornography is controlled locally through city ordinances, at the state level through Criminal Codes, and also by federal inter-state and postal laws (the Comstock laws). Certain limits are placed upon the state's ability to legislate because of the freedom of speech provisions of the first amendment to the American Constitution. Although in the case of *Roth* v. *United States* the Supreme Court of the U.S. held that obscenity was to be excluded from protection under the first amendment, at the same time the Court developed a strict interpretation of what constituted obscenity. Obscenity was defined as "material which deals with sex in a manner appealing to prurient interests." Reference was to be made to "contemporary community standards" and consideration given to whether the material had "even the slightest redeeming social importance."

In 1966, three important cases further defined the test to be used at that time. The first, involving the publication of *Fanny Hill,* outlined the following three-part test:

(a) The dominant theme of the material taken as a whole appeals to a prurient interest in sex;

(b) The material is patently offensive because if affronts contemporary community standards relating to the description or representation of sexual matters; and

(c) The material is utterly without redeeming social value....

A second case, *Ginzburg* v. *United States* held that the manner of publishing and marketing was relevant in determining whether a work was obscene. There, the manner of advertising placed the sole emphasis on sexually provocative aspects of the material. A third case, also involving Ralph Ginzburg, held that material which was not otherwise obscene would become so if it was intended for a juvenile audience. A later case, *Stanley* v. *Georgia,* held that the private possession of obscene materials could not be prohibited by state laws. Subsequent cases, however, have established an extremely narrow definition of what constitutes private possession, and the definition of "private" is now unlikely to extend outside of one's own home.

The current U.S. test was formulated in the 1973 case of *Miller* v. *California*, which involved an appeal from a conviction under a California law prohibiting the unsolicited mailing of obscene material. It was decided that the test to be applied in a mailing case was whether a significant danger existed of offending the sensibilities of unwilling recipients or of exposure to juveniles. At the same time, the U.S. Supreme Court stated a new standard as follows:

(a) Whether "the average person applying contemporary community standards" would find that the work, taken as a whole, appeals to the prurient interest....

(b) Whether the work depicts or describes, in a patently offensive way, sexual conduct specifically defined by the applicable state law; and

(c) Whether the work, taken as a whole, lacks serious literary, artistic, political or scientific value.

The case has three important aspects. Firstly, it rejects the earlier requirement that a work must be "utterly without redeeming social value." Secondly, community standards did not mean the national community, as in Canada, but rather state, local, or even town standards. Thirdly, despite this application of local standards, the ability of states to legislate was restricted by the requirement that only sexual conduct could be prohibited.

It is apparent that the Supreme Court considers only hard core pornography to be obscene, and consequently subject to regulation by the states. In fact, the Court has reversed several lower court decisions because they believed the material was not hard core pornography, and not patently offensive, by using their ability to guarantee the safeguards provided by the first amendment.

Flag Desecration

The first amendment protections have also been extended to cases involving flag desecration. In the U.S., desecration of the flag is prohibited by both state and federal legislation. The federal statute reads as follows:

Whoever knowingly casts contempt upon any flag of the United States by publicly mutilating, defacing, defiling, burning, or trampling upon it shall be fined no more than $1,000.00 or imprisoned for not more than one year, or both.

State laws generally conform to the Uniform Flag Act which prohibits desecration in similar language to that of the federal statute and also contains a provision regarding "improper use" of the flag by such things as affixing any "word, figure, mark, picture, design, drawing, or advertisement of any nature" on the flag or displaying it in public when it has been altered in this way.

During the 1960's, artists began to encounter problems

through violation of these statutes. Many "pop" artists were using the flag and it appeared frequently in the works of artists such as Jasper Johns and Robert Rauschenberg. At the same time, artists were using their media to make political protests against the war in Vietnam. The most famous case arose in regard to three-dimensional works by Mark Morrel exhibited in a New York Gallery.

The sculptures included depictions of the flag as an octopus, as a body being hung by a noose, and in the form of an erect penis "protruding from the upright member of a cross." Radich, the owner of the gallery, was convicted of flag desecration under New York law, and the court of appeal upheld the verdict. In the U.S. Supreme Court, in 1971, Justice William O. Douglas abstained, resulting in an equal division of the court. This impasse meant that the conviction in the lower court was affirmed. A rehearing was denied at the time, but ultimately the case was heard again in 1974, at which time the court decided that freedom of speech was more important than laws prohibiting flag desecration. They stated the following:

The flag and that which it symbolizes is dear to us, but not so cherished as those high moral, legal and ethical precepts which our Constitution teaches. When our interests in preserving the integrity of the flag conflict with the higher interest of preserving, protecting and defending the Constitution, the latter must prevail, even when it results in the expression of ideas about our flag and nation which are defiant, contemptuous or unacceptable to most Americans.

The feelings of the courts and the American public are clearly different in peace time than during the period of war. In the absence of American involvement in a new war, artists are expected to be allowed a good deal of freedom in this area.

Problems with the American Law

The most important problem with the American law is in the application of local standards. These standards can make it very difficult for an art exhibition or a play on tour, since a variety of different standards would be applied depending upon the location. Secondly, difficulties similar to those encountered in the interpretation of the Canadian Code exist in determining "serious artistic value." As well, public nuisance laws have been used at the local level to enforce standards and prohibit shows and exhibitions where obscenity laws fail. On the other hand, certain safeguards do exist in regard to the seizure of material. A hearing must be held to decide whether grounds exist for seizure and such a pre-seizure hearing at least allows an individual time to obtain a lawyer. The American law may be more restrictive than that in Canada by virtue of its narrow definition of what constitutes a private place, but the *Ginzburg* case seems to indicate that consideration will be given to the manner and circumstances of exhibition and the intended audience.

FUTURE DIRECTIONS IN CANADA

Amendments to the Criminal Code have been proposed which would expand the definition of obscenity to include "the undue degradation of the human person," and add a provision prohibiting depiction of totally or partially nude children (defined as actually or apparently under the age of 16) engaged or participating in acts of masturbation, intercourse, gross indecency, buggery, bestiality or "unduly displaying any portion of his or her body in a sexually suggestive manner."

Of more consequence for visual artists, is a change in the wording of section 159(8) *from* the following:

(8) For the purposes of this Act, any *publication* a dominant characteristic of which is the undue exploitation of sex, or of sex and any one or more of the following subjects, namely, crime, horror, cruelty and violence, shall be deemed to be obscene.

To this:

(8) For the purposes of this Act, a *matter or thing* is obscene where (a) a dominant characteristic of the *matter or thing* is the undue exploitation of sex, violence, crime, horror or cruelty or the undue degradation of the human person; or (b) the *matter or thing* unduly depicts a totally or partially nude child....

The importance of this change involves the interaction of section 159(8) with the provisions of section 159(1)(a) which reads as follows:

Everyone commits an offence who (a) makes, prints, publishes, distributes, circulates, or has in his possession for the purpose of publication, distribution or circulation any obscene written matter, picture, model, phonograph record or other thing whatsoever....

Cases have held that in regard to such things as "obscene" photographs made for *private use,* prosecution was prevented only because the present definition in section 159(8) requires some element of "publication" before a work is deemed obscene. The proposed change in wording from the phrase "any publication..." to merely "a matter or thing..." would create a theoretical danger of prosecution for an artist who makes a picture or a printer who produces a work, as well as anyone who makes a photograph for private use. In other words, this means that a work would not have to be publicly displayed to result in a prosecution for obscenity. A work which never left an artist's studio could still be found obscene.

Whether or not these new provisions are enacted, it seems clear that the trend in Canada is toward tightening rather than liberalizing the obscenity laws. Despite the problems associated with the present confusing obscenity laws, artists may be forced to lobby for the status quo.

NOTES

NOTES

NOTES

NOTES

NOTES

NOTES

NOTES

NOTES

NOTES

NOTES

NOTES

NOTES

NOTES

NOTES

NOTES

NOTES

INDEX

DESIGN AND TYPOGRAPHY
Peter Durham Dodd

COVER DESIGN
David Wyman

PRODUCTION COORDINATION
Helen Wooldridge

ASSEMBLY
Maria Arshavsky

EDITOR
Linda Davey

RESEARCH
Made possible by the Canada Council

ART
Pink Top by Jack Bush
by permission of The Jack Bush Estate

TYPESETTING
Expertype Graphics Ltd.

BINDING
Arthurs-Jones Lithographing Ltd.

PAPER
Warrans Cameo Dull (outer pages)
Curtis Tweedweave Lugo Gray (inner pages)

TYPEFACE
Souvenir